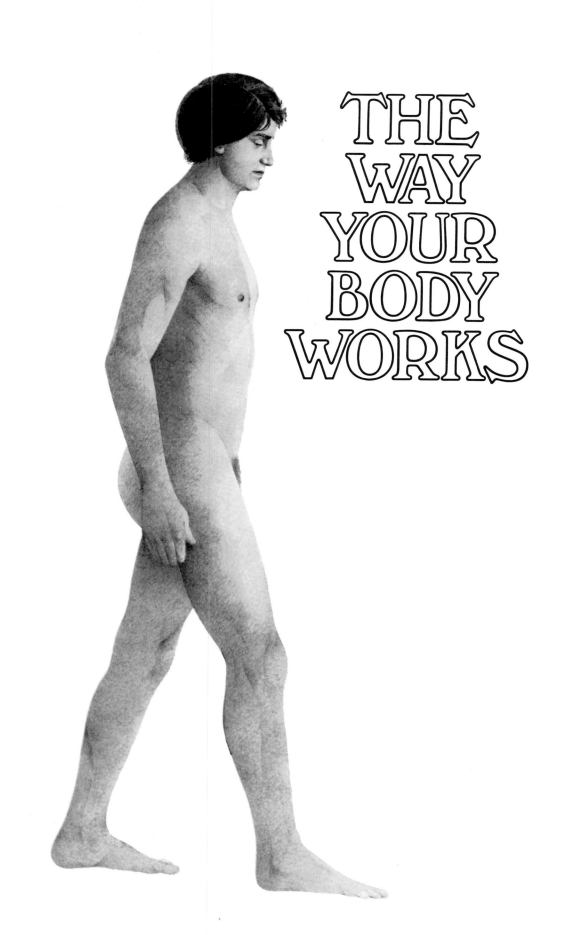

THE WAY YOUR BODY WORKS

THE WAY YOUR BODY WORKS

Chief contributor
Dr Bernard Stonehouse

BONANZA BOOKS
New York

THE WAY YOUR BODY WORKS
Edited and designed by Mitchell Beazley International Limited
14-15 Manette Street, London W1V 5LB

Chief contributor and consultant
Bernard Stonehouse, D.PHIL, MA, BSC
Contributors John Brotherhood, MB, BS
Rosalind Ridley, BA

Editor David Williams
Art editor Jim Bulman
Art assistant Julia Einhorn
Editorial assistant Vivianne Croot

Editorial director Bruce Marshall
Managing editor Frank Wallis

Published 1985 by Bonanza Books
distributed by Crown Publishers Inc.

Library of Congress Cataloging in Publication Data
Stonehouse, Bernard
  The Way Your Body Works

  Includes Index.
  1. Human Biology. I. Brotherhood, John
  II. Ridley, Rosalind. III. Title
  QP 38.586 1985 612 84-21617
  ISBN 0-517-467178

  h g f e d c b a

Printed in Portugal by Printer Portuguesa L.D.A.

The Publishers acknowledge the work of the
following artists: Bob Abrahams (House of Wizzard),
Nick Bantock, Ron Boardman, Giovanni Caselli,
Terry Collins, Clare Davies, John Davis,
Don Dawson, Brian Delf, Jennifer Eachus,
Jean George, Colin Gray, Bryon Harvey,
Trevor Hill, Peter Lampert (A.I. Studios),
Jack McCarthy, Annabel Milne, Charles Raymond,
Michael Stanhope, Harry Titcombe, Mary Waldron,
Martin White, Sidney Woods.

Thanks are also due to the Department of
Anatomy, University College, London.

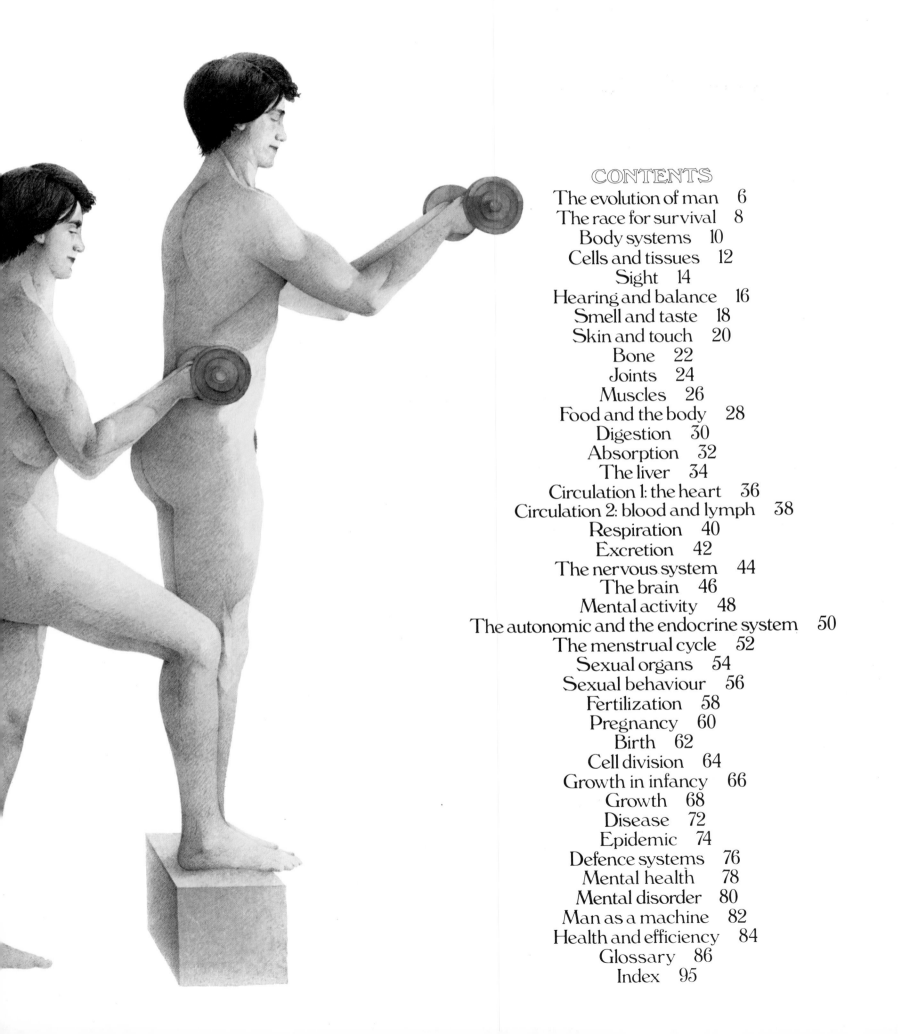

CONTENTS

The evolution of man

Man is a mammal. In common with other mammals he has warm blood and a hairy skin, maintains constant body temperature, produces his young alive and feeds them on milk produced by special glands of the skin. He is related to other mammals in the group known as primates—distantly to moles and shrews, more closely to lemurs, tarsiers and bush-babies and closest of all to monkeys and apes. He has evolved from insignificant, insect-eating ancestors in the geologically brief period of about 70 million years.

This was the period known to geologists and archaeologists as the Eocene period of the Tertiary era. Before it was the age of the great reptiles and dinosaurs, the Mesozoic era, which lasted about 225 million years. Earlier still, the Paleozoic era had lasted about 375 million years, right from the appearance of the earliest forms of animal life.

The first step was taken between 60 million and 70 million years ago, when small, shrew-like ancestors left the ground and took to hunting their insect prey among the leaves and branches of trees. They developed long, clinging fingers, large forward-facing eyes with sharp sight, and, perhaps, a long, balancing tail. Tree-shrews living today suggest what these early ancestors may have looked like. Modern lemurs and tarsiers, though not directly ancestral to man and far evolved along their own paths to specialization, indicate how the first primates may have appeared after several million years of tree-top life. Thirty to forty million years ago further enterprising groups of primates appeared, evolved from the lemur-like stock. The fossil record is far from complete, but these earliest anthropoids—direct ancestors of monkeys, apes and men—almost certainly had long, prehensile fingers, limbs freely jointed at hip and shoulder and a grasping tail which helped them to swing and leap through the tree-tops rather than crawl along the branches.

They probably resembled modern monkeys, with short, expressive faces, rounded rather than pointed lower jaws and square-cut molar teeth suitable for grinding a wide variety of foods.

Hominoids—which include only apes and men—branched from the primate stock 25 to 30 million years ago. At a time when the climate in many warm or temperate forested areas became cooler and drier, open grasslands gradually replaced the forests and several different kinds of mammals adapted to the new habitat. The earliest apes were monkeys that came down from the trees and took to living on the plains, much as baboons do today. They probably moved on all fours, perhaps running on hind legs but supporting their weight on the knuckles, occasionally standing upright to peer over the long grass.

Hominids—man and his immediate ancestors —are first identifiable as ape-like fossils four to five million years old. Though many names have been given to them, some authors place them all simply in the one genus *Australopithecus* (meaning southern ape). The earliest ones appear only in Africa. Small, lightly-built ape-men, they walked upright, and ate a variety of foods which probably included meat. They may well

have been hunters as well as gatherers of food, and lived in social bands. Later forms, better known from extensive deposits of fossil bones, had a humanoid hand with short opposable thumb, capable of gripping with power but not yet with the precision of a human hand. Their cranium was small, with a volume of up to 700 millilitres—about half that of modern man— and a low forehead with prominent brow ridges. Early ape-men broke stones to make simple tools; later ones made a range of tools from stone flakes and bones.

Man evolved from this condition to his present state over the last million years, a time-span known as the Pleistocene period. It covers the four glaciations of the Ice Age, the fluctuations of which were important in the development and migration of humans. During the first of the three glacial periods, ice covered Scandinavia, northern Germany and the Alps. Then the temperature rose and the ice retreated. It returned to cover much the same area three times more, with a long warm period of about 200,000 years between the second and third glaciations. During this time man developed steadily. The temperature during the fourth glaciation fluctuated comparatively frequently, but the ice finally retreated

during a warm period about 30,000 years ago.

The first large-brained hominid, *Homo erectus*, is known from Africa, China and Java in deposits under a million years old. This early kind of man, taller than *Australopithecus*, with a brain of 1,000 millilitres or more, seems to have spread widely and to have replaced the earlier ape-men completely. *Homo erectus* flourished during the second glaciation of the Ice Age, and was the first creature to have the truly human characteristics of firm and balanced upright stance, long legs and relatively short arms, the horseshoe-shaped array of teeth and the greatly developed skull. In *Homo erectus* the face is flattened, since the sense of smell and the need to pick things up with the teeth are no longer of prime importance to survival. The brain case is much larger than in any other branch of the hominids, and the mechanisms of symbolizing and complex vocal communication must have been established.

Homo erectus was replaced by a taller form with an even larger brain, *Homo sapiens*, which includes modern man. The earliest forms of *Homo sapiens*, including Swanscombe, Steinheim and Neanderthal man, are usually regarded as sub-species separate from each other and distinct from modern forms. They first appeared a quarter of a

million years ago, possibly slightly longer, and were unmistakably human. They made elaborate tools, hunted communally in bands (possibly using traps), cooked their food, and may have been cannibal; later forms made delicate arrowheads, chisels and knives from flint, buried their dead, drew and painted pictures, and lived in temporary or semi-permanent settlements. Modern man—our own sub-species of *Homo sapiens*—first appeared in Europe about 35,000 years ago, spreading rapidly to replace the other forms of man on all the habitable continents.

Anthropologists today distinguish three broad racial types of human being—Caucasoid, Negroid and Mongoloid—typified respectively by the peoples of Europe, West Africa and China. All other subdivisions of the human race are believed to be blends or fragments of these basic groups. Caucasoids vary considerably—from blond Nordic people, blue-eyed and pale-skinned—to dark-skinned Tamils and olive-skinned Mediterranean peoples. Negroids, brown or black of skin, and with thick lips and curly dark hair, originated in tropical Africa and spread to reach India, Papua, New Guinea and Australia. Mongoloids, with yellowish skin, sparse dark hair and slanting eyes, outnumber all other racial types.

The race for survival

Until about 10,000 years ago, the world population of human beings is unlikely to have exceeded 15 million. The men of the New Stone Age, who settled and began farming 8,000 to 10,000 years ago, probably created higher population densities in the fertile areas which they cultivated; the world population of humans may have reached 100 million or more. Civilization—the growth of cities, trading, law and social organization—brought further growth. About 1500 years ago, the world supported between 200 and 300 million people, a number which remained fairly steady over the centuries of pre-industrial civilization. From about 1500 AD population in the industrializing countries of Europe began to increase at a steadily accelerating rate.

At the present time the world's population is increasing by 50 million every year. Throughout the world, roughly 300,000 babies are born every day. Though the industrialized nations have in the past contributed hugely to human population growth, their present contribution is relatively small. Most of the increase is occurring now among the poorer nations—those whose resources and levels of social organization are least well equipped to cope with this tremendous problem.

In primitive populations with reasonable levels of prosperity, birth rates of thirty to forty per thousand head of population each year are not unusual. In the poorest populations living closest to subsistence level even higher rates are possible; only prolonged malnutrition seems to reduce fertility, though many infants born to underfed mothers die shortly after birth.

Medical science has reduced death rates substantially in all kinds of populations over the last three or four centuries. From the middle ages onwards, doctors and others concerned with the health of individuals and of the public at large have striven to heal the sick and stamp out the causes of illness and early death. They were conspicuously successful in the civilized countries, bringing under control plague, smallpox, diphtheria, tuberculosis, malaria, poliomyelitis, bronchitis and many other killing diseases, extending life expectancy by three decades or more, and reducing death rates to their present levels of nine or ten per thousand. They have also been successful in the under-developed countries, controlling many debilitating or fatal tropical diseases. Helped by agricultural experts, who have raised food productivity far above traditional subsistence levels, they have reduced death rates from above 30 to below 20 per thousand, extending life expectancy accordingly.

However, medical and agricultural success has left in its wake the problem of population—a small problem in rich countries, but a crippling problem in poor countries which are trying to develop their resources. In many developed countries, birth rates have fallen spontaneously during the last century, as more and more people have decided that small families are preferable to large ones, and contraceptives have become more readily available. For many of these favoured

communities, the birth rate now stands between eight and fifteen per thousand, usually only a little above the death rate. But birth rates have not fallen to the same degree in the underdeveloped countries, where many parents still feel the need for large families to help them prosper and insure against poverty in old age. There often remains a wide discrepancy between birth and death rates in the poorer countries, and their populations continue to rise at increasing rates.

Some governments have decided that it is not in the interests of their nation to reduce the rate of increase of their population; others have introduced campaigns to limit family size, trying with varying degrees of success to overcome traditional attitudes among their people. In the long term, prosperity itself seems to solve the problem; it is the prosperous nations alone which have reduced their birth rates and death rates to comparable levels and are keeping their rates of population growth within manageable bounds.

Body systems

The human body is a dazzlingly complex machine, an apparatus of intricate, interlocking systems, with millions of moving parts. But despite its complexity, its mechanisms function with inimitable efficiency and precision and its basic structure is relatively uncomplicated.

The body is composed of microscopic cells, more than fifty thousand million of them. Though the cells are chemically autonomous, groups of them function in concert as tissue to perform important tasks in the body. Muscles consist of rows and sheets of many millions of cells. The brain, spinal cord and peripheral nerves are networks of complex, interconnected cell tissue. Blood is tissue whose cells constitute a liquid. Covering (*epithelial*) tissues include skin, the lining of the gut, and membranes encasing internal organs. Tendons and ligaments are among the many categories of connective tissue.

Groups of tissues, congregated in a single functional body unit, form an organ. For example, the biceps muscle, a key organ of the arm, consists of muscle tissue, artery tissue, capillaries and veins, and strands of nerve tissue, banded together by connective tissue and encased in a tough tissue sheath. The stomach contains muscle tissues for churning food; it is lined with secretory tissue which produces mucus and digestive juices; it is held together by sturdy connective tissue; and it is controlled and serviced by nerve tissue and blood vessels.

The body systems are composed of organs serving a common function or purpose. The framework of the body, the structure which holds everything together, is the skeletal system, an edifice of articulated blocks and rods. The skeleton's bone and cartilage offer anchorage for muscles, provide leverage for mechanical efficiency, and serve as protective cages for internal organs. Equally vital is the linked system of connective tissue, including tendons, ligaments, and wrapping sheaths which link muscle to bone, hold bones in alignment, control movement at joints and keep organs in place.

Muscles are the body's motors, its instruments of motion and activity. They propel the body through its external environment and make possible the concerted internal interaction of bodily organs. There are three kinds of muscles, with different functions. Those which clothe the skeleton are *voluntary*, striated muscles which act under instruction from the central nervous system, though not always with our conscious knowledge. To move an arm or a leg is usually a deliberate decision; but we are usually unaware of the manipulation of many of the individual muscles involved in carrying out that decision. *Involuntary* smooth muscles are distributed throughout the body, working entirely beyond our awareness, controlling the diameter of arteries, the output of secretory glands, the focal length of the eye lens, and a vast catalogue of other vital unconscious functions. The third

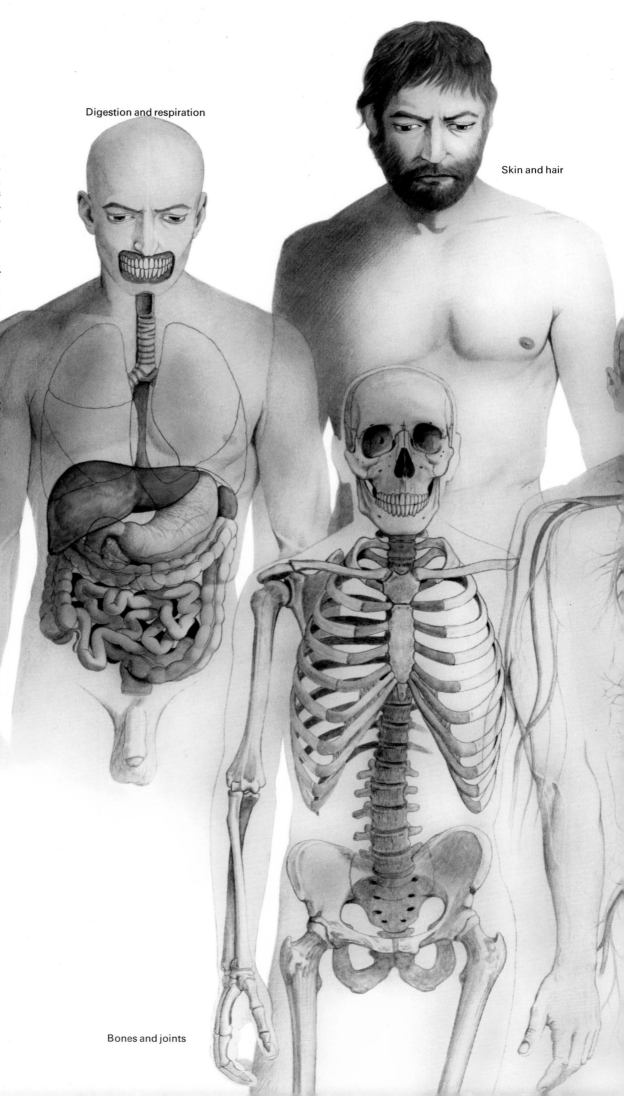

Digestion and respiration

Skin and hair

Bones and joints

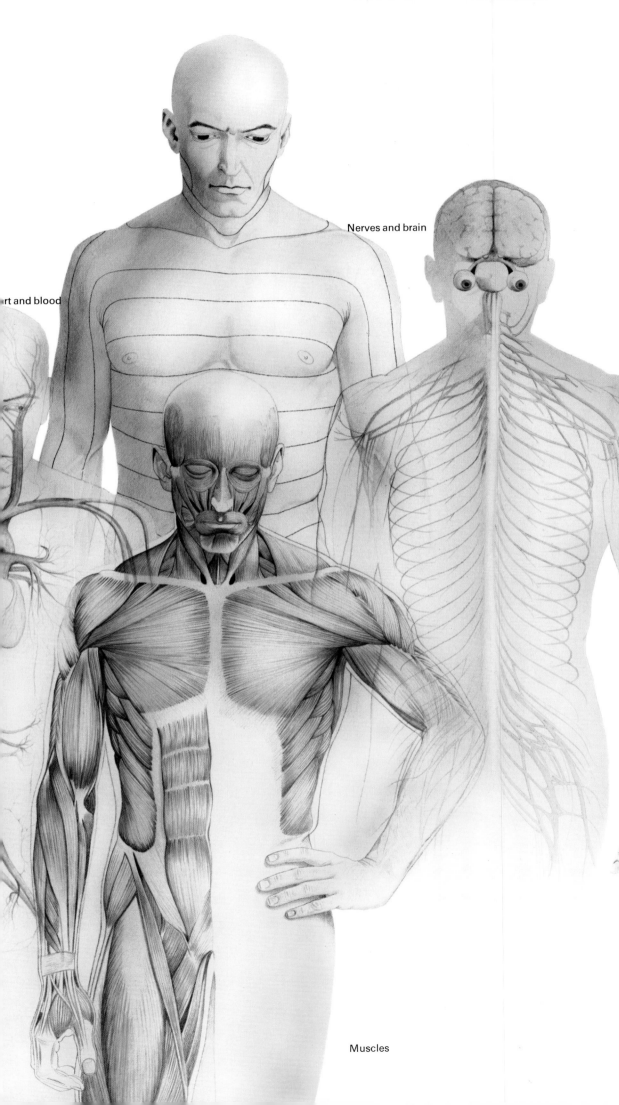

Nerves and brain

rt and blood

Muscles

category of muscle, *cardiac*, also *involuntary*, forms the substance of the heart.

The skin, the only organ system normally visible, is a tough, leathery container that guards the body against external injury, germs and other environmental dangers. It maintains a battery of nerve-end sensors that alert the body to touch, pressure, temperature change and other warning stimuli. The skin has a remarkable capacity for self-repair after damage and, through its small blood vessels and sweat gland pores, constitutes the body's most important instrument for cooling.

The digestive system, extending from the mouth to the anus, is the body's mechanism for sustenance, for absorbing nourishment. Equipped with cutting and grinding teeth, muscles for churning and pulverizing food particles, banks of cells producing digestive enzymes, the role of the digestive system is to distil nutrients from food intake and absorb them into the body for fuel. Each of its components—mouth, oesophagus, stomach, small intestine, colon and rectum—has its own special function in the processing of food.

The respiratory system deals with the air we breathe, breaking it down to supply oxygen to the body and to dispose of carbon dioxide. It includes the lungs and the windpipe (*trachea*). It also includes the rib-cage and diaphragm which alternately expand and contract, forcing air into and out of the lungs.

The body's circulatory system is a labyrinthine plexus of thousands of miles of tubes, most of them infinitesimal in width. This network, powered by the beating of the heart, conveys blood to all parts of the body. Aside from the heart, the major components of the circulatory system are arteries and arterioles, veins and venules. The tiny capillaries, less than a hair's-breadth wide, are woven among the tissues to carry blood to each individual cell. Liquid exuded from the capillaries bathes the cell walls with nutrients and oxygen and absorbs waste matter. This liquid collects in the lymphatic system and returns to the bloodstream for reconstitution.

The urinary system—kidneys, ureters, bladder and urethra—rid the body of waste matter. Kidneys serve as pressure filters which cleanse the blood through a process which isolates concentrated urine and dispatches purified blood back through the circulatory system.

Cells reproduce themselves continually, but the construction of new individuals is the task of the special reproductive system located in the pelvic region. Male and female produce reproductive cells which, when they meet in the female reproductive tract, fuse to form a single cell which then develops in the mother's body.

The co-ordinated functioning of the body as a whole is the responsibility of two elaborate control systems, the nervous system and the endocrine system. The nervous system includes the brain, spinal cord and nerve network which receives and responds to all pertinent internal or external stimuli requiring either conscious or unconscious response. The endocrine system operates through chemical messengers (*hormones*) produced by glands and released into the bloodstream to regulate the body's development, including growth and sexual maturity. Links between the nervous and endocrine systems retain and restore the body's equilibrium and performance capacity.

Cells and tissues

Though dozens of different kinds of cell make up the billions in the human body, all share a similar basic structure and conduct their business in strikingly similar ways. The outer wall of each cell is typically a delicate membrane seven to eight millionths of a millimetre thick, made up of a double layer of fat molecules sandwiched between two layers of protein. Flexible but firm, it is dotted with deep cavities and sometimes has finger-like villi, which increase its surface area and help to absorb nutrients selectively from the surrounding liquid. The cavities deepen and bud inwards, carrying nutrients in solution from the surface to every part of the cell; the villi wave, exposing a relatively large surface area for the absorption of molecules. Waste materials diffuse outwards into the surrounding fluid, where they are swept away to join the bloodstream for disposal through lungs, skin or kidneys.

The *nucleus* of the cell is densely packed with the genetic material *chromatin*, which organizes itself into chromosomes when the cell divides. The nucleus contains one or more *nucleoli*, centres which are responsible for the production of *ribosomes* and other forms of ribonucleic acid (RNA) which are involved in protein synthesis. Surrounding the nucleus is a thin membrane, perforated to allow constant interchange of materials between nucleus and *cytoplasm*, the jelly-like bulk of the cell.

The wall of the nucleus is arranged in extensive, irregular folds—the *endoplasmic reticulum*—lying within the mass of cytoplasm. These folds are dotted on the outer surface with thousands of ribosomes—tiny granular centres of chemical activity ten millionths of a millimetre in diameter. Ribosomes, which in many cells are also scattered throughout the cytoplasm, are made largely of RNA; they are the sites within the cell where proteins are manufactured from component amino acids. Some proteins are used within the cell; others are secreted by the cell as enzymes, hormones, and other products.

Golgi bodies are stacks of thin, flat, saucer-shaped sacs which originate as part of the endoplasmic reticulum. Their function is not entirely clear, but they seem to accept newly-created protein from neighbouring ribosomes and convert it to glycoprotein by the addition of carbohydrate molecules. Not surprisingly, the Golgi apparatus is especially prominent in cells which secrete mucus and other glycoprotein solutions. New products are accumulated in *microsomes*, small particles of the Golgi apparatus itself, and are expelled through the cell wall into the surrounding fluid.

Mitochondria are sausage-shaped organelles about three thousandths of a millimetre long, containing an elaborately folded membrane. The surface of the membrane appears to be covered with tiny stalked granules. All cells contain mitochondria, but they are most abundant in spermatozoa, muscle fibre, and other especially active

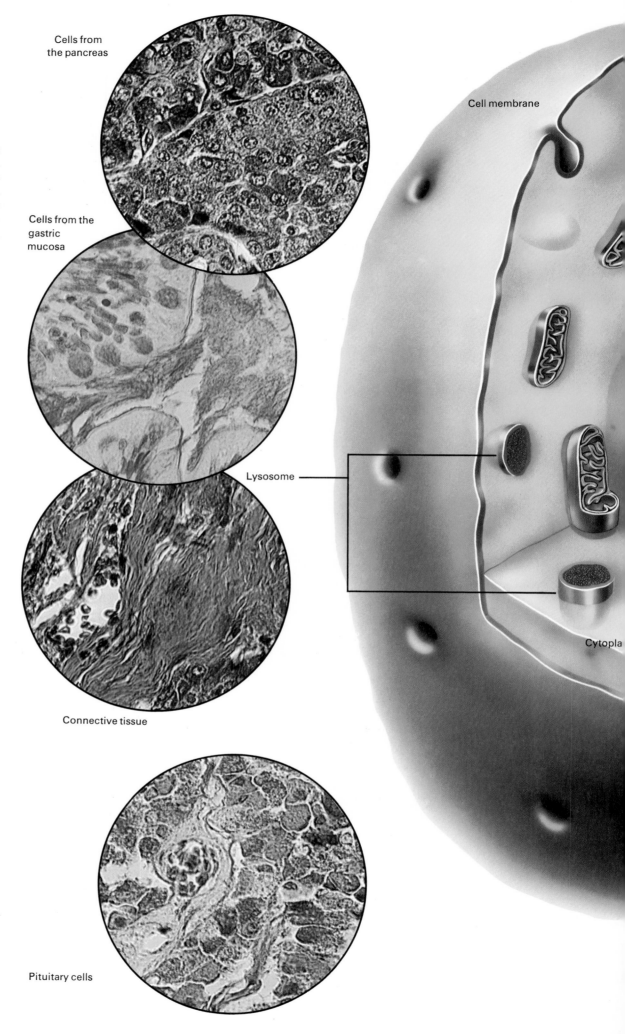

Cells from the pancreas

Cells from the gastric mucosa

Connective tissue

Pituitary cells

Cell membrane

Lysosome

Cytopla

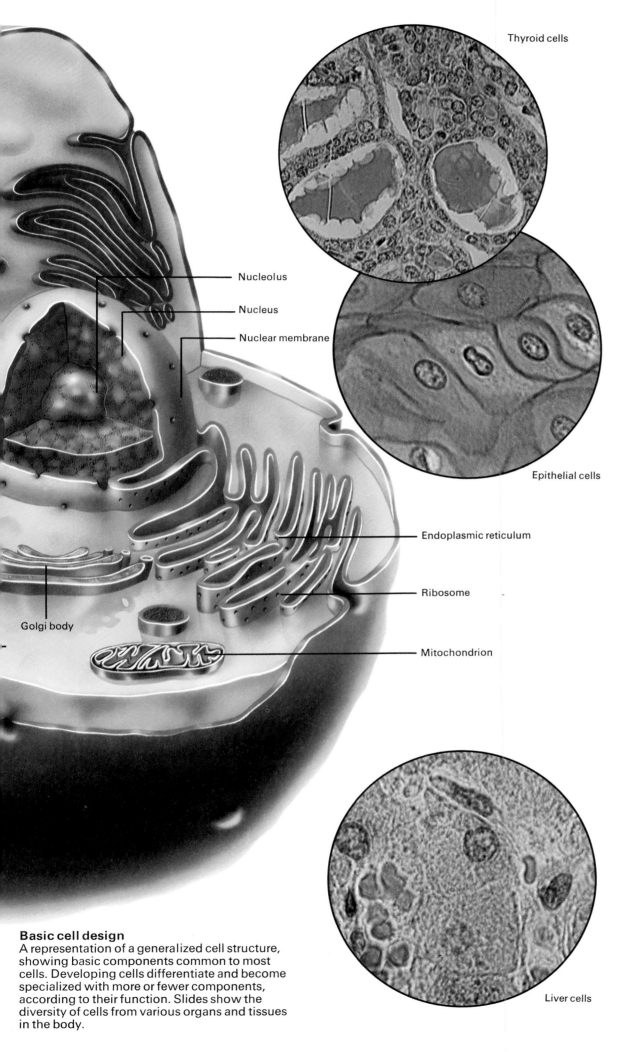

Thyroid cells

Nucleolus

Nucleus

Nuclear membrane

Endoplasmic reticulum

Ribosome

Golgi body

Mitochondrion

Epithelial cells

Liver cells

Basic cell design
A representation of a generalized cell structure,
showing basic components common to most
cells. Developing cells differentiate and become
specialized with more or fewer components,
according to their function. Slides show the
diversity of cells from various organs and tissues
in the body.

cells. They are the site of respiratory activity
within the cell.

Lysosomes are sacs of powerful digestive enzymes
which break down large molecules. The products
of this breakdown can then be used in chemical
processes by other parts of the cell. Cytoplasm
contains many other tiny organelles, including
fragments of protein, vacuoles of waste material
and mysterious tunnels and cavities of unknown
function. It also contains fat globules, crystals
and other chemical substances which contribute
to its granular or foamy appearance.

Tissues are groups of similar cells, combining
for a particular purpose. Usually their cells are
specialized in function, having surrendered some
of the characteristics of a generalized cell to take
on the special properties required for their
particular task.

Epithelial cells generally have the function of
covering surfaces, and vary in structure according
to where they are found. Those of the skin are
tightly-packed, box-shaped cells which form
layers, the outer layer presenting a resistant
covering which is constantly shed, and renewed
from underneath. By contrast, the cells of the
skin lining the mouth are soft and transparent,
forming a flexible membrane. Epithelial cells
covering the gut exude liquid which lubricates
all the internal surfaces and allows the organs to
move freely upon each other. Those lining the
stomach and duodenum secrete a range of
digestive enzymes which help to break up food,
and those lining the intestine absorb dissolved
nutrients. Cells lining the nasal cavity carry cilia
which, waving in unison, keep up a continuous
movement of the film of mucus secreted by
neighbouring cells.

Nerve cells, neurones, are perhaps the most
highly specialized of all the body's cells. They
consist of a cell body and one, two or many exten-
sions, dendrites and axons, which conduct signals
to or from the cell body. Nerve tissue consists of
many thousands of neurones organized in inter-
connecting lattice-works and extending into long
nerve fibres. Impulses which begin in receptor
organs or nerve endings, often in the skin or
muscles, travel along the fibres and are transmitted across the gaps or synapses between the
cells by chemical action. Muscle tissue has the
special ability of contraction. Individual cells,
muscle fibres, shorten when stimulated; arranged
in banks, they combine to cause powerful contractions which are the main motive power of the
body. Connective and skeletal tissues have a wide
range of important functions. Some produce
bone; others produce cartilage, the softer, more
resilient skeletal material which lines the joints
and supports the ears and nose; and yet others
produce the various protein threads which combine to make tendons, ligaments and sheets of
connective tissue.

Throughout the body as a whole, some three
hundred million cells are estimated to die every
minute, most of them to be replaced immediately
by the constant divisions of neighbours. Though
stained microscopic preparations and the detailed
photographs taken through an electron microscope give an impression that cells are fixed and
inert, in life they are constantly moving: cytoplasm streams and shifts, vacuoles circulate, grow
and explode through the cell wall, and the whole
cell pulsates with vitality.

Sight

Sight is one of the most precious, and remarkable, of all our senses. With it we are able to appreciate, not just what is happening in the immediate vicinity, but events many miles away—in fact many millions of miles away. Our eyes are highly specialized organs that respond to electromagnetic radiation of certain wavelengths—light—and turn its energy into meaningful images from which we can glean information.

Many simple animals possess light-receptor organs capable of distinguishing between light and dark, but the human eye also discriminates between wavelengths in the visible spectrum, giving us colour vision, and can adjust its focus for near and far vision. Because we have two receptors, with overlapping fields of vision, we have also the advantage of being able to estimate relative distances and see objects as three-dimensional realities.

The eye is a jelly-filled globe with an outer layer of tough, opaque fibrous material—the *sclera*, or "white" of the eye—embedded in a protective layer of fat and muscle within a forward-facing bony orbit in the skull. At the front of the eyeball is the *cornea*, a transparent window which bulges forward slightly. The cornea is covered with a thin, transparent, protective skin, the *conjunctiva*. This is in turn protected by the eyelids, which are operated by both voluntary and involuntary muscle. We can blink at will, but most of our blinking is a reflex action. A large lacrimal gland in the upper eyelid supplies a saline, bactericidal liquid which lubricates and helps to protect the conjunctiva. This drains into the inner corner of the eye, and through the naso-lacrimal, or tear duct, into the nasal cavity. Six small muscles move the eye in its socket; the two eyes move together in following a distant object, but may also converge or diverge to remain focused on objects which are approaching or receding.

Behind the cornea lies the *iris*, a thin, circular diaphragm of muscle coloured blue, green, grey, brown or a mixture of these colours, depending on the amount and dispersion of pigment present. A central hole, the pupil, lets light into the main chamber of the eye. The iris spreads and contracts under the direction of autonomic nerves, regulating the amount of light entering the eye; in bright light, the iris constricts, diminishing the size of the pupil to avoid glare and permit the sharpest possible focus; in dull light, the iris expands, dilating the pupil to admit as much light as possible.

Behind the pupil is the soft transparent lens, layered like an onion, and slung by suspensory ligaments from a ring of ciliary muscles which can be controlled by the autonomic nervous system. When the muscles tighten, the suspensory ligaments slacken, and the lens bulges, shortening its focal length. Constant adjustment of this system allows us to shift the focus of the eyes, so that we can see distant objects clearly one moment, and re-focus to see close objects equally sharply a second later. The front chamber of the eye is filled with a watery jelly (*aqueous humour*)

which, together with the cornea, forms an additional lens system. This lens cannot be adjusted. If it alters shape, which may happen during growth or with age, the adjustable lens within may compensate up to a point; thereafter we have to use additional, artificial lenses to make up for the deficiency. The main chamber of the eye is filled with a denser jelly (*vitreous humour*) under slight pressure, which contributes to the firmness and shape of the eye.

Lining the sclera is the *choroid*, a layer of blood vessels which bring nourishment to the structures inside the eye and carry away metabolic wastes. Within the choroid is the many-layered *retina*, with its all-important sensory cells to detect light and transform light energy into nervous impulses. The retinal cells (called *rods* and *cones*, because of their distinctive shapes) have black pigment underneath to prevent the scattering of light inside the eye, and above them the nerve cells that transmit impulses from the

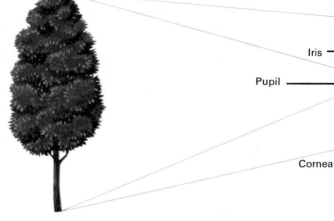

rods and cones to the brain. Light entering the eye is focused on the retina by the lens system. The retinal cells are stimulated, and signals from them are transmitted along each optic nerve back to the brain.

Retinal cells are minute and tightly packed; there are some 140 million rods and cones in each eye, with rods outnumbering cones by about fifteen to one. Both kinds of cell contain pigments which decompose as soon as light falls upon them, and re-form immediately with the help of enzymes and vitamin A. Rods contain *rhodopsin*, a reddish pigment (visual purple) which decomposes very readily, even in dull light, liberating energy which triggers off the cell and generates a nerve impulse.

Rods, which are most plentiful around the sides of the eye, are more sensitive than cones to dull light, but cannot distinguish one colour from another—in the late evening, we tend to see everything in tones of grey. Cones are of three kinds, containing different pigments which are sensitive to blue, red and green light. These work best in strong light and their varied sensitivities analyse light, between them conveying the whole colour range of the visible spectrum. Cones increase in density towards the back of the eye, and are particularly tightly packed in the area called the *fovea* or yellow spot. This is a small area of retina, diametrically opposite the pupil, which is especially discriminating, not only because it is packed with cones, but also because its cells are connected individually, rather than

in groups like most other other retinal cells, with nerve fibres to the brain. Both rods and cones are missing from the *blind spot*, the area of the retina on which nerve fibres and blood vessels converge to form the optic nerves, which leave from the back of the eye. The two optic nerves meet each other at the *optic chiasma*. About half the nerve fibres from each eye here cross over and join those of the other side, so that each side of the brain receives messages from both eyes through the *optic tracts* which the nerves now form. In the *visual cortex*, at the very back of the brain, the impulses are interpreted to give a three-dimensional visual sensation, helping us to respond both physically and aesthetically to our environment.

Ciliary body

Lens

Aqueous humour

Iris

Pupil

Cornea

Conjunctiva

Suspensory ligament attached here

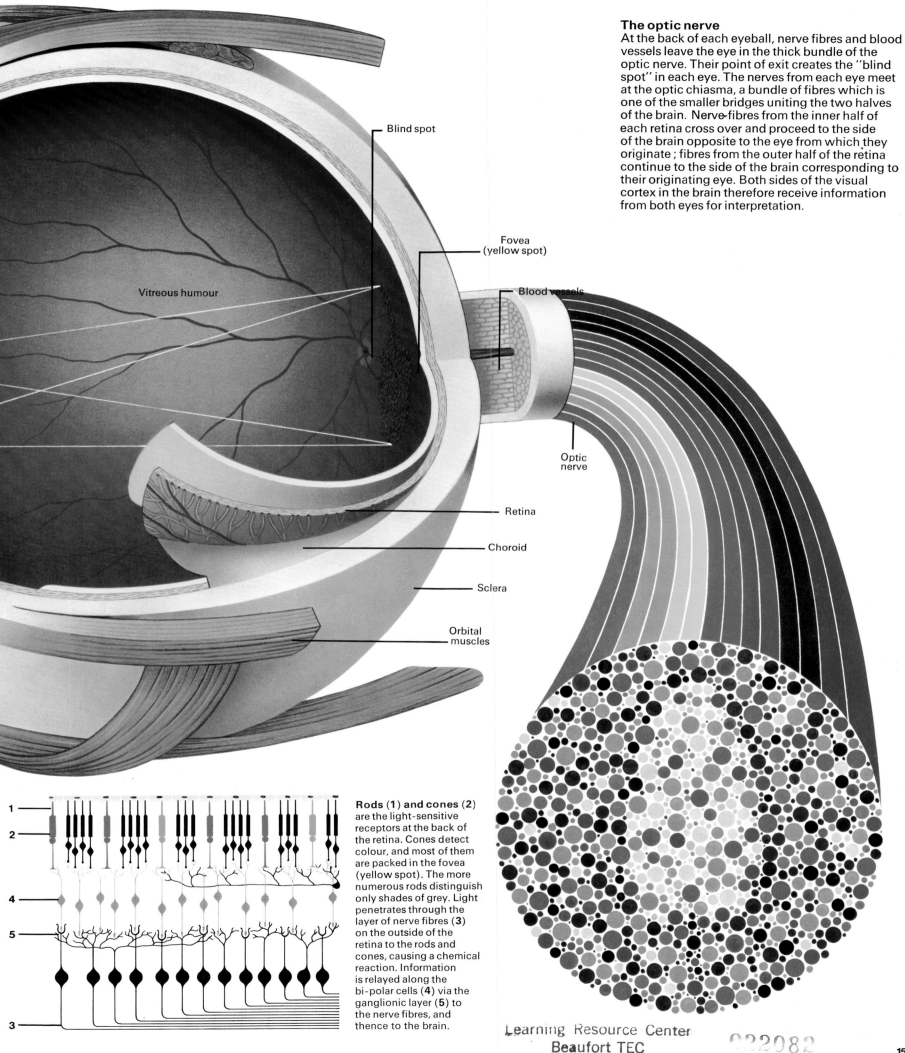

Blind spot

Vitreous humour

Fovea (yellow spot)

Blood vessels

Optic nerve

Retina

Choroid

Sclera

Orbital muscles

The optic nerve
At the back of each eyeball, nerve fibres and blood vessels leave the eye in the thick bundle of the optic nerve. Their point of exit creates the ''blind spot'' in each eye. The nerves from each eye meet at the optic chiasma, a bundle of fibres which is one of the smaller bridges uniting the two halves of the brain. Nerve-fibres from the inner half of each retina cross over and proceed to the side of the brain opposite to the eye from which they originate ; fibres from the outer half of the retina continue to the side of the brain corresponding to their originating eye. Both sides of the visual cortex in the brain therefore receive information from both eyes for interpretation.

Rods (1) and cones (2) are the light-sensitive receptors at the back of the retina. Cones detect colour, and most of them are packed in the fovea (yellow spot). The more numerous rods distinguish only shades of grey. Light penetrates through the layer of nerve fibres (3) on the outside of the retina to the rods and cones, causing a chemical reaction. Information is relayed along the bi-polar cells (4) via the ganglionic layer (5) to the nerve fibres, and thence to the brain.

Hearing and balance

The visible ear, a flap of skin-covered cartilage guarding the entrance to a narrow tube, is only the outer portion of a complex, convoluted, triple-purpose organ set deep in the side of the skull. To anatomists, the flap and the passage leading from it make up the *outer ear*. Within lie the hollow chamber of the *middle ear* and the coiled tubes and canals of the *inner ear*. Ears are organs of balance, posture and hearing, which detect and analyse air-borne vibrations.

We cannot hear vibrations lower in frequency than some 16 per second or higher than about 40,000 per second. But anything within that range can be picked up by our ears and, at least in youth, interpreted as sound by our brain. Sensitivity to the lower end of the scale remains constant throughout life. Beyond adolescence, sensitivity to the higher frequencies falls rapidly, the upper threshold dropping by half or more by middle age. We may be sensitive to very high frequencies, which we hear but cannot interpret. To very low frequencies we are relatively insensitive. In soft notes the amplitude of the vibrations is small, so that very little energy is available to trigger the mechanisms of the ear. Loud notes have greater wave amplitude and more energy, perhaps enough to bring pain or damage to our ears. Noise is a random, discordant combination of tones.

Sound waves falling on the outer ear are deflected into the auditory canal, which is protected by hairs and a wax secretion from the casual invasion of bacteria, insects and other potentially dangerous lodgers. The eardrum, a tough skin stretched across the inner end of the canal, vibrates in response to a wide range of frequencies. Its movements are transmitted across the chamber of the middle ear by three linked ossicles or tiny bones—the *malleus* (hammer), *incus* (anvil) and *stapes* (stirrup)— which are slung from the roof of the chamber by minute muscles and ligaments. During transmission through this lever system sound waves are intensified into shorter, more powerful vibrations. So the stapes, farthest from the eardrum, moves with the same frequency as the drum, but with a force more than 20 times greater. The flat footplate of the stapes, welded to a membrane across the opening of an oval window in the side of the chamber, transmits the vibrations to fluid filling the cochlea, in the inner ear.

The cochlea is a spiral chamber in the solid bone of the skull. From its central pillar a tapering, spiral shelf juts out into the chamber; from the edge of the shelf extends the complex basilar membrane, which divides the chamber into upper and lower galleries (the *scala vestibuli* and *scala tympani*), and carries along its full length a pressure-sensitive strip—the *organ of Corti*. Pressure waves pass through the fluid in the scala tympani to the basilar membrane, setting different areas vibrating according to their

frequency. High notes evoke vibrations towards the lower end, low notes towards the higher end. Wherever the membrane vibrates, it stimulates the sensitive cells of the organ of Corti to send signals along the auditory nerve to the brain. Over 30,000 separate fibres make up the auditory nerve—hence our remarkable ability to analyse sound into its component frequencies, and relay them separately to the brain. A round membrane-covered window in the wall between middle and inner ears bulges to absorb the pressure waves transmitted through the fluid.

Not all the sounds we hear enter via the outer and middle ears. Vibrations also reach the cochlea directly through the bones of the skull. If the middle ear is diseased, sounds can sometimes be diverted by a hearing aid to reach the inner ear through the bones in which it is embedded.

The inner ear also helps us maintain posture and balance. The three semicircular canals, set at right angles to each other, contain fluid which swirls when the head moves. Movement in a horizontal plane causes swirling in the horizontal canal; vertical movement causes swirling in both vertical canals, according to the direction of movement. The ampullae, small, flask-like chambers at the ends of the canals, contain tufts of fine hairs, the tips of which are embedded in a gelatinous capsule. Liquid swirling in the canals displaces the capsules and hairs, triggering signals in fine nerve-endings which weave among the hair roots. The utricule and saccule are two liquid-filled chambers, lined with epithelium,

which include many hair cells. Like the hairs of the ampullae, they are embedded in gelatinous material, which appears in this case to be weighted with *otoliths*—crystals of calcium carbonate. Any change in position of the head is recorded by a shift in distribution of the weight of the membrane, and picked up by nerve ends winding among the hairs. Thus the canals detect movement, the utricule and saccule record posture. Signals from their nerve endings pass down the vestibular nerve, which is made up of almost 20,000 fibres. This joins the cochlear nerve, leaving the ear as the auditory nerve. Fibres from the vestibular nerve pass to the vestibular nuclei of the cerebellum, where movements of eyes, limbs, and muscles of the neck and trunk are co-ordinated.

Auricle

Outer ear

Malleus

Tympanic membrane

(Eardrum)

The hearing pathway

Cortex

Auditory nerve

Middle ear

Eustachian tube

Pharynx

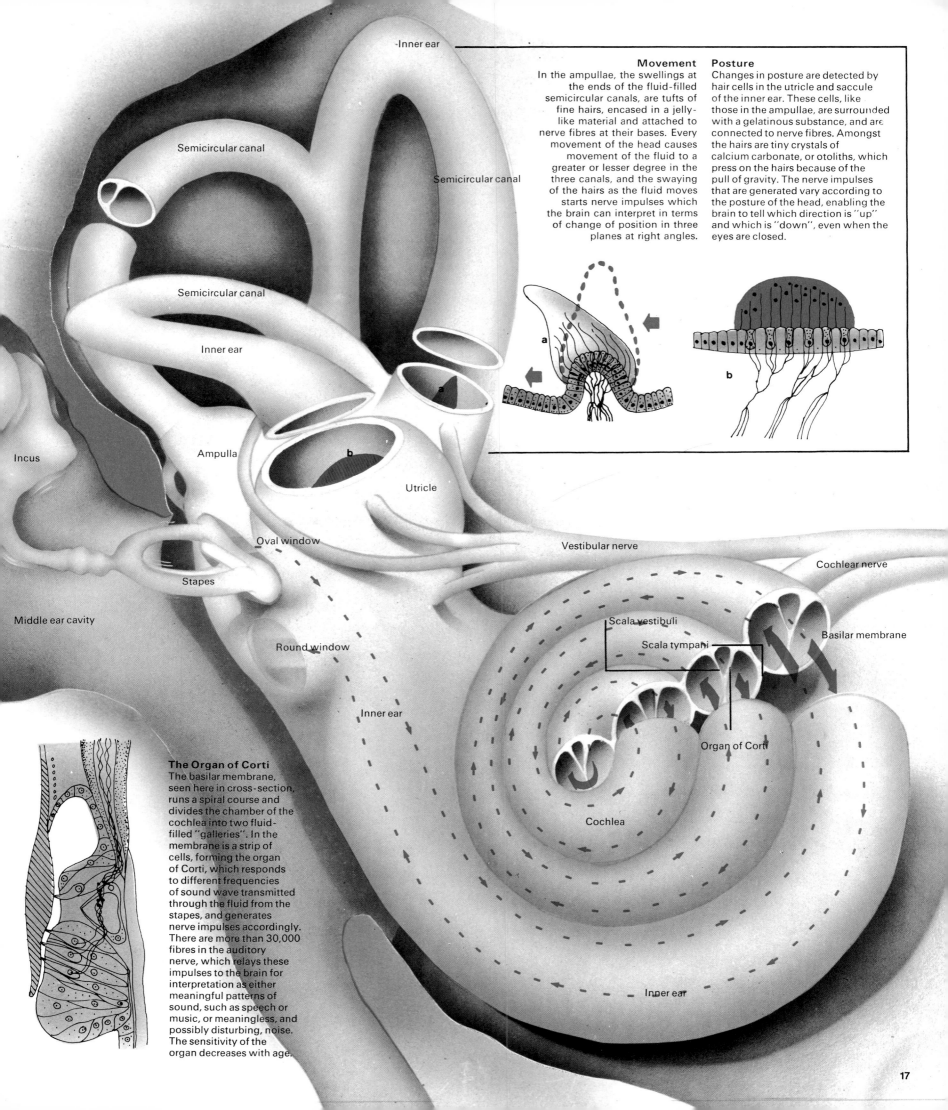

Semicircular canal

Semicircular canal

Semicircular canal

Inner ear

-Inner ear

Incus

Ampulla

a

b

Utricle

Oval window

Stapes

Round window

Middle ear cavity

Inner ear

Vestibular nerve

Cochlear nerve

Scala vestibuli

Scala tympani

Basilar membrane

Organ of Corti

Cochlea

Inner ear

Movement
In the ampullae, the swellings at the ends of the fluid-filled semicircular canals, are tufts of fine hairs, encased in a jelly-like material and attached to nerve fibres at their bases. Every movement of the head causes movement of the fluid to a greater or lesser degree in the three canals, and the swaying of the hairs as the fluid moves starts nerve impulses which the brain can interpret in terms of change of position in three planes at right angles.

Posture
Changes in posture are detected by hair cells in the utricle and saccule of the inner ear. These cells, like those in the ampullae, are surrounded with a gelatinous substance, and are connected to nerve fibres. Amongst the hairs are tiny crystals of calcium carbonate, or otoliths, which press on the hairs because of the pull of gravity. The nerve impulses that are generated vary according to the posture of the head, enabling the brain to tell which direction is "up" and which is "down", even when the eyes are closed.

a

b

The Organ of Corti
The basilar membrane, seen here in cross-section, runs a spiral course and divides the chamber of the cochlea into two fluid-filled "galleries". In the membrane is a strip of cells, forming the organ of Corti, which responds to different frequencies of sound wave transmitted through the fluid from the stapes, and generates nerve impulses accordingly. There are more than 30,000 fibres in the auditory nerve, which relays these impulses to the brain for interpretation as either meaningful patterns of sound, such as speech or music, or meaningless, and possibly disturbing, noise. The sensitivity of the organ decreases with age.

Smell and taste

Like sight and hearing, the senses of smell and taste form part of our environmental monitoring system, which samples the world about us and submits its reports to the brain. Smell and taste are chemical senses, separate but closely linked. They are perhaps the oldest and most primitive of our sensory systems, and their roles have varied considerably during our evolution. Bony fish, with whom we share ancestors, have chemo-receptor organs scattered all over their body, "smelling" and "tasting" the water in which they live. Air-breathing animals separated the two senses, housing them close together in the front cavities of the skull but drawing different information from them. The sense of smell, centred on two small patches of olfactory epithelium in the nasal cavity, detects air-borne odours from sources both far distant and close. The sense of taste, centred in the tongue, detects chemicals only in the mouth. The two senses are still closely interconnected; a foul smell can leave a nasty taste in the mouth, and enjoyment of food is a complex response to sensations from tongue, palate and nose.

The olfactory epithelia are housed in the roof of the nasal cavity, the narrow, lofty chamber of the nose. The floor of this cavity is the hard palate (roof of the mouth), its ceiling is the braincase, and into it protrude down-curving bony shelves (the *conchae* or turbinate bones) from the side walls. The whole cavity is lined with mucous membrane, a soft, warm skin well supplied with blood vessels. Glands in the skin secrete a film of mucus, the watery fluid which keeps internal surfaces of the cavity moist. Cilia—microscopic hairs growing from the epithelium—waft the mucus continually back towards the throat; sniffing and swallowing help it down the throat for disposal in the stomach.

Air drawn in through the nostrils is first filtered by a network of guard hairs, then warmed and partly cleansed by its passage over the sticky surfaces of the nasal cavity. Flowing back towards the lungs which are drawing it in, the air passes over the two small patches of sensory epithelium in the roof of the chamber. These are made up of many thousands of cells, most of which are grouped together in secretory glands, producing a dense, yellowish mucus. But scattered among them are the sensory cells, deeply embedded and linked to the surface by long rods which end in bundles of hairs. The hairs, and the cells surrounding them, have the truly remarkable capacity for discriminating between chemicals that dissolve in the layer of mucus—the sense of smell.

Taste receptors

The tongue has four kinds of taste receptor for the four fundamental taste sensations—acid (or sour), bitter, salt and sweet. The receptors are located in taste buds, mainly at the front, back and sides of the upper surface of the tongue. Sweet and salt are detected at the front, sour along the sides, and bitter at the back.

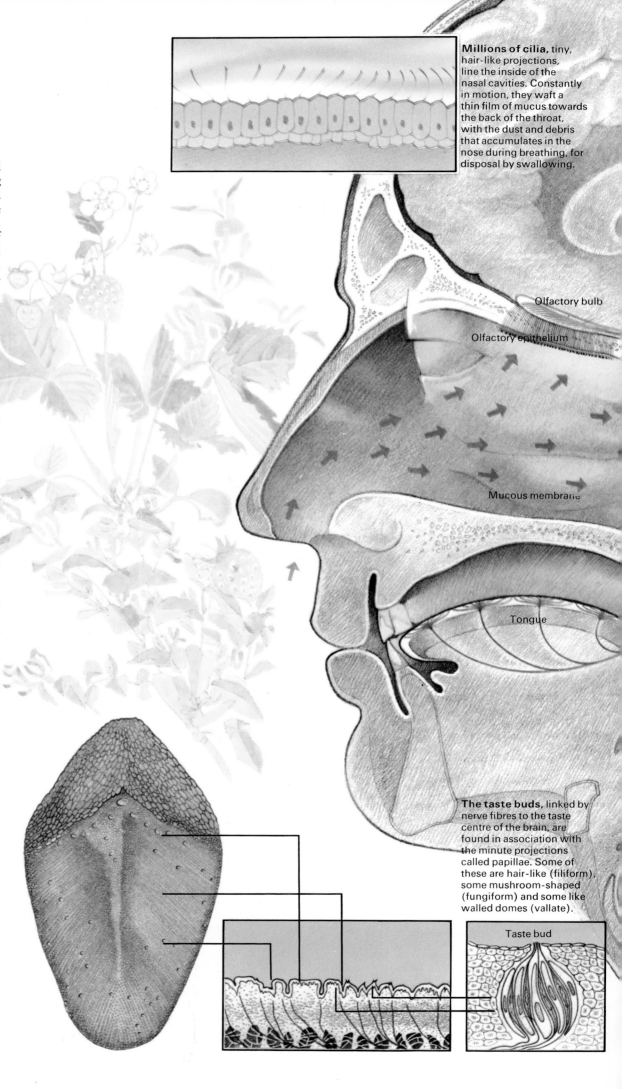

Millions of cilia, tiny, hair-like projections, line the inside of the nasal cavities. Constantly in motion, they waft a thin film of mucus towards the back of the throat, with the dust and debris that accumulates in the nose during breathing, for disposal by swallowing.

Olfactory bulb

Olfactory epithelium

Mucous membrane

Tongue

The taste buds, linked by nerve fibres to the taste centre of the brain, are found in association with the minute projections called papillae. Some of these are hair-like (filiform), some mushroom-shaped (fungiform) and some like walled domes (vallate).

Taste bud

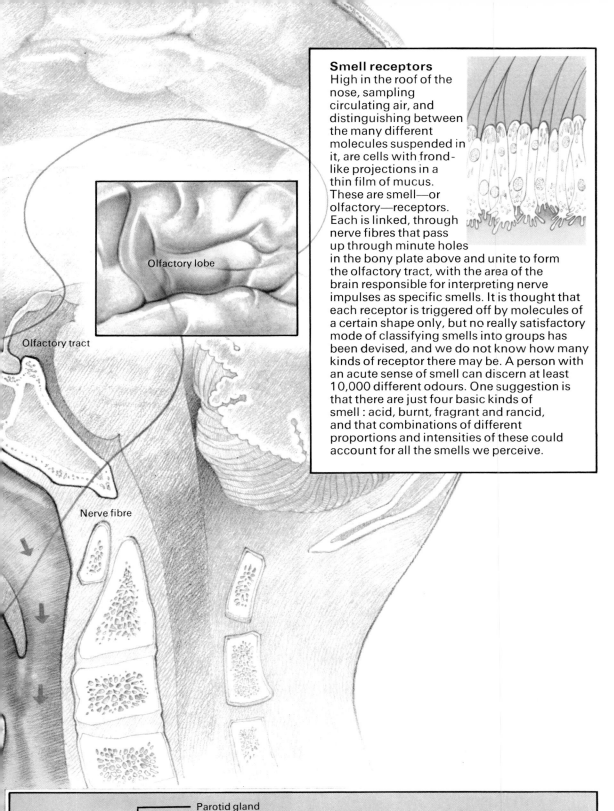

Smell receptors

High in the roof of the nose, sampling circulating air, and distinguishing between the many different molecules suspended in it, are cells with frond-like projections in a thin film of mucus. These are smell—or olfactory—receptors. Each is linked, through nerve fibres that pass up through minute holes in the bony plate above and unite to form the olfactory tract, with the area of the brain responsible for interpreting nerve impulses as specific smells. It is thought that each receptor is triggered off by molecules of a certain shape only, but no really satisfactory mode of classifying smells into groups has been devised, and we do not know how many kinds of receptor there may be. A person with an acute sense of smell can discern at least 10,000 different odours. One suggestion is that there are just four basic kinds of smell : acid, burnt, fragrant and rancid, and that combinations of different proportions and intensities of these could account for all the smells we perceive.

Olfactory lobe

Olfactory tract

Nerve fibre

Mixed sensations

Parotid gland

Our senses of taste and smell are closely, and sometimes confusingly, interlinked. In a hungry person the smell and sight of food produces a flow of saliva from the salivary glands. When food is taken into the mouth, further stimulation is given by its chemical components as they dissolve and trigger the taste buds (insoluble substances cannot be tasted). But at the same time the smell sensation is reinforced when odours rise from the mouth into the nasal cavity. What is interpreted by the brain as taste may in fact be smell. Only when a cold or hayfever blocks olfactory sensation do we realize how much the "taste" of food is really its smell. Even a wine "taster" relies far more upon olfactory receptors than on taste buds.

Sublingual gland
Submandibular gland

How the system works is not known. It seems probable that molecules of chemical vapour carried in the airstream are deposited on the mucus and in some way sensitize the hairs; these communicate with the cell body beneath them, which initiates an impulse in associated nerve fibres. The fibres pass from the olfactory membrane through the floor of the cranium to the olfactory bulbs, which link directly with a reception centre in the brain.

Compared with many other kinds of animals, our sense of smell is poorly developed. We cannot even imagine the olfactory sensations of a trained tracker dog, which is capable of following the invisible trail of a fugitive over miles of rough ground, or of a male moth scenting a female of the same species several hundred metres away upwind. In developing acute vision, hearing and the elaborate apparatus of our forebrain we lost some of the need for chemoreception, and parts of our brain which were once associated with scent are now put to other, more important uses. Yet our sensitivity to many organic odours is still remarkable; some we can detect and identify in minute concentrations, perhaps from the stimulus of only a few individual molecules.

Comparatively speaking, our sensitivity to flavours is poor and curiously undiscriminating. Taste receptors are groups of minute, sausage-shaped cells—taste buds—which are clustered on the papillae of the tongue, and to a lesser extent on other surfaces of the mouth. The receptor cells, stimulated by contact with chemicals in solution, cause signals to be transmitted to the brain along two of the twelve pairs of cranial nerves—a pathway completely different from the signals triggered by odours. Taste receptor cells distinguish only four "flavours"—sweet, salt, acid and bitter. Different kinds of cells are involved, and they are distributed patchily over the tongue, making different parts especially sensitive to different flavours.

Food would be dull indeed if our enjoyment of it depended only on stimuli received from the tongue. Normally we are stimulated first by its aroma, received through our nostrils. Then we receive further olfactory stimulus while the food is being chewed, so that much of what we regard as taste is in fact smell. We are reduced to tasting alone when hay fever or a bad cold swells the mucous membranes of the nasal cavity, putting the olfactory epithelia out of action. Then the true tastelessness of food becomes apparent, and we realize how closely the two senses are linked in normal life. Apart from its chemical sensitivity, the tongue is also sensitive to heat, cold, pressure and irritants (e.g. pepper and other strong condiments).

Because stimuli from the tongue pass along cranial nerves to the hindbrain and are only indirectly involved in the higher brain centres, taste plays little part in our lives except in direct relation to food. Stimuli from the olfactory mucosa by contrast feed through the olfactory lobes into the forebrain—effectively into the centre of the elaborate computer which associates and assimilates stimuli from all over our body, and accommodates thought processes, reasoning and memory. So odours play an important part in our lives, blending with other sensations and helping us to remember events, feelings and emotions which might otherwise be forgotten.

Skin and hair

Your skin is the largest organ in your body. Tough, flexible and self-replacing, it has a total area of more than one and a half square metres and weighs nearly twice as much as the brain. The thinnest skin, of the eyelids and penis, is only half a millimetre thick; the thickest, under the feet, may be more than 5mm in depth and even thicker in protective corns or callouses. The skin's first responsibility is to protect the body from damage and the invasion of parasites. It is also waterproof, an important sensory organ, has a range of secretory and excretory functions, and plays a key role in stabilizing body temperature.

The two main layers of skin, the thin *epidermis* and the thicker underlying *dermis*, fit tightly together at a corrugated peg-and-socket interface. Pinch the skin on the back of your hand and you lift both layers. The dermis is connected loosely to underlying muscles with elastic fibres. Skin itself stretches only slightly, but can readily be distorted and pulled into different shapes, recovering when the tension is removed. Young people have a snug-fitting skin, but in old age the skin sags and wrinkles as the fibres lose their elasticity. The subdermal space, between the skin and muscle, contains fluid and fat cells, which serve as food stores, insulate the body, and round off body contours.

In the epidermis, some five different cell layers can be distinguished; cells at the bottom gradually rise to replace those lost from the surface. The *stratum basale*, or Malpighian layer, is made of tightly packed, actively growing cylindrical cells, firmly fixed to the upper surface of the dermis. By constant division, they provide a steady supply of new cells, forming the *stratum spinosum*, five to ten cells thick. As these are pushed up from the dermis, and so away from the supply of blood and nutrients, they gradually fill with granules of protein waste and die, forming first the *stratum granulosum*, later the clear, almost transparent *stratum lucidum* and finally, flattened and loaded with keratin (the tough protein of hair, horn and nails), a thick, dead, impervious layer, the *stratum corneum*. Dead skin cells are rubbed or washed away in flakes from the surface all the time.

The colour of the skin and hair is decided by how much *melanin* they contain. Melanin is a dark pigment laid down in fine granules, in greater or lesser quantities, within the epidermis and in the hair. Dark skins have a great deal, fair skins only a little. Strong sunlight stimulates the skin to produce more melanin, and the tan that results gives some protection against harmful ultraviolet rays. Tanned skin is also thicker than normal skin.

Built around a network of tough protein fibres, the dermis gives the skin its bulk, pliability and tensile strength. It is well supplied with blood, and has numerous nerve endings, glands and hair follicles (which are actually epidermal cells) embedded in it.

(1) Epidermis, the tough waterproof and germproof outer skin made up of densely packed layers of specialized cells. Millions of dead, horny cells are shed and worn away from the surface every day, making way for growing cells pushing up from layers beneath.

(2) Dermis, the fibrous, flexible, deeper skin layer, packed with blood vessels and nerves. The whorls and lines of fingerprints are due to ridges in the dermis.
(3) Fat stored below the dermis insulates and pads the body.

(4) Blood vessels bring fuel and oxygen and remove wastes.
(5, 6, 7, 8) The four types of **sensory receptor.**
(9) Hair growing from follicle.
(10) An associated **sebaceous gland,** which secretes oily sebum to lubricate both hair and skin.

(11) Sweat glands excrete water, salt and waste materials through tiny ducts opening on the surface as pores **(12).** Evaporation of sweat cools the skin.

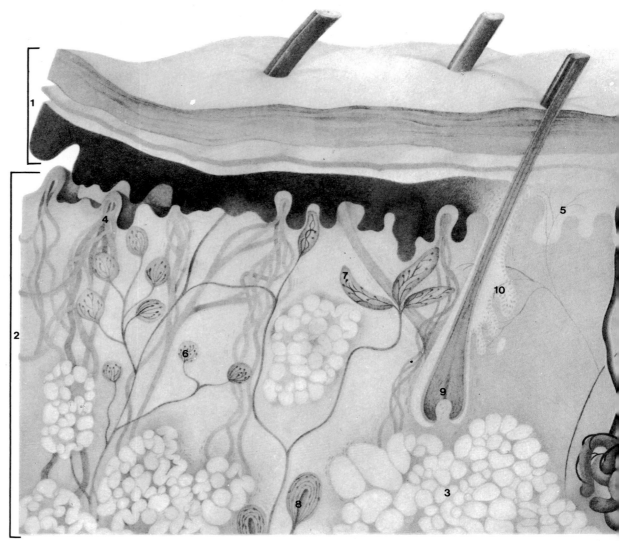

The finest branches of the blood vessels—capillaries—fill the corrugations and dome-shaped papillae immediately below the epidermis. They provide nourishment for the growing skin, and are also important in heat regulation. When they are expanded, blood flows freely through them, and the skin blushes and warms, giving out heat. When they are constricted, blood bypasses them, flowing through deeper, wider vessels. Pallid and cold, the skin then loses little heat.

Hair grows from follicles, tubelike growths of cells with a bud-like papilla at the base, supplied with blood vessels and nerves. A tube of dead keratin is pushed up from this "root" to form the hair shaft. Hair colour depends upon the amount of the pigment melanin it contains (and, in red hair, another pigment); in old age less pigment is formed, and minute bubbles of air give a grey or white appearance. Tiny muscles attached to the hair follicles are capable of erecting each hair. The autonomic nerve system is in control of this response to cold or alarm—

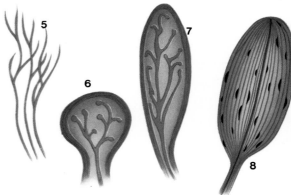

Sensations in the skin
Four kinds of sensory receptor are distributed through the skin. Some are bare nerve endings; some are cocooned in corpuscular envelopes.
(5) Naked nerve endings sensitive to light pressure and pain.

(6) Bulbous corpuscles sensitive to cold.
(7) Oval corpuscles sensitive to warmth or touch.
(8) Lamellated corpuscles sensitive to pressure. Excessive stimulation of any receptor will be sensed as pain.

Hair is made of keratin, a protein produced and pushed outwards by special cells grouped to form a sac or follicle. At the base lies the hair root, living cells supplied with nerves and blood vessels. The keratin forms a fine but tough shaft, with an inner layer or medulla, and an outer, scaly cortex. Different parts of the body produce distinctive kinds of hair. Pubic and armpit hair is coarser than scalp hair. Eyebrows and eyelashes are short, curved and tapered. Body hair varies greatly in distribution and texture from person to person. Hair colour depends upon the amount of pigment, mainly melanin, dispersed in the keratin. In old age minute air bubbles in the hair shaft make hair grey.

Skin colour depends upon the pigment melanin, laid down by special epidermal cells, densely in brown skins, sparsely in white. Albinos have none. Patchy distribution gives freckles and moles. Sunlight boosts melanin production, giving a protective tan.

"gooseflesh" and a prickling sensation in human beings are the equivalent of a bird fluffing out its feathers, or a cat's fur standing on end.

Numerous nerve endings are found in the skin, giving sensitivity to temperature, pain and touch, and to pressure. There are free nerve endings, and others with endings in the shape of bulbs and corpuscles or capsules. Most of the specialized nerve endings accommodate rapidly to repeated or constant stimulation by "switching off"; we feel our clothes in the morning when we first put them on, but soon ignore them.

Several kinds of gland are found in the dermis, liberating their products on to the skin surface. *Sebaceous glands* in the sides of hair follicles produce an oily secretion, *sebum*, which greases the hair and surrounding skin. *Sweat glands* are of two kinds. *Eccrine* glands, widely distributed, produce the dilute salt solution that pours from us in the hot sun. Sweat has an important cooling function, but is also a means of excreting small quantities of urea and lactic acid, which are waste products. *Apocrine* glands are concentrated in the armpit, anal and genital regions; they produce a much thicker secretion, especially when stimulated by adrenaline in the blood.

Skin secretions help to keep the skin supple, and, by absorbing some radiation, help to prevent sunburn. They provide a medium in which many different bacteria can grow. Fortunately, most of these are harmless, and their presence may actively discourage other, more harmful, bacteria, which might otherwise cause infection.

The breast, which stays rudimentary in the male, is a collection of special secretory glands deep within the skin, and protected by fatty tissues. Each gland is made of lobes, and secretes milk when active after childbirth. This is collected by a network of lactiferous sinuses and taken to the nipple. Sebaceous glands to lubricate the nipple are found in the surrounding areola, and are seen as tiny swellings. The areola darkens during pregnancy, and remains pigmented in women who have borne children.

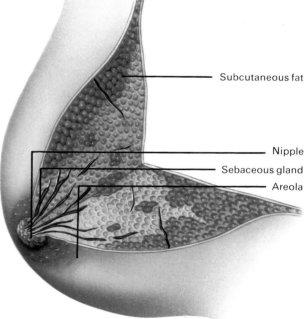

Subcutaneous fat

Nipple

Sebaceous gland

Areola

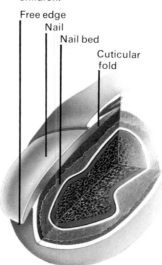

Free edge
Nail
Nail bed
Cuticular fold

Nails, at the ends of fingers and toes, are made of keratin, and give a protective, and useful, covering for the end of each digit. The crescent of paler colour is due to the presence of air in the developing transparent plate, which is laid down upon the epidermis by special germinative cells in an infolding from the surface at the nail root.

Bones

Within your body lies the mobile supporting framework that is your skeleton, vastly different in life from the assortment of dry, rattling bones that you might see in a museum. Bone, although hard, is a living, growing and continually changing material. It is just one of the tough tissues that together support and shape your body, protect its vital organs, and enable muscles to produce movement. Blocks, struts and jointed, lever-like rods of bone form a dynamic scaffolding, clothed in, and moved by, muscle.

Integrated with the bony skeleton, and equally important, are *connective tissues*; strong and supple *ligaments* link bone to bone, springy *cartilage* lines and cushions the joints where bones meet, and fibrous, inelastic *tendons* (sinews) are cables attaching muscles to the levers that they move. Connective tissues of different types are found throughout the whole body, within and enclosing organs. All assist the skeleton in maintaining the body's shape.

The hardness of bone is due to its high mineral content. Minute crystals of a special form of calcium phosphate called calcium hydroxyapatite, calcium carbonate and fluoride, and some magnesium chloride, are arranged layer upon layer within a regular meshwork, or matrix, of strong, pliable protein threads. If a long bone is soaked in acid, so that the minerals are dissolved away, the remaining protein framework is so pliable that it can be tied in a knot. If, on the other hand, a bone is heated strongly, destroying the protein, the remaining mineral structure is rigid and brittle. The combination of these qualities gives living bone its unique nature. It has strength and rigidity, with resilience and the ability to withstand bending and crushing forces. Most of the bones in your body began as rods or blocks of cartilage, the tough, elastic tissue that forms a temporary skeleton for the foetus developing in the womb. Some, notably those forming the roof and walls of the skull, began as sheets of membrane. During growth, bone-producing cells called *osteoblasts* invade the tissues and lay down mineral—the process called *ossification*. Crystalline plates are built up into thick-walled tunnels of bone, in the centre of which run blood vessels supplying nutrients to the tissues through their many fine branches. Osteoblasts wall themselves in as they deposit bone about them, and become immobile; they maintain contact with their neighbours through tiny canals in the bone. At this stage they are called *osteocytes*, or simply bone cells.

Growing bones retain bands of cartilage near their ends, separating, in long bones, the shaft or *diaphysis* from the cap-like *epiphyses*. Here growth can take place without interfering with joint movement. Growth ceases in the late teens or early twenties, when the cartilage ossifies, and the epiphyses fuse with the diaphysis.

The skull is a thin, bony vault, housing and protecting the all-important brain, the sense organs of the head, and the entrances to the respiratory and digestive systems. The portion that encloses the brain is called the *neurocranium*.

The bones of the skeleton

Traditionally there are said to be 206 different bones making up the human skeleton. In fact, there may be more or less; individuals vary. Some people are born with an extra vertebra, and some with extra toes or fingers, and sometimes small extra bones develop in soft tissues subjected to pressure or wear. Again, some bones fuse during growth—the sacrum could be looked on as either one bone, or five vertebrae. The "normal" complement is a matter of opinion.

Largest of the body's bones is the femur, or thigh bone; smallest are the tiny ossicles of the middle ear, carrying sound waves to the inner ear from the eardrum.

The bones form a living, working foundation for the body. Their main function is to support muscles, giving them anchors to pull against and levers to magnify their movements. But the skeleton is also protective, encasing the central nervous system in bony blocks, and heart and lungs in a bony cage. The bones are also important for the storage of minerals, particularly calcium and phosphorus. These stores are constantly "quarried" for use in tissues elsewhere in the body, and to maintain correct chemical balance.

At the front are the bony cavities that contain the eyes—the orbits—and suspended below, held in place by ligaments and the powerful muscles of mastication, is the *mandible*, or lower jaw. Below the orbits in front are the bones that form the upper jaw, or *maxilla*. The skull is lightened by the presence of air-filled cavities within some of its bones. Largest of these *sinuses* are the maxillary sinuses, within the cheekbones.

Supporting the skull, and the arms and legs (the *appendicular skeleton*), is the central *axial skeleton*. The spine is made up of thirty-four *vertebrae* (seven in the neck, twelve in the thorax, five forming the small of the back, five in the sacrum and five forming the tail, or coccyx, at the end of the spine). The spine is a flexible column with a double bend, supporting, at the *pectoral girdle*, or shoulder framework, the weight of the arms. Below the pectoral girdle is the rib cage, enclosing and protecting the heart and lungs, and forming an attachment for the muscles and ligaments of the abdominal wall. Below, the spine meets the other bones of the *pelvic girdle*, which transmits the body's weight to the legs.

Discs of fibrocartilage separate the vertebrae, allowing them to move slightly upon one another, and strong ligaments bind them to maintain the strength of the column. The spinal cord—the main cable of the central nervous system—occupies a canal formed by the bony arches at the backs of the vertebrae, and is further protected by surrounding muscle masses and spinal ligaments.

The pectoral girdle comprises paired *clavicles* (collar bones), and paired *scapulae* (shoulder blades). It fits loosely over the ribcage, with joints with the *sternum* (breastbone) at the front. The head of the *humerus* (upper arm bone) fits into

The atlas and axis
Supporting the skull on the spine is the first vertebra, or atlas, at a joint that allows nodding movements. The atlas has a socket into which a peg from the second vertebra, or axis, fits, allowing tilting and rotation between the two bones.

a shallow socket on the scapula, allowing wide movements of the arms at the shoulder joint. The clavicles act as struts to prop the shoulders back.

The pelvic girdle is a more massive framework, formed of three bones, the *ilium*, *ischium* and *pubis*, on each side, joined firmly to the fused sacral vertebrae. The two pubic bones arch round to meet in front, so that the pelvis forms a basin to support the intestines and other internal organs. The flanges of the ilium form attachments for the major leg muscles, and the head of the femur is bound firmly into a cup-shaped cavity at the junction of the three bones on each side, the *acetabulum*.

Arms and legs, hands and feet, are built to similar specifications. A single, sturdy upper limb bone (*humerus*, *femur*) forms a lever for thinner, parallel bones (*radius* and *ulna* in the forearm, *tibia* and *fibula* in the lower leg) which, because they can twist around each other, allow hand and foot a considerable degree of rotation. Wrist and ankle, fingers and toes, are made up of equivalent bony elements. Boxlike *carpals* in the wrist, and *tarsals* in the foot give attachment to *metacarpals* and *metatarsals*, and through them to the thinner *phalanges* of the fingers and toes.

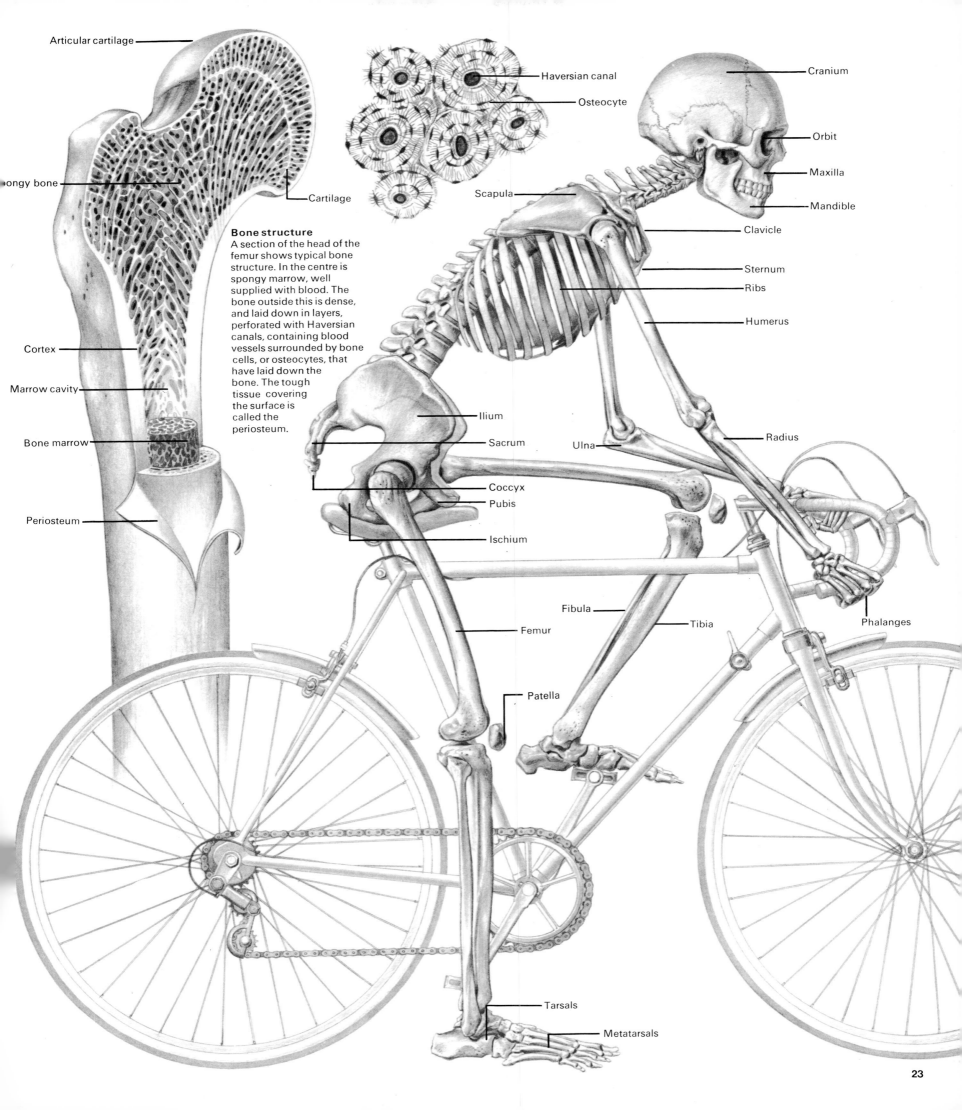

Articular cartilage

Haversian canal

Osteocyte

Cranium

Orbit

Maxilla

Mandible

Spongy bone

Cartilage

Scapula

Clavicle

Sternum

Ribs

Bone structure
A section of the head of the femur shows typical bone structure. In the centre is spongy marrow, well supplied with blood. The bone outside this is dense, and laid down in layers, perforated with Haversian canals, containing blood vessels surrounded by bone cells, or osteocytes, that have laid down the bone. The tough tissue covering the surface is called the periosteum.

Humerus

Cortex

Marrow cavity

Bone marrow

Radius

Ilium

Ulna

Periosteum

Sacrum

Coccyx

Pubis

Ischium

Fibula

Tibia

Phalanges

Femur

Patella

Tarsals

Metatarsals

Joints

Wherever in the body one bone meets another, there is a joint. The joints are of many different patterns, and each allows a range of movements suiting it to a particular function. At some joints there is in fact no movement at all, while at the other end of the scale are joints where movement is so free that they are virtually universal joints.

Engineers would recognize in the skeleton typical joint types—hinges, pivots and ball-and-socket joints—and perhaps envy the qualities of the bearing surfaces, and the lubricants which keep them working, constantly and efficiently, for decade after decade. Many of the body's joints are more complex, and permit movement in more planes, than their equivalents in the world of engineering. Nevertheless, by imitating these structures in metal and plastic, biomedical engineers can now make acceptable substitutes, for the replacement of living joints which have been irreparably damaged by accident or disease. Cartilage, tough and springier than mineral-filled bone, plays a vital part in joint function. Most of the bones in the body begin as cartilage, which becomes ossified as growth proceeds. At the ends of the bones, however, where they meet and articulate with others, the cartilage remains unossified. In joints where there is relatively little movement, as between the bodies of the vertebrae (except between the atlas and axis in the neck) and between the pubic bones meeting at the front of the pelvis, pads of cartilage unite bone directly with bone. Such joints are known as *cartilaginous joints*. Between the bony plates of the skull, formed by the ossification of membranes, and dovetailed together, there is virtually no movement. Fibrous tissue knits the bone edges into tight *sutures*. These are *fibrous joints*.

Freely movable joints have a complicated structure, because of the extra problems posed by mobility. Where there is movement between two bones there is friction, and if the joint is also weight-bearing, then there are the added stresses and strains caused by the jolting movements of walking, running, jumping or climbing stairs. Each bone has its own cap of cartilage, covering the bearing surface and acting as a buffer. This is *articular cartilage*; it bears the brunt of the wear and tear in joints, and its surface is constantly replaced.

For continuing efficiency, any joint needs to be lubricated to reduce friction. In the freely movable joints of the body the lubricant is a fluid, runny like thin syrup, called *synovial fluid*. The fluid is secreted by a membrane, the *synovial membrane*, which encloses the joint and is attached to each bone where the cartilage caps it. The synovial membrane is the lining of the joint capsule. Outside it are ligaments, strengthening, protecting and stabilizing the joint, and the tendons of the muscles that move its bones. Pads of fatty tissue give added protection, and in large joints, such as the knee, sacs of fluid called *bursae* cushion the structures and facilitate the movement of one tissue against another. The swelling of the joint in "housemaid's knee" is due to inflammaton of bursae at the kneecap.

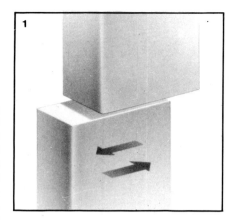

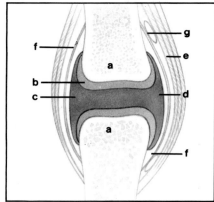

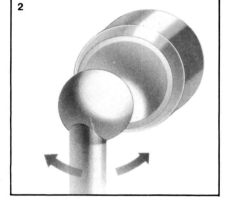

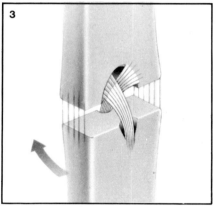

Synovial joints contain fluid, secreted by the synovial membrane, as a lubricant for the wearing surfaces—tough caps of cartilage covering the bone itself. Ligaments and tendons support and give protection to the capsule, aided by fat and bursae.

a Bone
b Cartilage
c Synovial fluid
d Synovial membrane
e Tendon
f Ligament
g Bursa

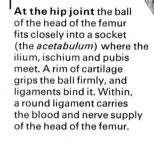

At the hip joint the ball of the head of the femur fits closely into a socket (the *acetabulum*) where the ilium, ischium and pubis meet. A rim of cartilage grips the ball firmly, and ligaments bind it. Within, a round ligament carries the blood and nerve supply of the head of the femur.

Simplest of the freely movable joints are gliding joints (1), which allow one surface to slide over another to a greater or lesser degree. Examples of gliding joints are those between the carpal bones at the wrist, between the tarsal bones in the foot, and between the ribs and the vertebrae. Movement at these joints is restricted by the ligaments that bind bone to bone.

Ball-and-socket joints (2) are found in the hip and shoulder. At the hip the ball of the top of the femur fits snugly into a cup, called the acetabulum, formed by the junction of the ilium, ischium and pubis. A rim of cartilage helps to grip the ball firmly, assisted by external ligaments and a special internal ligament (the *ligamentum teres*), which also carries nerves and blood vessels into the head of the femur. The hip joints between them support the full weight of the body.

The shoulder joint is also of the ball-and-socket type, but the socket, a specially shaped part of the scapula, is much shallower than that of the hip, allowing the humerus a great deal of play—but also more liable to dislocation.

Internal ligaments (3) also play an important part in stabilizing the knee joint, where the lower end of the femur articulates with the upper end of the tibia. Ligaments uniting the bones actually cross over in the centre of the joint, enclosed in synovial membrane.

Pivot joints (4) are found where the atlas and axis articulate, and between the head of the radius and the upper end of the ulna. A peg of bone sticks up from the axis, and can rotate within the socket formed by the ring-like atlas. This allows turning of the head. At the elbow the peg is the head of the radius, rotating within a loop of ligament attached to the ulna, and allowing twisting movement in the forearm.

Hinge joints (5) allow movement in only one plane; examples are the joints between humerus and ulna at the elbow, between the bones of each finger and each toe (the *phalanges*), and the ankle.

A saddle joint (6) has articular surfaces so shaped that combinations of movements in two different planes can be performed, but one bone cannot rotate upon the other. A good example is the joint at the base of the thumb, where its metacarpal meets the carpal bone, called the trapezium. The joint allows the thumb to be *opposed*, or moved across the palm of the hand.

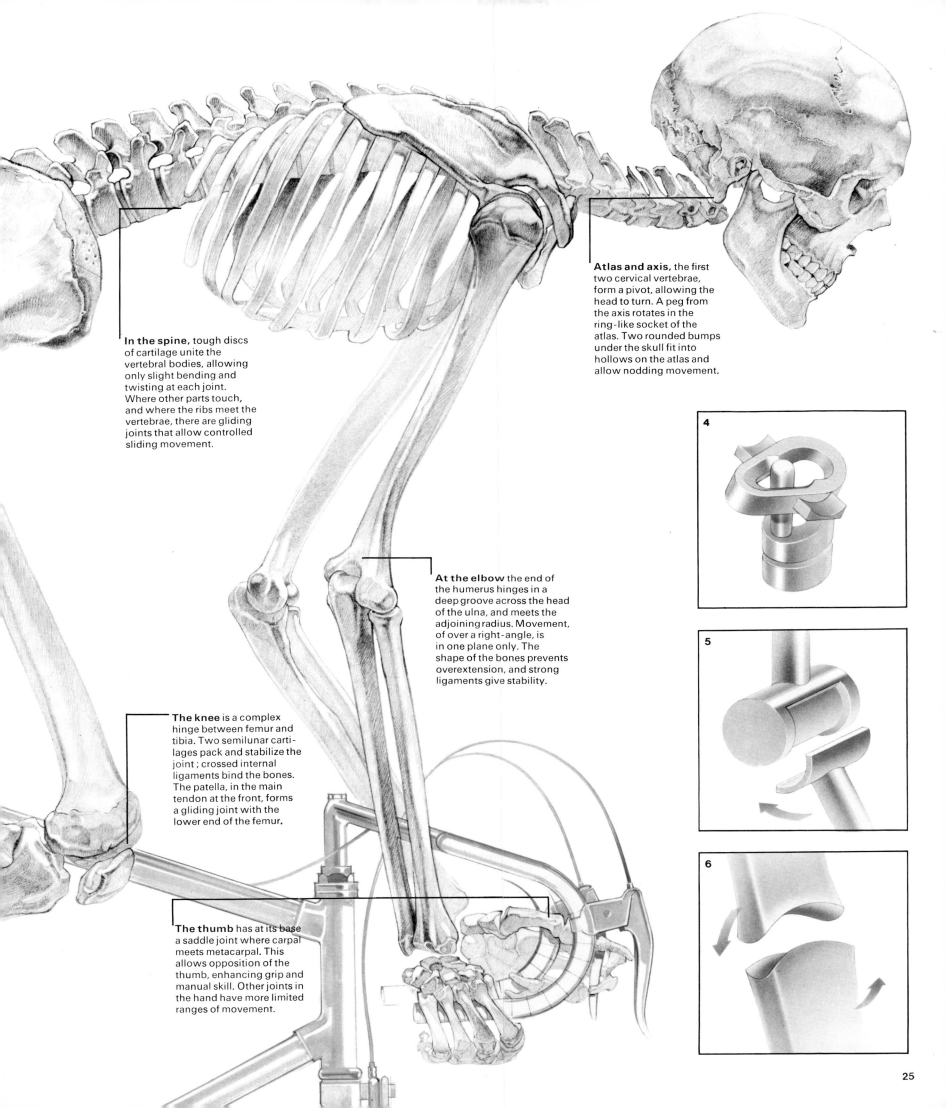

In the spine, tough discs of cartilage unite the vertebral bodies, allowing only slight bending and twisting at each joint. Where other parts touch, and where the ribs meet the vertebrae, there are gliding joints that allow controlled sliding movement.

Atlas and axis, the first two cervical vertebrae, form a pivot, allowing the head to turn. A peg from the axis rotates in the ring-like socket of the atlas. Two rounded bumps under the skull fit into hollows on the atlas and allow nodding movement.

At the elbow the end of the humerus hinges in a deep groove across the head of the ulna, and meets the adjoining radius. Movement, of over a right-angle, is in one plane only. The shape of the bones prevents overextension, and strong ligaments give stability.

The knee is a complex hinge between femur and tibia. Two semilunar cartilages pack and stabilize the joint; crossed internal ligaments bind the bones. The patella, in the main tendon at the front, forms a gliding joint with the lower end of the femur.

The thumb has at its base a saddle joint where carpal meets metacarpal. This allows opposition of the thumb, enhancing grip and manual skill. Other joints in the hand have more limited ranges of movement.

4

5

6

Muscles

Six hundred or more skeletal muscles clothe the skeleton. Each has its own name, usually in anatomists' Latin, and its own function, which is often specified within the name. Thus the *extensor carpi radialis brevis* is the short muscle which, extending·between the radial bone of the forearm and the wrist, helps to extend or straighten the wrist. *Extensor* muscles straighten a joint, *flexor* muscles bend it. *Abductors* pull a limb or other part of the body away from the main axis. *Protractors* move a limb forward, *retractors* pull it back, and *rotators* twist it about its own axis. *Sphincter* muscles form a ring round a tube or opening, tightening up on themselves to reduce or seal the aperture. Most skeletal muscles are attached at either end to bones, directly or through tendons. Some surface muscles, including many which give expression to the face, link bone to skin. A few are attached to the fibrous covering of other muscles, reinforcing their efforts or helping them to maintain shape when relaxed.

Skeletal muscle is one of three kinds of muscle in the body; the other two kinds—*cardiac* and *smooth* muscle—are found respectively in the heart, and in the gut, arteries and other internal organs. Skeletal muscle alone is controlled directly by the central nervous system; for this reason it is sometimes called *voluntary* muscle. It is known also as *striped*, or *striated*, muscle, because its fibres appear striped under the microscope. The special quality of every muscle fibre is its ability to contract along its own length when stimulated. A muscle, made up of thousands or millions of fibres, contracts because its fibres are stimulated together. Energy is released and heat generated during contraction. For this to happen time after time, fuel and oxygen must be supplied in abundance by the blood stream, and waste products (including heat) resulting from chemical changes must be swept away. For this reason every skeletal muscle is well endowed with arteries and veins, to provide a steady flow of blood at high pressure through its fibres.

Each fibre of a skeletal muscle is controlled by an individual nerve ending. The nerve endings, which may all originate in a single nerve trunk, are stimulated by signals from the brain or spinal cord. Their response on stimulation is to release minute amounts of a chemical—acetylcholine—which causes the individual muscle fibres to contract. A weak signal may stimulate only a few nerve endings, and cause no more than a faint twitch in the muscle. Strong signals cause synchronous contraction of many or all of the fibres, and the massive contraction of the muscle. Contracted fibres cannot expand by their own efforts. They can be extended only by the pull of opposing muscles, or by gravity or other external forces. So skeletal muscle is usually arranged in opposing or antagonistic blocs—flexors pulling against extensors, abductors against adductors and protractors against retractors. In the normal relaxed body the blocs pull gently against each other all the time; even in sleep we retain some degree of muscle tension or *tone*. In standing we increase tone, strengthening the opposing pulls and keeping the muscles firmly tensed against the additional pull of gravity. Constant adjustments, based on information from sensory organs in the muscles themselves, and controlled from centres in the brain stem, keep the levers, muscles and weights in balance and hold the body erect. Tense muscles do no external work, but their pull against each other involves energy expenditure; this appears as heat, and contributes to man's high body temperature.

Some of the many muscles important in athletic activity :

(**1**) Biceps brachialis

(**2**) Quadriceps femoris

(**3**) Triceps

(**4**) Rectus abdominis

(**5**) Pectoralis major

(**6**) Soleus

(**7**) Deltoid

(**8**) Peroneus longus

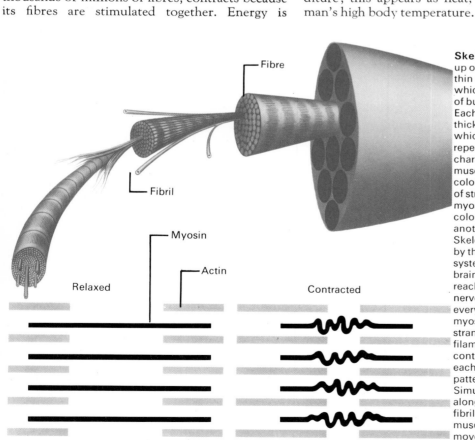

— Fibre

— Fibril

— Myosin

— Actin

Relaxed

Contracted

Skeletal muscle is built up of bundles of long, thin strands or fibres, which are in turn built of bundles of fibrils. Each fibril consists of thick and thin filaments which overlap to form the repeating striped pattern characteristic of skeletal muscle. The thick, dark-coloured filaments are made of strands of the protein myosin ; the thin, light-coloured ones are made of another protein, actin. Skeletal muscle is controlled by the central nervous system. Messages from the brain or spinal column reach the muscles through nerve endings attached to every muscle fibre. The myosin and actin protein strands within each filament are stimulated to contract, sliding against each other and altering the pattern of the striations. Simultaneous contraction along the length of every fibril in every fibre of a muscle results in muscular movement.

Muscles in co-ordination

Even when the body is thought of as being completely relaxed—as in deep sleep—in fact there is a great deal of co-ordinated muscular activity going on. Cardiac muscle in the heart is contracting and relaxing in regular cycles, the smooth muscle of the gut is contracting in rhythmic waves as digestion proceeds, and the muscles of the diaphragm and rib cage are alternately contracting and relaxing to produce the automatic, unconscious movements of respiration. During consciousness, in vigorous physical activity, virtually every muscle in the body may be brought into play, voluntarily or reflexly. As one muscle, or group of muscles, contracts, so another relaxes, to produce a balanced movement. The actions desired and initiated by the brain are translated into co-ordinated muscular activity. Voluntary muscular contraction is accompanied by appropriate reflex relaxation in the opposing muscle groups, to allow a smooth response.

Movement of an arm or leg results from a controlled imbalance of antagonistic blocs of muscles. In raising the forearm, nerve signals pass from the brain to the fibres of the flexor muscles (biceps and brachialis), causing a firm, progressive contraction. At the same time signals pass from the brain to the fibres of the antagonistic extensor muscles (triceps), inhibiting it from contracting and causing it to slacken at a corresponding rate. So the flexors take up the strain smoothly against reducing opposition, and the forearm rises. Additional signals, of which we are normally quite unaware, pass from the control centre of the brain to the muscles of the shoulder, tensing them to hold the upper arm steady while biceps and brachialis pull against it.

Many other simple movements involve our automatic use of unexpected blocs of muscles in faultless co-ordination. In bending the fingers, muscles on the underside of the forearm pull hard on the web of tendons which cross the palm of the hand, while the corresponding extensors relax. So hard is the pull that the whole hand and wrist tend to be drawn into the movement. To counter this tendency we automatically tighten the extensor muscles on the upper side of the

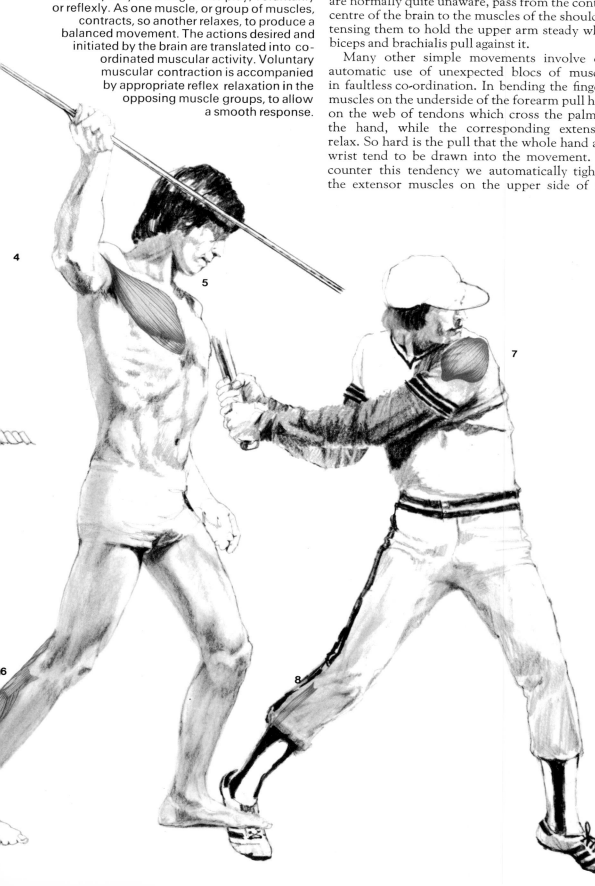

forearm, which together help to keep the wrist straight. Turning and lowering the head in a single, controlled movement involves co-ordinated action from the many muscles of the neck. If at the same time we keep our eyes fixed on a distant object, twelve further muscles—the six that control movements of each eye—are brought effortlessly into play. The smooth, controlled actions of threading a needle, tying a knot or playing the piano are everyday miracles of co-ordination, involving dozens of muscles, thousands of muscle fibres and millions of nerve cells in the control centres of the brain.

Contracting muscle fibres shorten to varying degrees, some to one-third of their original length on full contraction. Many muscles have the fibres running parallel to each other and to the main direction of muscle contraction. This provides the greatest possible shortening, but not necessarily the strongest pull. Stronger muscles, from which shorter, more powerful contractions are demanded, often have their bundles of fibres arranged oblique to the line of pull, like the vanes of a feather. Whether short or long, the pull of a powerful muscle is usually magnified by the skeletal system of levers. So a small contraction of the deltoid muscle of the shoulder raises the arm several inches from the side, and a tiny contraction of the biceps, magnified by the long lever of the forearm, causes a much more extensive movement of the hand. Most lever systems of the body are arranged in this way to provide magnified movements rather than weight-lifting efficiency. In this they differ from most man-made lever systems, where "mechanical advantage" implies a small movement of a heavy body in exchange for a wide sweep of a lever arm.

Eighty per cent by weight of a large skeletal muscle is water, and eighty per cent of the solid remaining is protein. Much of the protein is in the form of tiny threads, packed tightly within the fibres. The exact mechanism of contraction is unknown, but, as the fibre shortens, neighbouring threads of two different proteins (actin and myosin) slide against each other, altering the microscopic pattern of striations across the fibre. One-twentieth by weight of the muscle is fats, sugars, salts and other substances involved in the chemical changes accompanying contraction.

Muscle fibres derive their energy from *glycogen*, a complex starch manufactured in the liver from sugars contained originally in food. Within the muscle fibres, glycogen is broken down to the simple sugar glucose, which in turn is split to form pyruvic acid and lactic acid, with the liberation of a little energy. During prolonged, strenuous exercise, when the muscles are working hard and the blood cannot maintain an adequate supply of oxygen, much of the energy is obtained in this way. Because lactic acid accumulates in the muscles and inhibits their action, the athlete or hard worker who cannot maintain his rapid intake of oxygen soon tires and loses efficiency. In steadier work, when breathing keeps pace with muscular effort, the steady flow of oxygen converts lactic acid through a complex cycle of reactions to carbon dioxide and water, with the release of sixteen times as much energy as before. So the tortoise catches up with the hare, the jog trotter with the sprinter, and all ultimately wring full value from every molecule of fuel.

Food and the body

We are what we eat. Every part of each of our tissues has been built up by shuffling and rearranging chemical building blocks provided by foodstuffs. The overall changes in the body—the breaking down of food materials into units that can be burnt for fuel, and the building up of other units for cell growth and repair—are called *metabolism*. Any breaking-down process is said to be *catabolic*, and any building-up process *anabolic*. The body never ceases changing.

What is food, and how does it turn into living, growing tissues, and provide energy for the body? The three main components of food are *proteins*, *fats* and *carbohydrates*, but a balanced diet, as well as providing quantities of each of these, must contain *vitamins*, *minerals* and *water*. You can survive without food for a month or more—without water only a matter of days. Each kind of food material is put to a different use.

Proteins, found in meat, fish, eggs and cheese, and peas and beans, are chemical compounds of carbon, hydrogen, oxygen and nitrogen. Some also contain sulphur. They are very large molecules, built up from smaller units called amino acids, linked together to form a chain. There are about twenty different amino acids; variation in both the proportion of different kinds, and the order in which they are arranged in the chain, means that thousands and thousands of different proteins can be built up from the same building blocks. So chicken meat looks and tastes different from whale meat, or bacon, and all are different from human muscle, despite containing the same units.

Fats, made of carbon, hydrogen and oxygen, are built from molecules called fatty acids, linked to glycerol molecules. Different fats contain different fatty acids, and so vary from animal to animal, and plant to plant, much in the way that proteins vary. Some are liquid (oils), and some more solid, as in butter and lard.

Carbohydrates, in sugary and starchy foods, are built from simple sugar units called monosaccharides, molecules of either six carbon atoms in a ring (hexoses) or five carbon atoms (pentoses), with hydrogen and oxygen attached. Two units linked make a disaccharide, and a chain of many, possibly branching, is a polysaccharide. Starches are polysaccharides, and so is cellulose; cellulose, the chief structural material of plants, cannot be broken down in the body as can starches, and remains as roughage.

Before the body can make use of food that is eaten, digestion must take place—the breaking down of food, physically and chemically, into its component units. Only small molecules can be absorbed from the intestine into the blood, for distribution to the body's tissues. Chemicals called *enzymes*, produced by the body, do the splitting in the intestine; other enzymes are responsible for the building up of the food units into body structures, and the "burning" of food in the tissues to provide energy.

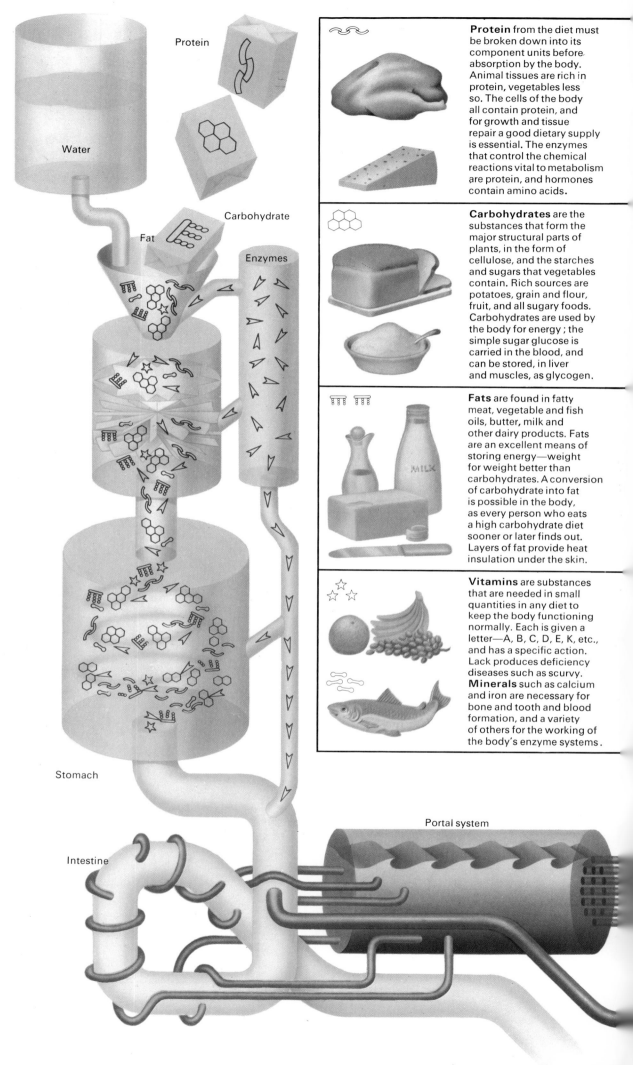

Protein from the diet must be broken down into its component units before absorption by the body. Animal tissues are rich in protein, vegetables less so. The cells of the body all contain protein, and for growth and tissue repair a good dietary supply is essential. The enzymes that control the chemical reactions vital to metabolism are protein, and hormones contain amino acids.

Carbohydrates are the substances that form the major structural parts of plants, in the form of cellulose, and the starches and sugars that vegetables contain. Rich sources are potatoes, grain and flour, fruit, and all sugary foods. Carbohydrates are used by the body for energy; the simple sugar glucose is carried in the blood, and can be stored, in liver and muscles, as glycogen.

Fats are found in fatty meat, vegetable and fish oils, butter, milk and other dairy products. Fats are an excellent means of storing energy—weight for weight better than carbohydrates. A conversion of carbohydrate into fat is possible in the body, as every person who eats a high carbohydrate diet sooner or later finds out. Layers of fat provide heat insulation under the skin.

Vitamins are substances that are needed in small quantities in any diet to keep the body functioning normally. Each is given a letter—A, B, C, D, E, K, etc., and has a specific action. Lack produces deficiency diseases such as scurvy. **Minerals** such as calcium and iron are necessary for bone and tooth and blood formation, and a variety of others for the working of the body's enzyme systems.

Before proteins can be absorbed by the body and utilized, digestive juices containing "proteolytic", or protein-splitting, enzymes must get to work. Long protein molecules are broken down in stages into smaller and smaller and smaller fragments, called proteoses, peptones and peptides, and eventually into the units called amino acids. These are small enough to be taken up by the intestinal wall.

Breakdown of carbohydrates starts in the mouth, but is mainly carried out in the intestine. Enzymes split polysaccharides into simpler and simpler units, the final result being the simple sugars called hexoses and pentoses, which can be absorbed into the blood through the gut wall and distributed round the body. Cellulose cannot be broken down by human enzymes.

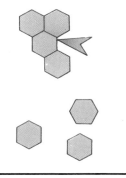

Fats are digested into a mixture of fatty acids and glycerol, by the enzymes called lipases aided by the salts found in the bile from the liver. Bile salts help to turn fats into an emulsion of very fine globules which enzymes can attack more effectively. Fatty acids and glycerol can be absorbed into the blood, but microscopic fat globules also find their way into the lymph system.

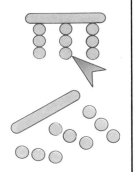

Water is all-important in the body, as a general solvent permeating all cells and tissues. All the body's chemical reactions take place in aqueous solution, and waste products are removed from the body in water, as urine and sweat. We need a constant intake to maintain water balance. Water is present in the diet, not only in drinks, but in all but the very driest of foods. You are 60% water.

Liver

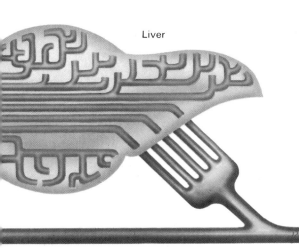

Protein forms a basis for the soft tissues of your body, and even bones have a protein meshwork in which mineral salts are laid down. Each protein has its own pattern of amino acids; brain protein differs from muscle protein, and muscle protein from that in the blood, in the way the building blocks of amino acids are put together. Starting with the amino acids taken into the bloodstream, the body builds up its own specific proteins for different functions. So chicken meat, or bean protein, can be reassembled into human nerve cells, blood cells, muscle fibres or skin.

Carbohydrates play little part in the structure of the body. They are used to provide energy; the simple sugar glucose is carried by the blood to wherever there is activity—which means in every living cell—and burnt as fuel. The body keeps the level of sugar in the blood remarkably constant, by means of a complex hormonal control system. If there is an excess of sugar provided by the diet, then it can be stored as glycogen, or help form fat. The liver is the main organ where the processing of carbohydrates occurs, but muscles also store glucose as glycogen.

The distribution of substances taken into the body after the digestion of food is carried out by the bloodstream. Sugars, from carbohydrates, amino acids, from proteins, and fatty acids and glycerol, from fats, all circulate in the blood. Blood rich in foodstuffs passes from the intestinal wall, through the hepatic portal vein to the liver. Here some material may be stored, and some allowed to pass into the circulation, while other substances will be used for the synthesis of urgently needed structural compounds. Blood from the liver passes to the heart for distribution.

The minerals that are taken into the body include common salt (sodium chloride), the calcium abundant in milk products, meat, peas and beans, phosphates in cheese, liver and eggs, and iron in green vegetables and liver. These are all necessary for healthy bone and tooth formation, energy transfer in every cell, blood formation, and the working of enzyme systems. The greatest accumulation of calcium salts is of course in the bones. Sodium and potassium are found throughout the body's cells and fluids, and iron forms an important part of the haemoglobin found in every red blood cell.

Fats are used as fuel by the body, and provide an even greater source of energy than carbohydrates. Tiny globules of fat are distributed in the bloodstream, and the building blocks of fat—fatty acids and glycerol—also circulate freely. If there is too much fat for immediate use as fuel, then it is stored in fat cells in the tissues, notably under the skin. Here it forms an insulating layer, gives the roundness of the body's contours and provides an easily tapped reserve of energy for bodily activities.

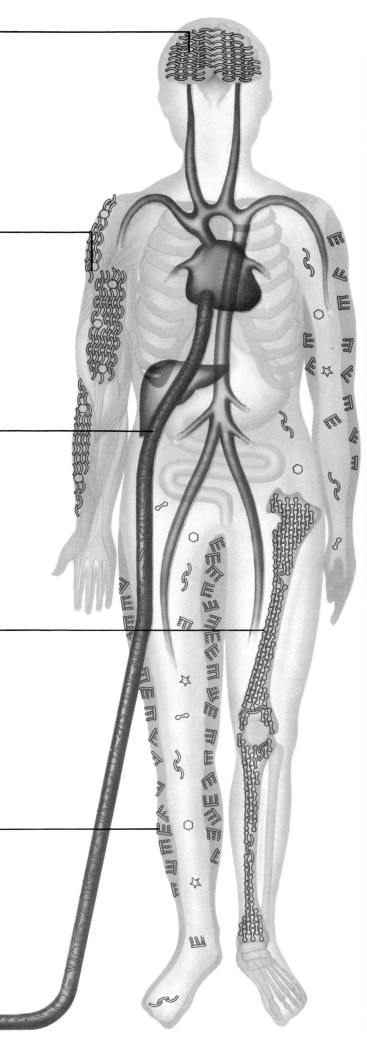

Digestion

Though probably descended from insect-eating ancestors, man is today an omnivore—an unspecialized feeder—happy to tackle anything from abalone to zebra steak. An astounding variety of food disappears into his mouth to be chopped, ground and forwarded for dunking in the strong chemical solutions of the stomach. The first stage of digestion is chewing, or mastication, which breaks chunks of food, whether carbohydrate, protein or fat, into manageable fragments. Physical breakdown gives more surface area for enzyme-laden digestive juices to penetrate; chemical breakdown splits large, often insoluble, molecules into soluble ones small enough to be absorbed. Once through the wall, food units are used either for cell growth and repair, as immediate fuel, or stored in the liver and other tissues.

Digestion begins in the mouth; the tongue rolls the food around, repeatedly presenting it to the mill of the teeth and keeping itself out of the way by an elaborate reflex action. Saliva helps to soften, mix and lubricate the food, forming it into a bolus or ball of convenient swallowing size. At the same time the salivary enzyme *amylase* starts breaking starches into sugars. When suitably softened, the bolus is thrown against the back of the pharynx by a reflex action that also causes the flap of the epiglottis to close the windpipe, letting the bolus slide safely past into the *oesophagus*.

The oesophagus is a short, thin-walled tube made of layers of circular and longitudinal smooth muscle and lined, like the rest of the gut, with mucus-secreting cells for protection and lubrication. Slow, *peristaltic*, waves of contraction surge along it about every eight or nine seconds, delivering the bolus to the stomach, where its arrival starts churning movements.

The thick-walled, elastic sac of the stomach also includes layers of smooth muscle. Entrance and exit are guarded by upper (cardiac) and lower (pyloric) sphincters—rings of muscle. The stomach secretes gastric juices at the direction of both nerves and hormones. If you are hungry, the very sight and smell of food are enough to start this secretion. Impulses pass down the vagus nerve and stimulate the gastric glands. A pool of strongly acidic gastric juice collects in the stomach, ready to receive the first boluses. Amino acids, released from protein in food, cause the lower stomach wall to secrete minute amounts of the hormone *gastrin*, which stimulates the gastric glands in the upper stomach to secrete more digestive juice. So the juices continue to flow long after the last mouthful has been swallowed.

Blended and homogenized by the combination of chemical breakdown and churning, the stomach content (now called chyme) is ready for the next part of its journey. It passes in spurts through the relaxed pyloric sphincter into the duodenum, where the digestive process will continue. Only water, salts, glucose and alcohol are absorbed directly from the stomach, and possibly some drugs.

Four kinds of teeth make up the adult complement of 32. Each kind functions in a different way to break up food in the first stage of digestion. Incisors (**1**) are grouped in two sets of four at the front of the upper and lower jaw. The upper set fits over the lower, cutting up food in a scissor-like movement. Incisors are flanked by canines (**2**)—often known as eye-teeth—sharp, pointed teeth designed to tear into tough food like meat. Behind these are the premolars (**3**) and molars (**4**), large, square teeth which grind together like millstones. Working together, the teeth quickly reduce food to a moist pulp, aided by the action of the tongue and the saliva poured from the salivary glands.

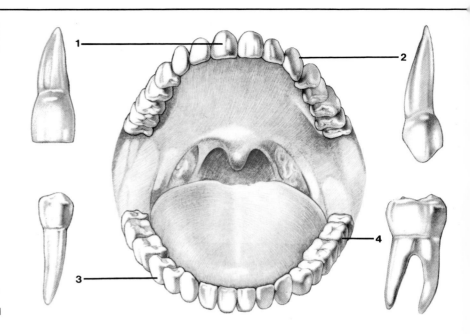

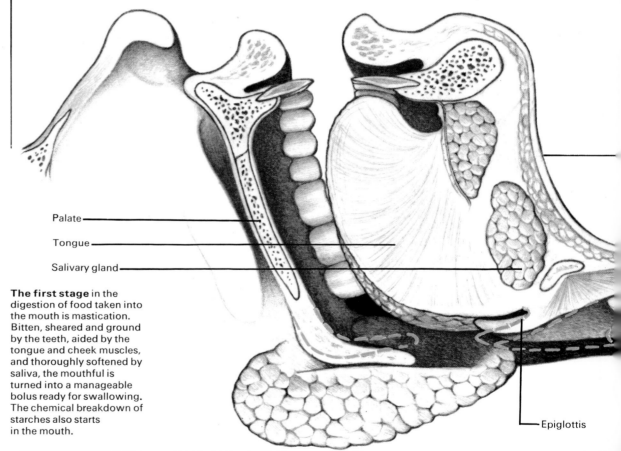

Palate

Tongue

Salivary gland

Epiglottis

The first stage in the digestion of food taken into the mouth is mastication. Bitten, sheared and ground by the teeth, aided by the tongue and cheek muscles, and thoroughly softened by saliva, the mouthful is turned into a manageable bolus ready for swallowing. The chemical breakdown of starches also starts in the mouth.

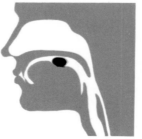

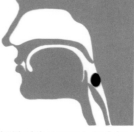
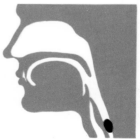

Swallowing, deglutition, starts as a voluntary action, but then becomes reflexly controlled. The bolus is thrown backwards by the tongue into the

pharynx, and the soft part of the palate lifts to prevent the food passing up into the nasal cavity. Simultaneously, the larynx and pharynx are drawn up

behind the tongue, and the flap-like epiglottis moves forward to bar entry of the bolus into the larynx and trachea. The food is propelled down behind the

epiglottis, and enters the upper end of the oesophagus. Waves of contraction in the oesophageal wall—peristalsis—now squeeze the bolus downwards.

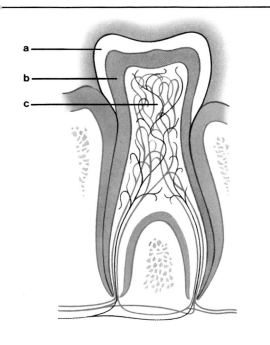

Gastric secretions
The lining, or mucous membrane, of the stomach has a honeycomb appearance. It has numerous small depressions, called gastric pits, less than half a millimetre across, and at the bottom of these pits lie the glands that pour out the gastric digestive juices. Different cells are responsible for the production of the hydrochloric acid, enzymes and mucus that are mixed with the food as the stomach churns and liquefies its contents. The mucus has a protective function, and prevents the gastric juices from attacking the lining of the stomach itself. Any break, or erosion, in the mucous membrane allows the acid and enzymes to eat into the underlying tissues. The result is a painful gastric ulcer (this, like a duodenal ulcer, can also be called a peptic ulcer). The enzyme *pepsin* in gastric juice is responsible for the splitting of the proteins in food into smaller molecules—proteoses and peptones.

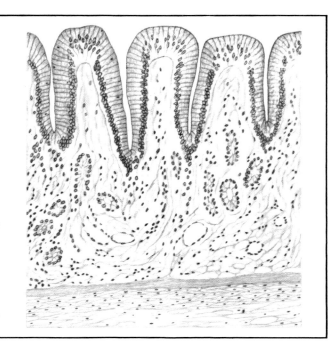

Tooth enamel (a) is the hardest of all body tissues, with a mineral content of 96 per cent. It covers the crown of the tooth—the part that projects above the gum—protecting the layer of dentine (b) underneath. Dentine is the living, bone-like part of the tooth.
Beneath the dentine is the sensitive "nerve" of the tooth, the dental pulp (c) containing blood vessels and nerve endings. The tooth narrows to enter the gum, in which it is rooted with bony, cement-like tissue.
All teeth except molars have a single root: molars divide into two or three cusps at the crown, and so are known as bi- or tricuspids.

Peristaltic movement
The propulsion of a bolus of food down the oesophagus and through the upper, or cardiac, opening of the stomach is accomplished reflexly. The walls of the oesophagus have two muscular layers—longitudinal and circular—which, by contracting in a series of waves starting at the upper end, squeeze the food steadily downwards. A wave of contraction is followed by relaxation of the muscle, in preparation for a further bolus. In normal circumstances gravity aids swallowing, but one can swallow solids, and drink liquids, even when lying down—or standing on one's head. Peristalsis occurs throughout the whole length of the gut. In the intestine, waves of contraction pass backwards and forwards rhythmically in different regions as digestion proceeds, but the eventual movement is always onwards.

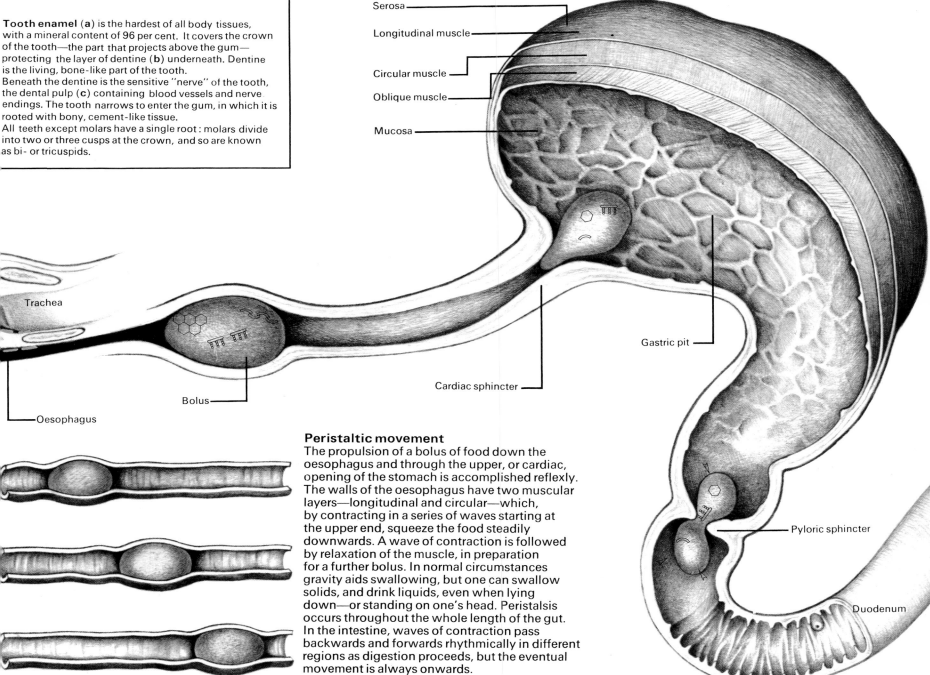

Serosa
Longitudinal muscle
Circular muscle
Oblique muscle
Mucosa
Gastric pit
Cardiac sphincter
Pyloric sphincter
Trachea
Bolus
Oesophagus
Duodenum

Absorption

Released through the pyloric sphincter, chyme passes into the short, curved tube of the duodenum and into the rest of the small intestine, comprising the jejunum and ileum. The surface of the intestine is corrugated with pits, and has finger-like projections called villi, which are in turn covered with microvilli. Villi and microvilli contain capillaries and lacteals, a network of lymph vessels. The total absorptive surface is therefore enormous and made even more effective by continual movement of the gut wall.

Peristaltic waves pass through the intestine every three seconds or so, urging the chyme on. More violent spasms intrude intermittently, temporarily sealing off small sections of gut in which the chyme is tossed and churned with new digestive juices.

The arrival of chyme in the duodenum stimulates the production of hormones which activate various organs around the gut. One inhibits the production of acid digestive juices by the stomach wall; others stimulate the production and release of juices from the liver, gall bladder, pancreas and intestinal wall.

While in the duodenum, chyme is also permeated with bile, a concentrated solution of salts and pigments derived from breakdown processes in the liver, which helps to digest fats. Most oils and fats are liquid at body heat; bile emulsifies the liquid into microscopic globules, providing a large surface area on which the fat-splitting enzyme, *lipase*, can work. Slightly alkaline, bile also neutralizes excess acid in the chyme, creating better working conditions for other intestinal enzymes.

Pancreatic juice is produced by the pancreas, a dual-purpose organ with two distinct secretory systems, exocrine and endocrine. Exocrine cells, which make up the bulk of the organ, are stimulated by hormones released from the duodenum to produce the juice, a watery solution which contains digestive enzymes to reduce protein chains to two-molecule blocks. Endocrine cells secrete hormones which control the blood sugar levels and have no direct effect on digestion (see p 50).

Juices produced by the intestinal wall contain more enzymes which complete the breakdown of remaining carbohydrate and protein units. By this stage all fats have been digested, and absorbed either directly as emulsion or, after splitting by lipase into fatty acids and glycerol, through the villi.

Carbohydrases split carbohydrates into their basic units, and *erepsins* resolve proteins finally into their component amino acids, for direct absorption. So after several hours nearly all digestible material has been absorbed through the gut, leaving only salts, roughage, dead cells from the gut lining, bile pigments, which give faeces their brown colour, and water.

Most of this water and some salts are re-absorbed along the length of the large intestine, or colon. Bacteria thrive on the indigestible waste, producing important vitamins and amino acids which are reabsorbed to the host's benefit.

Pancreatic enzymes

Filling the loop of the duodenum (**1**), the pancreas (**2**), is a diffuse gland containing both exocrine and endocrine cells. Stimulated by hormones released into the bloodstream by the duodenum, the exocrine cells secrete the enzyme-rich pancreatic juice, which flows into the intestine through the pancreatic duct (**3**), entering through the duodenal papilla (**4**). The enzymes *trypsin*, *chymotrypsin* and *carboxypolypeptidase* break proteoses and peptones, derived from proteins, into the paired amino acid blocks called dipeptides. The enzyme *deoxyribonuclease* splits DNA into amino acids, and pancreatic *amylase* and *lipase* split complex sugars into simpler sugars, and fats into fatty acids and glycerol, respectively.

Bile

Tucked under the edge of the liver, the gall bladder collects and concentrates bile, a yellow-green liquid containing bile salts and pigments, secreted by the liver. A hormone from the duodenum stimulates the release of bile through the bile duct, which shares an entrance to the intestine with the pancreatic duct, at the duodenal papilla. Bile neutralizes excess acid in the chyme, and helps the digestion of fats by aiding emulsification into droplets.

Intestinal enzymes

The wall of the intestine secretes the enzymes *sucrase*, *maltase* and *lactase*, which break disaccharides into monosaccharides, and *erepsins*, which convert dipeptides to amino acids.

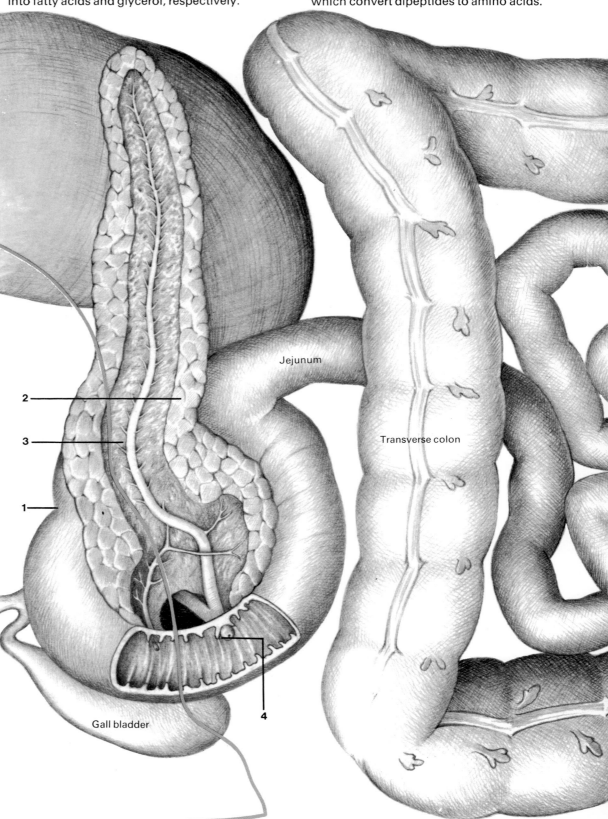

Jejunum

Transverse colon

2

3

1

4

Gall bladder

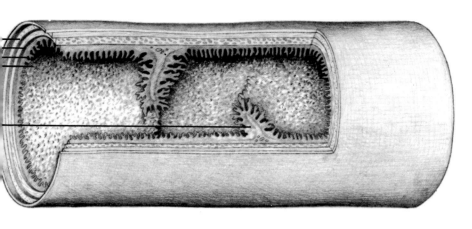

The intestinal wall has an outer layer, or *serosa* (**a**), longitudinal (**b**) and circular (**c**) muscle layers, and a lining of *mucosa* (**d**). The mucosa of the upper regions has numerous fine, finger-like projections, *villi* (**e**), through which digested food materials are absorbed into the bloodstream and lymphatics for processing by the liver and distribution to the body's tissues.

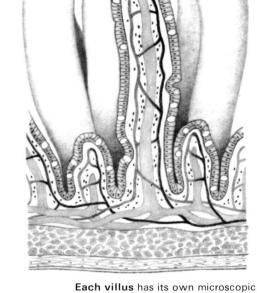

Each villus has its own microscopic projections, *microvilli*, further increasing the area of absorptive surface in the intestine. In section it is possible to see the fine network of blood vessels— capillaries—into which pass the small molecules formed by the breakdown of proteins (amino acids), carbohydrates (monosaccharides) and fats (fatty acids and glycerol). Fats, in the form of minute globules, are also taken up by the vessels called *lacteals*, which pass them, in milky suspension, through lymphatic vessels to join the bloodstream in the venous return to the heart.

Descending colon

Ileum

Rectum

Anus

Ascending colon

Caecum

Vermiform appendix

The large intestine

By the time that the contents of the small intestine reach the end of the ileum, most of the food material has been absorbed. The remainder, consisting of indigestible residues, including cellulose, passes through into the first, or ascending, part of the colon. At the junction of ileum and colon is the sac-like swelling called the caecum, with the short and apparently functionless appendix forming a cul-de-sac. The contents of the colon move up, across the upper abdomen in the transverse colon and down the descending colon, on the left side of the body, to the rectum and so to the anus. The main function of the colon is the absorption of water and salts from the food residues. Bacteria present in the colon may also produce quantities of vitamins and amino acids that can be absorbed through the wall and supplement dietary intake. Dead bacteria form a large percentage of the faeces.

The liver

Largest and most versatile of the body's internal organs, the liver is housed below the diaphragm in the right upper corner of the abdominal cavity. Sculptured to fit the space between stomach, diaphragm and ribcage, it has a small left lobe and a larger right lobe, which reaches down to the level of the lowest rib. As every cook knows, liver is bright red and well endowed with blood, with a spongy, uniform texture. Its rather sweet flavour, and reputation for richness in iron and vitamins, testify to one of its functions in life—it is a store for many commodities which have to be metered out to other tissues of the body, including sugars, minerals and vitamins A, D and B_{12}. The liver has scores of different functions, more than any other single organ of the body. It is a busy organ, with over a litre of blood passing through its tissues every minute. Much of the body's heat is generated in the liver, as a result of its many chemical activities.

So versatile an organ might be expected to be complex inside. In fact its cell layout is remarkably simple; all the complexity lies within the cells, rather than among them. Micro-sections show the liver to be made up of lobules, many thousands of roughly cylindrical or hexagonal units one or two millimetres across, each centred on a small branch of the hepatic vein. Lobules are made up of rows, chains and plates of cells, radiating out to an ill-defined edge. Between the rows are fine, blood-filled spaces (sinusoids). Between the lobules are further spaces, which contain branches of the hepatic artery, the hepatic portal vein (bringing blood laden with nutrients from the gut wall) and fine vessels—canaliculi—which collect bile and convey it to the gall bladder. The two blood vessels deliver their blood to the sinusoids, where it bathes the liver cells. Eventually the blood finds its way to the central vein of the lobule, and returns to the heart by the great hepatic vein.

All the many activities of the liver are carried out in the liver cells, which take what they need from the blood as it flows past them, and deliver to it their metabolic products. Only the bile takes a different route, collecting in tiny vessels which run among the cells and join each other in the interlobular canaliculi. This deceptively simple mechanism allows the liver to act as a clearing house, store, factory and chemical laboratory.

The functions of the liver can be summarized under the headings *synthesis, storage, metabolism, detoxication,* and the *processing of red blood cells.*

Synthesis. Bile salts are built up in the liver from cholesterol, a fat-based chemical which appears in cell membranes and forms the basis of many vitamins and hormones. Excess cholesterol, circulating in the blood, may give rise to fatty degeneration of arteries and the dangers of coronary thrombosis. Thus the liver converts a dangerous surplus to a useful aid to digestion. *Amino acids* and *proteins* are synthesized in the liver, including the proteins prothrombin and fibrinogen (important in blood clotting), albumins and globulins of the blood, and antibodies important in defence against disease. *Glycogen* (animal starch), a storage carbohydrate, is built up from sugars absorbed in the gut, and also from fats and proteins.

Storage. The liver acts as a store of glycogen, fats, amino acids, vitamins, metals (especially iron and copper) and other substances. It is able to release them quickly on demand, so that such specialized cells as those of the brain and nervous system, which have no store-room of their own, can be supplied from stock without delay. The liver processes fats for storage elsewhere (for example under the skin). Its stock of iron is recovered from the breakdown of the red blood pigment haemoglobin.

Metabolism. Glucose, glycogen, amino acids, fatty acids and glycerol are constantly being interchanged in the liver. Sugars surplus to requirements in the bloodstream are readily converted to glycogen, or broken down immediately to liberate heat, water and carbon dioxide. Fats and their breakdown products (fatty acids and glycerol) are also interconvertible, or may be altered to sugars. Neither proteins nor amino acids can be stored as such. Surplus amino acids in the blood are broken down in the liver to ammonia (a poison, which is converted immediately to relatively innocuous urea and excreted through the kidneys) and organic acids which can be stored or burnt like carbohydrates.

Detoxication. The liver has a special function of extracting and, where possible, neutralizing or destroying poisons that enter the body through

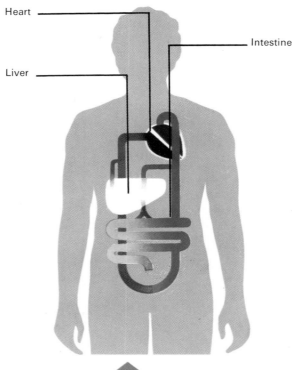

Heart

Liver

Intestine

Storage

Hepatic artery

Gall bladder

Portal vein

Small intestine

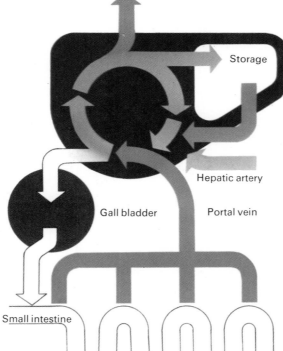

Although in close contact with the upper digestive tract, the liver has only a minor role in the digestive process : the secretion of bile to aid the emulsification of fats. Tucked under the front edge of the liver is the gall bladder, an enlarged side-shoot of the bile duct, where bile can be stored until required, and then released into the duodenum. All of the other functions of the liver are concerned with the processing of materials actually within the bloodstream—whether absorbed from the intestine or released into the circulation from the body's tissues.

The liver has a dual blood supply. Blood rich in food materials absorbed from the intestinal wall enters through the portal vein, and freshly oxygenated blood through the hepatic artery. Blood is returned into the circulation through the hepatic vein. Bile leaves the liver through the bile duct, and is either stored in the gall bladder or enters the intestine directly. Materials not immediately required may be temporarily stored in the liver's cells, or processed by enzyme action into other chemicals, and then released into the circulation.

Iron is recovered by the liver from outworn red blood cells that it breaks down. Only in foetal life does the liver actually produce new red cells.

the gut. It oxidises alcohol, nicotine and some barbiturates, and inactivates other poisons by linking them with carrier substances, which allows them to be excreted harmlessly. It also destroys certain hormones which, having circulated freely with the blood, are no longer needed.

Red blood cells. The foetal liver is a factory for red blood cells (*erythrocytes*). After birth this function is taken over by bone marrow, but the liver remains responsible, together with the spleen, marrow and lymph nodes, for destroying outworn cells. Much of the iron recovered in this process is lodged in the liver, and the protein residue of the haemoglobin molecule is converted to bile pigments, collected in the liver, and eventually disposed of through the bile duct into the duodenum.

In each of the liver's cells, which are arranged in angular columns, or lobules, all the many different functions of the organ are carried out simultaneously.

Blood enters each lobule, from both hepatic artery and portal vein, passes to the centre and leaves by a central vein. Bile leaves by canaliculi, which unite to form the bile duct.

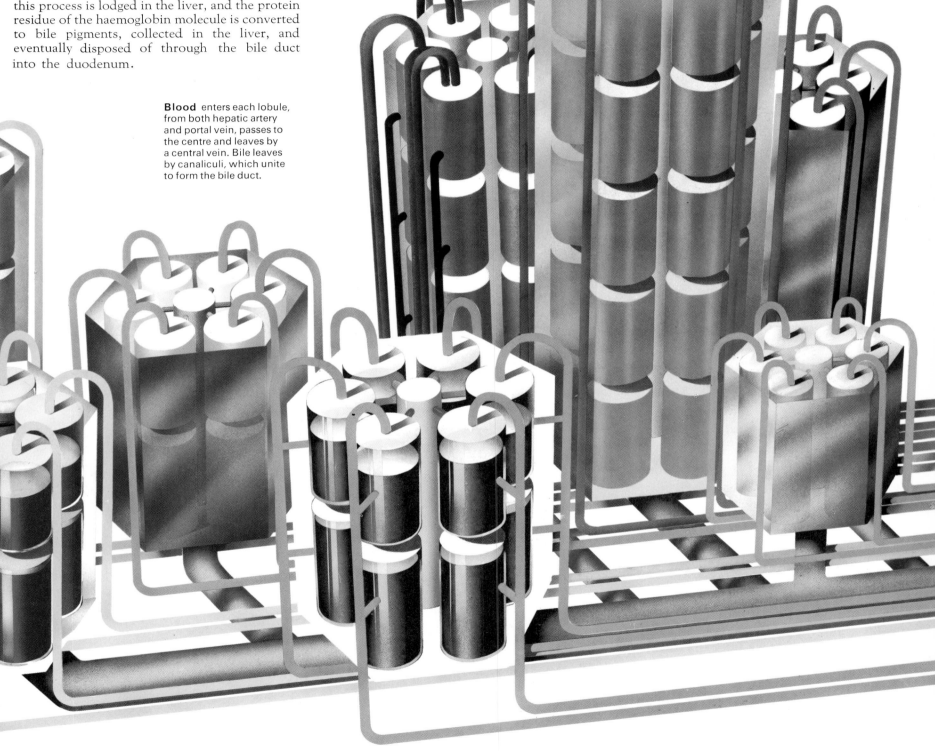

Bile pigments, from the protein residue of used red blood cells, are taken from the bloodstream and excreted into the intestine through the bile duct.

Vitamins, notably A, D and B$_{12}$, are stored in the liver, and released into the bloodstream when their levels in the blood fall below those necessary.

Poisons in the bloodstream may be rendered harmless in the liver—the process of detoxication. Unneeded hormones are also rendered inactive here.

Proteins such as blood albumins and globulins, and fibrinogen, are built up from amino acids, which may also be used to form sugars or burnt as fuel.

Fats and their component fatty acid and glycerol molecules may be used as fuel, converted to sugars or processed for storage elsewhere in the body.

Sugars absorbed from the intestine may be utilized immediately as fuel, stored as glycogen, or converted into other substances by complex enzyme reactions.

Circulation 1: the heart

The heart is a muscular pump weighing about one third of a kilogram. It begins work four weeks after conception—fully eight months before we are born—and continues without rest until we die. On average it beats 70 to 75 times per minute, but the rate can increase up to two and a half times in an emergency, the total output building up to 20 to 25 litres per minute—about four times that of the normal resting body. Athletes can increase output even further, but their heart rate seldom rises above the normal maximum of 170 to 180 beats per minute even during strenuous activity.

Heart muscle is made up of long, branched strands, striated like skeletal muscle, but different in appearance and performance. A regular, rhythmic beat is built in to the normal heart, which contains two centres of modified muscular tissue—the sino-atrial (SA) and atrio-ventricular (AV) nodes—which control the overall contractions and keep the heart beating as a unit. The SA node is the "pacemaker". Contractions within its fibres spread across the walls of the two atria, causing them to contract and drive blood down into the ventricles. The contractions spread to the AV node which, after a pause of a fraction of a second, stimulates a further, rapid tightening in, the thicker walls of the ventricles. This drives the blood almost simultaneously from the right ventricle into the lungs and from the left ventricle into the rest of the body. All this happens in the space of a heartbeat.

Chemical and nervous stimuli can affect the basic contraction rates of the SA and AV nodes, speeding or slowing the heartrate. Exercise or sudden fright causes the adrenal glands to secrete adrenaline, which reaches the nodes through the blood stream, speeding up the heart immediately "for fight, fright or frolic". Injected adrenaline (epinephrine) has the same effect. Shortage of oxygen, excess carbon dioxide, and a rise of body temperature also cause the heart beat to quicken. Raised blood pressure, detected by sensors in the carotid arteries, causes nervous signals to reach the heart through the brain and vagus nerve, slowing the beat and reducing pressure. When the pressure is too low, the sympathetic nervous system alerts the heart to increase both beat and pressure, to maintain an adequate blood supply to body tissues.

Four and a half to five litres of blood circulate in the human body through an immense complexity of tubes and tubules whose total length is measurable in kilometres. Veins and arteries, the largest tubes of the blood system, are the major routes to and from the heart—like motorways linking a capital city with its satellite towns. Arterioles and venules are smaller vessels which ramify in muscles and organs, but the greatest length and bulk of the blood system is made up of the capillaries. These are fine tubules averaging one millimetre in length and less than one hundredth of a millimetre in diameter, which weave their way into every corner of every organ and tissue, carrying blood to within a fraction of a hair's-breadth of every living cell.

Arteries are strong, triple-walled vessels which conduct oxygenated blood under pressure away from the heart. The pulmonary artery alone carries dark, de-oxygenated blood to the lungs for recharging. Ranging in diameter from 25mm to 0.5mm, arteries tend to run deep in the tissues where they are safe from superficial damage, as pressure within them is high. A punctured aorta emits a jet of blood almost the height of a man, and a disastrous amount of blood can be lost within seconds from a severed artery. The slightly elastic arterial walls expand a little at each heartbeat, helping to smooth the blood flow from the pump. This can be felt as the pulse, faithfully echoing the heartbeat at the neck, wrist and other places where arteries run close to the body surface.

Arteries divide into arterioles—tubes with

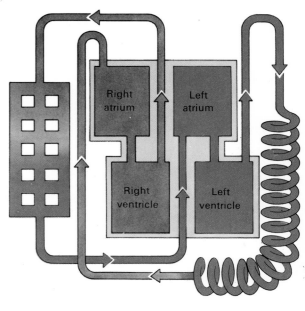

60,000 miles of tubing supply blood to every part of your body. Arteries carry oxygenated blood from the heart to the tissues through the capillaries, and veins return stale blood, laden with waste, for re-cycling.

Oxygenated blood from the lungs passes through the left chambers of the heart and is pumped round the body. Stale blood goes back through the right chambers of the heart to be pumped back to the lungs for re-oxygenation.

Right atrium

Left atrium

Right ventricle

Left ventricle

Pulmonary artery

Capillaries

The pulmonary artery carries used, stale blood from the heart to the lungs. In the capillaries of the lungs it is relieved of waste carbon dioxide and picks up oxygen, returning as fresh blood along the pulmonary vein to the heart ready to be pumped around the body once more.

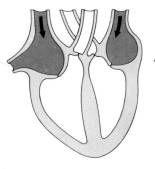
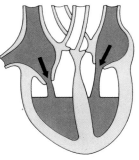
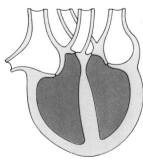
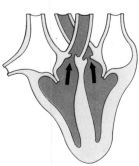
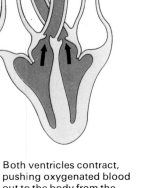

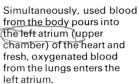

Simultaneously, used blood from the body pours into the left atrium (upper chamber) of the heart and fresh, oxygenated blood from the lungs enters the left atrium.

An impulse from the SA node, the heart's "pacemaker", causes both atria to contract, pushing the blood into the ventricles (lower chambers) through two valves.

For a fraction of a second, blood remains in both ventricles before an impulse from the AV node, the other half of the pacemaker, triggers a contraction.

Both ventricles contract, pushing oxygenated blood out to the body from the left side, and stale, used blood out from the right side to the lungs, where it is re-oxygenated.

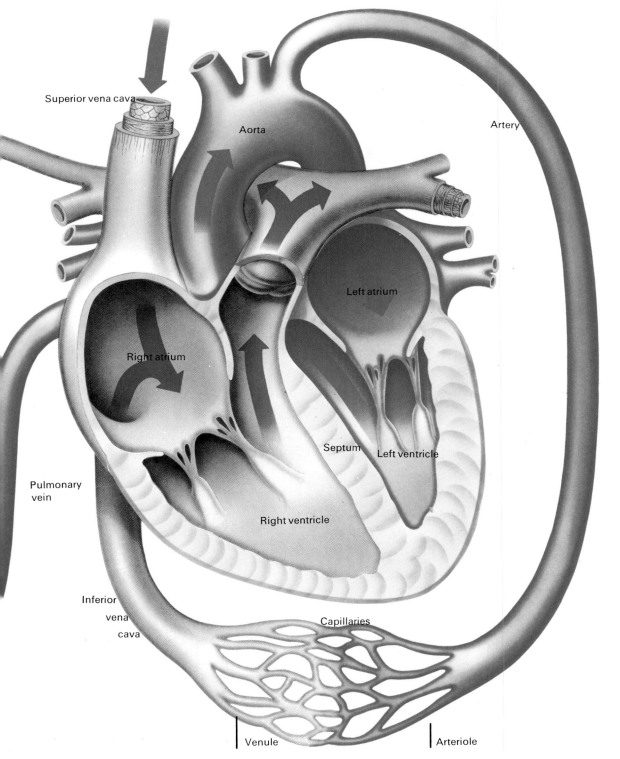

Superior vena cava

Aorta

Artery

Left atrium

Right atrium

Septum

Left ventricle

Pulmonary vein

Right ventricle

Inferior vena cava

Capillaries

Venule

Arteriole

thinner walls, containing layers and rings of smooth muscle which control the amount of blood entering the organ, and are themselves directed by the autonomic nervous system. They also respond to hormones and other chemicals in the blood. Thus, under stress, adrenaline in the blood causes arterioles in the skin and gut to contract and those in the skeletal muscle to expand, diverting blood from inessential organs to the muscles, for immediate action.

Arterioles in turn divide into capillaries, forming a dense network throughout the tissues. Capillary walls are made of endothelium, a membrane only one cell thick which lines venous and arterial vessels.

Now under only slight pressure from the heart, blood passes from capillaries to venules, thin-walled tubes of endothelium wrapped in connective tissue and muscle fibre, which lead in turn to stronger, thicker veins. Though nowhere as robust as arteries, veins form a coarse network of pipes which offer many alternative routes back to the heart. Pressure is low, but the tendency of blood to collect under its own weight in the lower extremities is normally counteracted by the massaging effect of neighbouring muscles, which keep the blood moving. Simple cup-shaped valves in the larger veins ensure that it only moves towards the heart. Though many veins are visible as a bluish network just below the skin, major veins tend to run deep in the tissues, like arteries, to protect them from damage.

The main blood vessel of the body is the aorta. Thick as a walking stick, it arches gracefully from the left ventricle of the heart; major arteries leave from the top of the arch for the arms and head; from the main length of the aorta, arteries lead off to the muscles of the spine and ribs, to the oesophagus and windpipe, diaphragm, gut, liver, spleen, kidneys and reproductive organs. At its lower end, the aorta divides to supply the leg and buttock muscles, the tiny remnant continuing into the pelvis taking blood to the last few vertebrae.

The venous return system follows a similar pattern. Veins converge on two major vessels, the inferior and superior vena cavae, which join above the heart and drain into the right atrium. The venous blood descends into the right ventricle and is pumped at each heartbeat through the pulmonary artery to the lungs. Here it is relieved of carbon dioxide and acquires oxygen, travelling rapidly through the lung capillaries to collect in the pulmonary vein for immediate return to the heart. It enters the left atrium and in a single heartbeat is on its way once again round the body, leaving through the aorta.

Capillaries
Most of the 60,000 miles of tubing in the circulatory system is taken up by capillaries, which spread in a network throughout the tissues carrying blood from the larger vessels to every part of the body. Arteries, carrying fresh, oxygenated blood under high pressure from the heart, branch into arterioles, which in turn subdivide into capillaries. Capillary walls are only one cell thick, allowing oxygen and nutrients to pass easily through, and waste material to diffuse back into the bloodstream. Now carrying de-oxygenated blood at a low pressure, capillaries join up to form venules which lead back into veins. Stale blood is thus conducted back to the heart.

Circulation 2: blood...

The blood and lymph circulatory systems form a vast interlinked network through which oxygen and food are distributed to each of the body's cells, and waste materials are removed. The lymph system returns fluid from the tissues into the blood, through lymph vessels interrupted by lymph nodes, which act as one of the body's defences against infection. Each node has its own blood supply and drainage, and is continuously active, filtering bacteria, foreign matter and cancer cells from the lymph; here also the cells called lymphocytes are produced. Lymphocytes play an important role in the development of immunity against infectious disease; when stimulated they turn into plasma cells, which form antibodies.

The cells in the blood

The vast majority of the cells of the blood are *erythrocytes*—red blood cells—with the vital function of transporting oxygen which has diffused into the plasma from the air in the lungs, and the removal of carbon dioxide formed by the tissues during metabolism. Each cubic millimetre of blood contains between four and a half and five and a half million erythrocytes. In the same volume there are also about seven and a half thousand white cells—*leukocytes*. These have a different function—that of protection against micro-organisms that have managed to enter the tissues. Leukocytes are of several different types, named from their appearance when stained and examined microscopically. *Neutrophils, eosinophils* and *basophils* contain granules, *lymphocytes* and *monocytes* do not.

Lymph node

Vein

Artery

Venous valve

Vein structure

Drawn fresh from a pin-prick, blood is a dense, slightly tacky red fluid which congeals and solidifies rapidly. Collected in bulk and spun in a centrifuge (or treated and allowed to settle), it separates to a pale, straw-coloured liquid (plasma) and a reddish-brown sediment of fine particles making up about 45 per cent of the total volume. Plasma is a solution of salts and proteins, not unlike the fluid content of living cells. Blood proteins, which account for up to nine per cent by weight of the plasma, contribute to its slightly syrupy texture and have important roles to play in nutrition and defence. *Serum*, the pale liquid that oozes from scraped skin, is plasma less *fibrin*, one of the proteins that help to coagulate blood.

The reddish-brown sediment is made up of red blood corpuscles (*erythrocytes*) in enormous numbers, and smaller quantities of white corpuscles (*leukocytes*) and platelets. Normally these circulate in suspension through the tissues; every drop of blood contains hundreds of millions of each; they can readily be examined on a suitably-stained slide under the microscope. Red corpuscles, which are only seven to ten thousandths of a millimetre in diameter, are by far the most numerous; there are normally about five million to every cubic millimetre, and some two million are created and destroyed every second. Formed in red bone marrow, they appear first as normal cells but soon lose their nuclei, harden, and become biconcave. This is the form in which they circulate. By weight they are about one-third *haemoglobin*, a purple-red compound of iron and protein which readily takes up oxygen to form the bright red, unstable *oxyhaemoglobin*.

While going through the lungs, where dissolved oxygen is plentiful, haemoglobin in the erythrocytes is converted to oxyhaemoglobin. Circulating to other tissues of the body, which demand oxygen for their minute-to-minute activities, oxyhaemoglobin breaks down to yield free oxygen and haemoglobin; the oxygen is absorbed immediately by the waiting cells, and the haemoglobin continues on its way for reconversion during its next passage through the lungs. Erythrocytes have an active life of about twelve weeks. When worn out, they are removed from circulation by *phagocytic* (cell-eating) cells in the liver, marrow and spleen. Their iron is stored and reused; their proteins are demolished and the residues become bile pigments.

White blood corpuscles (leukocytes) are two to three times the diameter of erythrocytes, but almost a thousand times less numerous. Normally colourless and transparent, they appear only in stained preparations, when both their nuclei and their cytoplasm take up colour. In life they circulate passively with the blood like erythrocytes, but are also to one degree or another active in themselves, squeezing into and out of blood vessels, creeping through tiny holes and cavities in the tissues like mites in cheese, and accumulating at trouble spots—especially wounds or sites of infection—where there is work for them to do, aiding the body's defences.

Platelets or *thrombocytes* are the smallest blood particles. They contain a chemical which, released at the site of an injury, converts the plasma enzyme *prothrombin* to an active form *thrombin*, which precipitates the protein *fibrin* and causes the blood to clot.

...and lymph

The very finest subdivisions of the circulatory network, the capillaries, are responsible for supplying the tissues of the body with food materials and oxygen, and removing from them the waste products, which would otherwise accumulate. For these materials to pass from and into the bloodstream it is necessary for them to dissolve in the blood plasma, and for the solution to cross the barrier formed by the capillary wall. At the arterial end of the capillary, blood pressure is high, squeezing fluid through the wall; at the venous end the pressure is lower, so that water is attracted back from the tissues into the now concentrated blood by the force called osmotic pressure.

Lymph is the transparent and almost colourless fluid exuded from the capillaries. It bathes the cells (where it is known as tissue fluid) and ultimately drains into a diffuse system of channels of its own—the lymphatic system. As might be expected, it is essentially plasma with only a low proportion of proteins, but lymph also contains high levels of waste materials, bacteria, dead cells, and other debris from the inter-cellular spaces of the tissues. Lymph channels are lined with thin epithelium and fitted at intervals with valves; like venous blood, lymph is pushed along one-way channels by pressure from the surrounding tissues. Most lymph vessels of the body converge on the thoracic duct, which runs along the spine between the dorsal aorta and inferior vena cava and drains into the left subclavian artery close to the neck. The right side of the head and chest, and the right arm and shoulder, drain into a separate channel, the right thoracic duct, which enters the right subclavian vein.

Lymph also plays an important part in the process by which fats are taken into the body and distributed around it. Within the villi of the intestinal wall are fine lymph vessels called lacteals, which take up microscopic globules of fat (*chylomicrons*) from the wall and pass them, in the form of a milky fluid, directly into the venous circulation.

Lymph nodes, strategically placed along the course of lymph vessels, filter debris from the liquid and manufacture phagocytic lymphocytes and monocytes; they also produce the globulins which are important in antibody formation, protecting the body against the invasion of foreign protein. Tonsils and adenoids are special concentrations of lymphatic tissue that produce lymphocytes in the throat region, and the intestine has patches of lymphatic tissue, similar in function, along its length. The thymus gland, large in infants but reducing in size and eventually almost disappearing after adolescence, is a source of protecting lymphoid cells and chemicals during the critical period of growth, when the young person meets new sources of infection every day. The spleen also produces phagocytic lymphocytes, and has the special additional function of destroying red blood corpuscles.

The lymphatic system has important protective functions. "Enlarged glands" appearing in the neck, armpit and groin during illness testify to its efficiency, for the glands—actually lymph nodes—are actively destroying bacteria, clearing the circulatory systems of harmful debris, and producing cells which attack sources of infection both physically and chemically.

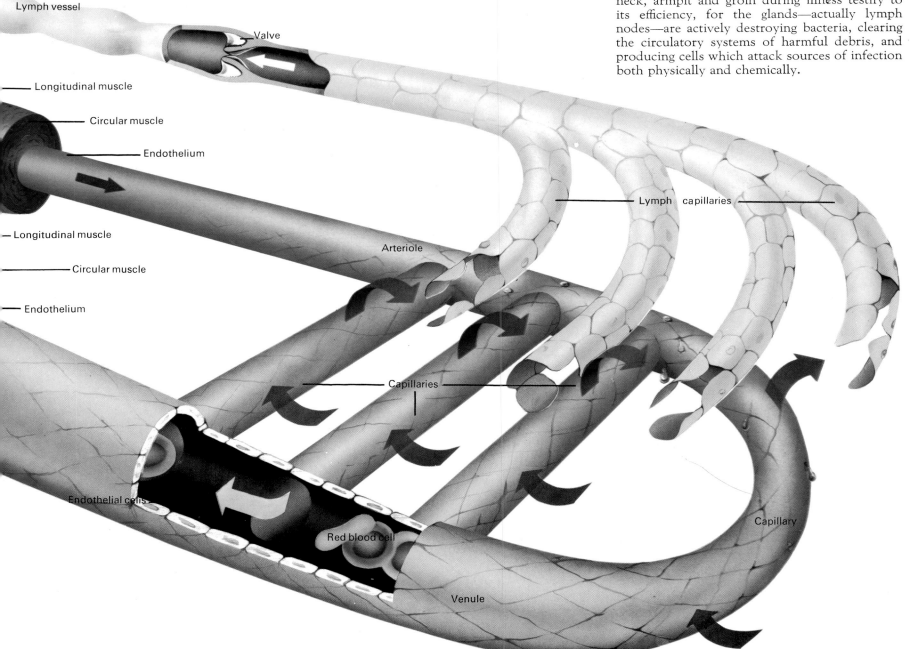

Lymph vessel

Valve

Longitudinal muscle

Circular muscle

Endothelium

Longitudinal muscle

Circular muscle

Endothelium

Arteriole

Lymph capillaries

Capillaries

Endothelial cells

Red blood cell

Capillary

Venule

Respiration

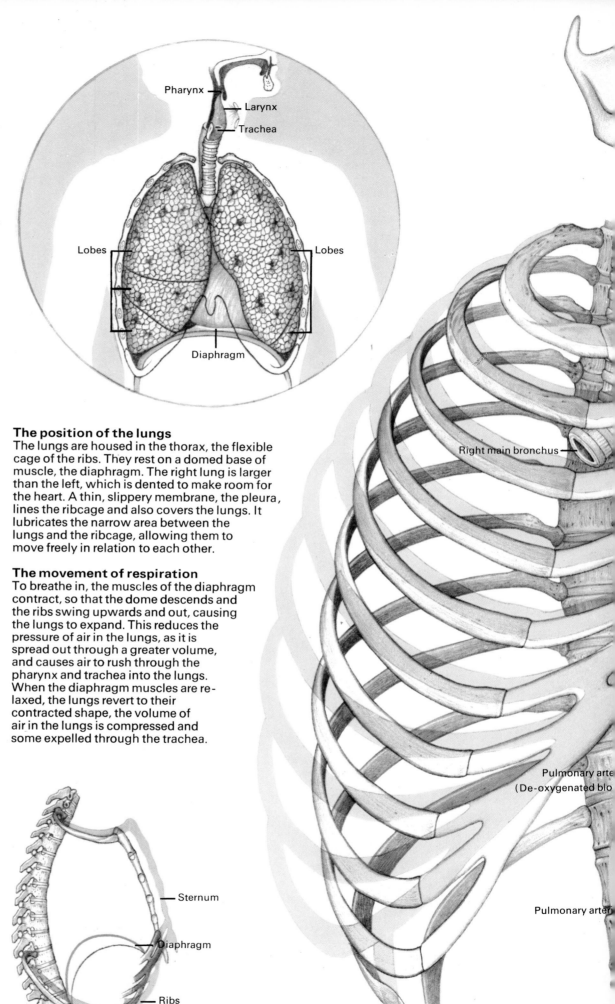

In ordinary language respiration is the simple, everyday matter of breathing in and out. To biologists respiration is the more complex business of releasing chemical energy from food, for the use of the body. Respiration includes breathing, which involves the chest and lungs and the bloodstream. But it also involves every other tissue of the body, for the release of energy occurs in the individual cells, at rates which match their needs and levels of activity.

The body surface is too small to absorb all the oxygen we need for the millions of cells all over the body, and so we have developed a special internal surface for breathing—one which we can keep permanently moist, safe from drying out and mechanical damage, and protected from invasion by bacteria, fungi and other disease-producing organisms. This is the lining of our lungs, a vast area of sixty to seventy square metres, over forty times the surface area of our body. Stowed away neatly inside its two springy sacs, the lining of the lung brings us into intimate contact with the outside world, but very much on our own terms. Thin as fine paper, and backed by a plexus of fine-walled capillaries, it absorbs oxygen readily into solution and transfers it rapidly to the haemoglobin of the blood. At the same time it allows carbon dioxide to escape from the blood into the air spaces of the lungs, and be blown out with the next breath.

The *trachea* or windpipe, which conducts air down to the lungs, begins at a narrow opening— the *glottis*—in the wall of the pharynx. This opening is protected by the *epiglottis*, a flap of cartilage and skin which closes at the critical movement of swallowing, helping to keep food out. Air enters the glottis from the nasal cavity or mouth, where it has been warmed and filtered, and passes through the *larynx* (voice box). The trachea itself is a flexible cylindrical tube about 25 cm long and 25 mm in diameter, clearly visible under the skin of the throat. Lined with ciliated epithelium, which constantly secretes mucus, it is strengthened and held in shape by C-shaped bands of cartilage. At the lower end, within the thorax, it forks to form left and right bronchi, which enter their respective lungs.

Weighing a little over a kilogram, the lungs fit neatly into the thorax, the flexible cone-shaped box formed by the rib-cage and domed, muscular diaphragm. The left lung, slightly smaller than the right, is deeply indented on its inner surface to make room for the heart. The lungs are covered, and the thorax is lined, with a damp, secretory membrane (*pleura*); apart from a thin film of liquid lubricating the pleura, there is no room for anything else in the thorax. Each lung is divided internally into nine segments, and each segment receives a separate sub-branch of the bronchus. Within the segments bronchi divide further into smaller bronchi and then into *bronchioles*, finally ending in over a quarter of a million respiratory bronchioles, each about 0.5 mm in diameter. Surrounded with smooth muscle and lined with thin epithelium, the respiratory bronchioles are covered with hollow,

The position of the lungs

The lungs are housed in the thorax, the flexible cage of the ribs. They rest on a domed base of muscle, the diaphragm. The right lung is larger than the left, which is dented to make room for the heart. A thin, slippery membrane, the pleura, lines the ribcage and also covers the lungs. It lubricates the narrow area between the lungs and the ribcage, allowing them to move freely in relation to each other.

The movement of respiration

To breathe in, the muscles of the diaphragm contract, so that the dome descends and the ribs swing upwards and out, causing the lungs to expand. This reduces the pressure of air in the lungs, as it is spread out through a greater volume, and causes air to rush through the pharynx and trachea into the lungs. When the diaphragm muscles are re-laxed, the lungs revert to their contracted shape, the volume of air in the lungs is compressed and some expelled through the trachea.

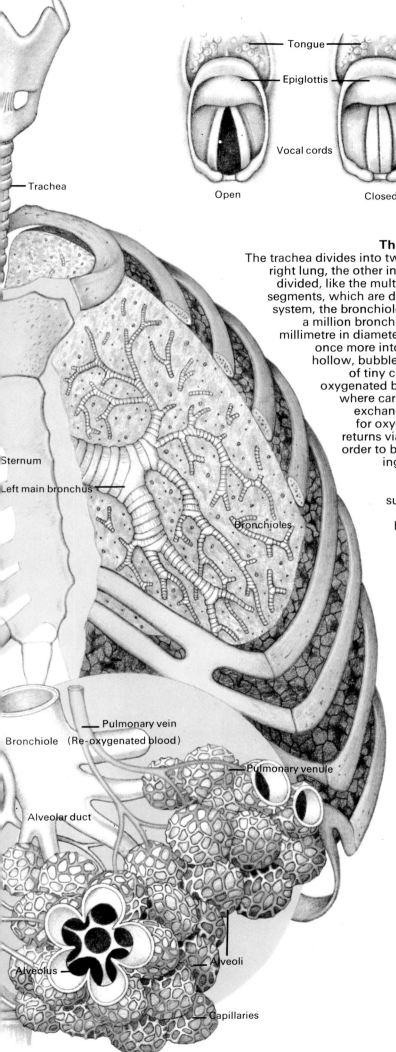

Trachea

Sternum

Left main bronchus

Bronchioles

Bronchiole (Re-oxygenated blood)

Pulmonary vein

Pulmonary venule

Alveolar duct

Alveoli

Alveolus

Capillaries

Tongue

Epiglottis

Vocal cords

Open   Closed

The larynx, which produces vocal sounds, consists of cartilage, ligaments and muscle. The vocal cords are fibrous strands stretched across the top of the trachea between the thyroid cartilage ("Adam's apple") and the arytenoid cartilage. The pitch of the voice is controlled by varying length and tension in the cords; timbre and resonance by the shape of the mouth and air passages; and volume by the pressure of air from the lungs.

The internal structure of the lung

The trachea divides into two bronchi, one carrying air into the right lung, the other into the left. Each bronchus is further divided, like the multiplying branches of a tree, into nine segments, which are divided again into the "twigs" of the system, the bronchioles. There are more than a quarter of a million bronchioles in the lungs, each about half a millimetre in diameter. These tiny bronchioles subdivide once more into alveolar ducts, which terminate in hollow, bubble-like organs, the alveoli. A network of tiny capillaries surrounds the alveoli. De-oxygenated blood is pumped into the capillaries, where carbon dioxide is extracted from it and exchanged through the walls of the alveoli for oxygen. The re-oxygenated blood then returns via the pulmonary vein to the heart in order to be pumped through the body, carrying oxygen to each cell. This complex structure, ending in the millions of alveoli, provides a large, protected surface area over which air can come into close contact with the body's bloodstream. Cells which are otherwise distant from the air and the essential oxygen it contains can be supplied with it when it enters the bloodstream through the walls of the alveoli. The internal surface area of the respiratory system, if laid out flat, would cover 60 to 70 square metres, many times the external surface area of the body. Even if we were able to breathe through the whole of our external body area, it would still not provide enough oxygen to refuel all the cells in the body.

The alveoli are grape-like structures, the end of the journey for the air drawn in at a breath. They are surrounded by a network of blood capillaries. The walls of the alveoli and the walls of the capillaries are each made of a single layer of cells, so that the distance between the pocket of air in the alveolus and the blood into which oxygen from the air has to pass is less than 0.005 of a millimetre. Oxygen and carbon dioxide are exchanged through the walls of the alveolus. Carbon dioxide is expelled, and re-oxygenated blood returns along the pulmonary vein to the heart, ready to be pumped around the body once again.

bubble-like *alveoli*, whose internal surface is the site of gaseous exchange within the lung. Capillaries of the pulmonary artery form a network over the alveoli, bringing blood very close to their surface. The alveoli secrete a thin film of liquid with low surface tension, through which the gas exchange takes place.

In breathing we increase the internal volume of the thorax, by tightening the muscles of the diaphragm (causing it to contract from dome to shallow-saucer shape) and tightening the muscles of the rib-cage, causing the ribs to swing upwards and outwards. When the thorax expands, the lungs must expand too, and the air in the lungs becomes rarefied, forming a low-pressure area. To restore pressure, air rushes down the tube of the trachea. The walls of the lungs are stretched by the expansion. When tension slackens in the muscles of diaphragm and ribs, the walls of the lungs revert to their normal or resting shape, pulling the thorax back to shape with them. This compresses the air in the lungs, forcing some of it out again through the trachea. At each normal breath we take in about half a litre of air. Of this about one-third remains in the bronchi and bronchioles, and only two-thirds finds its way to the alveoli.

Within the alveoli, oxygen is absorbed into the blood, and carbon dioxide passes from the blood (where it is held mainly in the plasma, but also partly on the erythrocytes) to be released into the air. Apart from its main function of bringing oxygen into the body and eliminating a poisonous waste product, this exchange restores the correct level of acidity to the blood. Rate of breathing is in fact controlled by acidity level, which is normally determined by the amount of bicarbonate (derived from carbon dioxide) present in the plasma. When we are breathing too slowly, carbon dioxide accumulates and causes our blood to acidify slightly. This change is detected by cells in the medulla of the brain, which are responsible for the movements of breathing. Acidification stimulates the cells which cause inspiration, making us breathe faster and more deeply. This rids us of the excess carbon dioxide and restores the blood to its normal level of acidity. There are additional monitoring cells in the walls of the aorta and the carotid arteries, with similar functions.

With so important a task to perform, the delicate alveolar membrane has to be protected rigorously from damage and other influences which would lower its efficiency. The alveoli themselves are cleaned by wandering phagocytes, which engulf dust particles and bacteria. The cilia lining the bronchi and tubules constantly waft mucus upwards from the base of the lungs to the trachea, carrying cell debris and foreign particles up to the throat; "phlegm" produced in this way is swallowed and disposed of in the stomach. Large foreign particles and other sources of irritation (including fungi and bacteria) cause over-production of mucus, which has to be coughed up. Both the coughing and the sneezing reflexes, which involve sudden, sharp exhalation, help to blow invading particles and other debris from the air passages, and so protect the lungs. Cold or dry air, which may upset the working of the alveoli, is warmed and moistened on its way down by the mucous membrane which lines the nasal cavity, pharynx and trachea.

Excretion

Like every other chemical factory with a wide intake of raw materials and extensive range of products, the body has a day-to-day problem of waste disposal. We have an urgent and constant need to shed the by-products of chemical activity—the waste materials of the system—which are mostly poisons and may kill if allowed to accumulate in the tissues. Excretion is the elimination of chemical waste products; we have several ways of doing this.

The most important waste products of metabolism are heat, carbon dioxide and water (derived from oxidation of carbohydrates and fats), bile salts and pigments remaining from the destruction of red blood corpuscles, mineral salts from the breakdown of other outworn tissues and from excess dietary intake, and urea—one end-product of protein breakdown. We lose heat through the skin by radiation, and heat and water through both skin and lungs by evaporation. Carbon dioxide is blown away through the lungs. Bile salts and pigments leave via the gut, serving a useful purpose as digestive agents on the way. Mineral salts (especially sodium chloride) leave through the skin during sweating, together with a little urea. Most urea, with a few selected mineral salts, leaves through the kidneys —our main excretory organs for non-gaseous wastes—in the form of urine.

Kidneys evolved in our aquatic ancestors as organs for eliminating excess water and simultaneously removing soluble waste materials from the body. These are still the most important functions of the kidney in man, though there is a change of emphasis. Living in air, we are more likely to run short of water than to become waterlogged, and our kidneys now emphasize water conservation, rather than water loss. In fact they maintain a state of balance between salts, proteins and water in the blood, continuing to remove soluble wastes at the same time. Firmly fixed to the back wall of the abdomen, slightly above waist level, the two kidneys are roughly the shape of a bean and the size of a child's fist. Each is supplied with blood by a large artery from the aorta, and drained by a vein of similar size to the inferior vena cava. The two kidneys together receive about one-quarter of the volume of every heart-beat—approximately one and one-third litres of arterial blood per minute. This they monitor, filter and process with incredible speed and accuracy. Waste products in solution drain away down the two ureters, which pass from the concave, inner side of the kidney to the bladder. All the blood passes through the kidneys almost twenty times each hour, though only about one-fifth of it is filtered at each circuit. Sliced open, the kidney reveals an outer *cortex* and an inner *medulla*, of a different texture.

The kidney contains about one million renal tubules or *nephrons*, each three to six centimetres long, with a cup-shaped mouth (*Bowman's capsule*) enclosing a *glomerulus*—a tiny knot of 40 to 50 minute capillaries carrying blood from the renal artery. Practically all of the nephrons lie with the capsule and glomerulus in the cortex,

The function of the kidneys is to remove soluble impurities from the blood and to maintain the balance of salts, water and protein in the bloodstream. Waste products are excreted in urine, which is produced in quantity and concentration according to how much fluid the body needs to lose to maintain water balance. The renal capsule covers the "rind" or cortex of the kidney. Embedded in the cortex are the nephrons, or renal tubules, which extend into the medulla. Urine drains from these tubules into ducts which lead into the pelvis of the kidney, through the ureter and collects in the bladder to be passed out of the body via the urethra. Blood is pumped into the kidneys through the renal artery, and leaves through the renal vein. About one-quarter of the volume of the blood pumped by each heartbeat passes directly to the kidneys. Approximately one and a third litres of blood per minute passes through the kidneys to be filtered and cleansed.

but the tubules bend and twist upon themselves, some locally, others extending like trombones into the medulla. Each tubule opens into a collecting duct in the medulla, and the many thousands of ducts drain into a collecting area (*hilum*) in the concave side of the kidney, where the ureter begins. Blood forced into the kidney through the renal artery is distributed between the million or so glomeruli. Because the venules that leave the glomeruli are narrower in bore than the branches of artery entering them, pressure in the glomeruli builds up until sufficient to force some of the plasma through the walls of the capillaries. The walls allow water, sugars, salts and urea molecules to filter through, but hold back large protein molecules and all the blood particles—including red and white corpuscles and platelets. The liquid filtrate collects in the cup-shaped opening of the nephron, which surrounds each glomerulus, and runs down the nephron tube. The remaining blood, concentrated by the loss of about a fifth of its plasma, passes through the glomeruli and into a network of vessels surrounding the tubules.

If all the filtered liquid were voided as urine, we would be seriously dehydrated in less than an hour. Instead the long kidney tubules undertake a recovery process which transfers water salts, and sugars back through their wall and into the bloodstream, leaving a concentrated solution of urea, together with a small amount of salts and other minor waste products, to collect in the hilum and find its way down the ureter to the bladder. Here it is stored until release.

The action of the kidneys is controlled by several hormones, mostly in response to changes in water content of the tissues. In

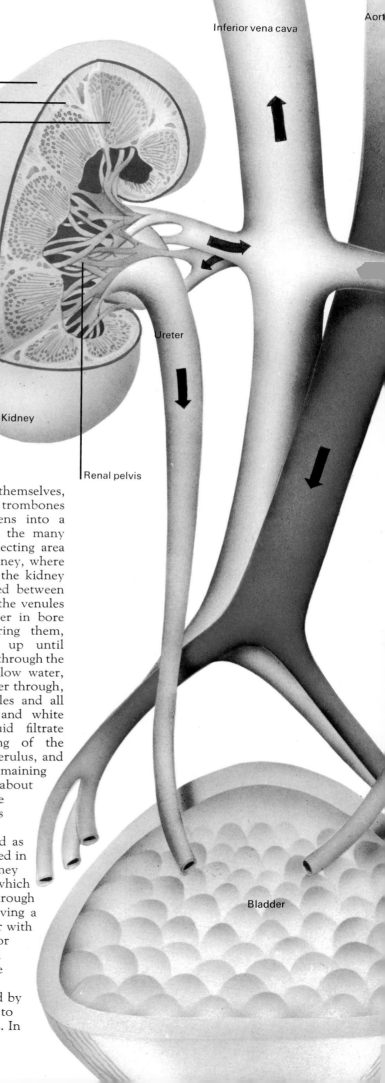

Inferior vena cava

Aort

Capsule

Cortex

Medulla

Ureter

Renal pelvis

Kidney

Bladder

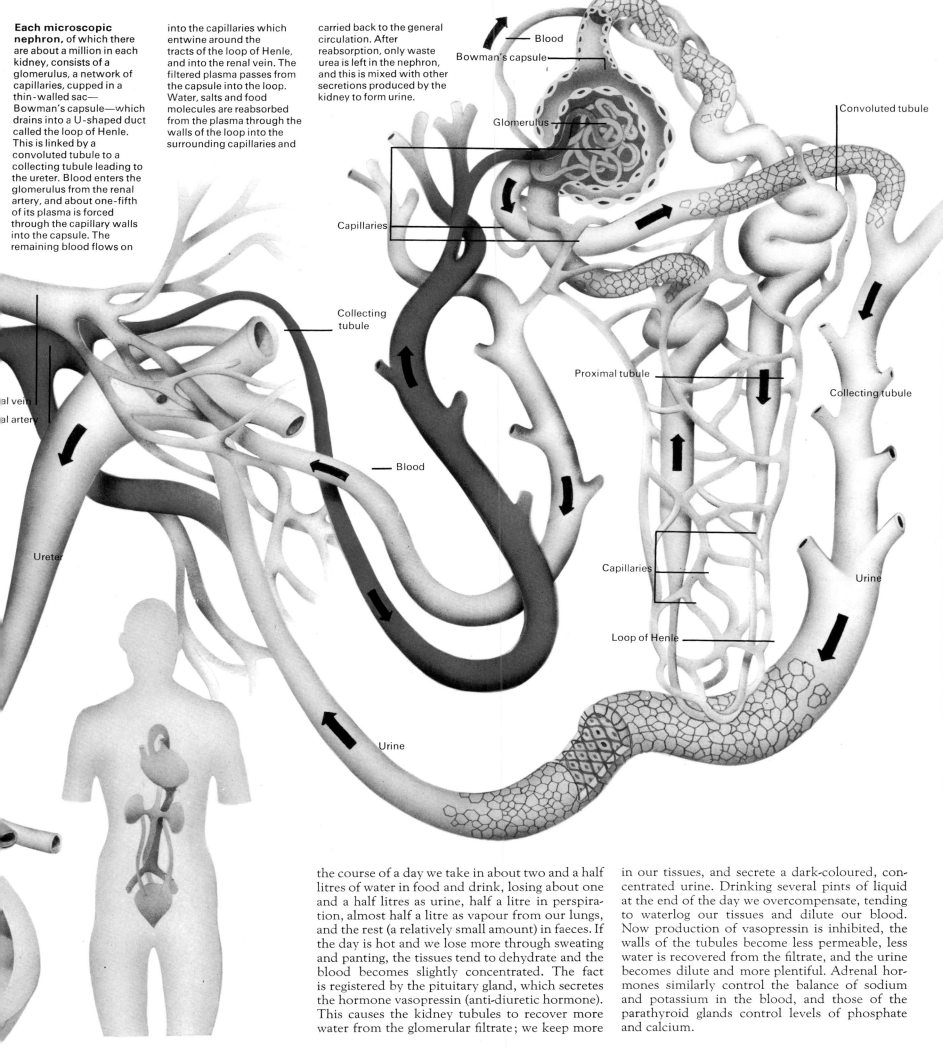

Each microscopic nephron, of which there are about a million in each kidney, consists of a glomerulus, a network of capillaries, cupped in a thin-walled sac—Bowman's capsule—which drains into a U-shaped duct called the loop of Henle. This is linked by a convoluted tubule to a collecting tubule leading to the ureter. Blood enters the glomerulus from the renal artery, and about one-fifth of its plasma is forced through the capillary walls into the capsule. The remaining blood flows on into the capillaries which entwine around the tracts of the loop of Henle, and into the renal vein. The filtered plasma passes from the capsule into the loop. Water, salts and food molecules are reabsorbed from the plasma through the walls of the loop into the surrounding capillaries and carried back to the general circulation. After reabsorption, only waste urea is left in the nephron, and this is mixed with other secretions produced by the kidney to form urine.

Blood

Bowman's capsule

Glomerulus

Convoluted tubule

Capillaries

Collecting tubule

Proximal tubule

Collecting tubule

Blood

Capillaries

Urine

Ureter

Loop of Henle

Urine

al vein
al artery

the course of a day we take in about two and a half litres of water in food and drink, losing about one and a half litres as urine, half a litre in perspiration, almost half a litre as vapour from our lungs, and the rest (a relatively small amount) in faeces. If the day is hot and we lose more through sweating and panting, the tissues tend to dehydrate and the blood becomes slightly concentrated. The fact is registered by the pituitary gland, which secretes the hormone vasopressin (anti-diuretic hormone). This causes the kidney tubules to recover more water from the glomerular filtrate; we keep more in our tissues, and secrete a dark-coloured, concentrated urine. Drinking several pints of liquid at the end of the day we overcompensate, tending to waterlog our tissues and dilute our blood. Now production of vasopressin is inhibited, the walls of the tubules become less permeable, less water is recovered from the filtrate, and the urine becomes dilute and more plentiful. Adrenal hormones similarly control the balance of sodium and potassium in the blood, and those of the parathyroid glands control levels of phosphate and calcium.

The nervous system

All living organisms, even the simplest single-celled animals, show the fundamental quality of *irritability*, or responsiveness to stimuli from the world about them. This quality allows animals to monitor their environment, detect changes in it, and respond in ways which help them to survive. In the course of evolution, progressing from single-celled to many-celled organisms, animals have developed a special system for receiving, processing and using information. This is the nervous system. Without it we would virtually be helpless. We would perceive nothing of the outside world or even of the world within us. Our muscles would not move, and the various organs of the body would be unable to work together in co-ordination.

The nervous system can be thought of as a number of separate but integrated sections which monitor the world and instigate and co-ordinate the body's multiple activities. The *central nervous system* (CNS) consists of the *brain* and *spinal cord*, which are enclosed within the skull and vertebral column. The *peripheral nervous system* is made up of *sensory nerves* which run from sense organs throughout the body to the CNS, *motor nerves* which originate in the CNS and run to the muscles, and *autonomic nerves* which originate in the spinal ganglia and are distributed to internal organs.

The nervous system is delicate and precious and, like any other precision instrument, must be carefully protected. The brain and spinal cord are wrapped in very tough membranes called *meninges*. They are bathed in a liquid—cerebrospinal fluid—which also fills the *ventricles*, or spaces in the middle of the brain, and the central canal of the spinal cord. Cerebrospinal fluid augments the supply of nutrients and oxygen provided by a copious blood supply, and adds an effective water cushion to the other defences (including skull, vertebral blocks and muscles) which protect the system against jarring. Individual nerve cells within the brain and cord are further buffered by *glial cells* (neuroglia), which are packed between them and support them. Peripheral nerves are surrounded by a protective membrane, the *perineurium*, and most nerve fibres are encased in modified glial cells (*Schwann cells*), which wrap around them like a roll of paper.

Nerve cells or *neurones* have a cell body containing the nucleus and a very long fibre or extension called an *axon*. On the cell body, and on the end of the axon are short branches called *dendrites*, which end in tiny *synaptic knobs*. The point where these knobs touch some part of another nerve cell is called a synapse; similar contact with a muscle cell is called a *neuromuscular junction*. Peripheral nerves consist mainly of axons which run the whole length of the nerve. The CNS consists of *nuclei* (which are groups of cell bodies) and *tracts* (made up of many parallel axons). Groups of cell bodies outside the CNS are called *ganglia*. The cell bodies of motor neurones are housed deep inside the spinal cord, while those of sensory neurones cluster in the *dorsal root ganglia*, just outside the spinal cord. Some autonomic nerves are connected to a chain of ganglia—the *sympathetic chain*—which runs parallel to the spinal cord in the abdominal and thoracic cavities, linking autonomic nerves which emerge between each pair of adjacent vertebrae. Most nerves and tracts of axons, wrapped in *myelin* (the fatty material of Schwann cells), appear white; myelinated tracts in the CNS are therefore called *white matter*. Cell bodies are not myelinated, and so form the *grey matter* of brain and spinal cord.

Nerves to the ears, eyes, nose, mouth and face leave the brain through holes in the skull. Nerves to the rest of the body leave the spinal cord through the spaces between the vertebrae. *Efferent nerves* (called *motor nerves*, because they control the skeletal muscles or motor system of the body) emerge from the ventral side of the vertebral column. *Afferent nerves* (called *sensory nerves*, because they link with sensory organs) enter the spinal cord on the dorsal surface. Between each pair of vertebrae, an afferent and an efferent nerve emerge on either side of the vertebral column, the two joining to form the paired spinal nerves.

Although nerves can be thought of as wires or telegraph cables carrying messages in the form of bursts of electric current, in fact a nerve impulse is more complicated than a surge of electrons travelling through a conducting material such as a copper wire. The transmission of an impulse through a living cell involves the movement of electrically charged particles—ions—across, and not along, a membrane.

At rest, a nerve cell is polarized—that is the outside of its membrane bears a different charge from the inside; this is because of the different concentrations of sodium and potassium ions within and without the membrane. Inside is a high concentration of potassium ions and a low concentration of sodium, and outside *vice versa*. When a nerve is stimulated, the arrangement of the molecules in the membrane is altered, allowing potassium ions to leak out, and sodium ions to leak in. At this point the nerve membrane becomes depolarized and the electrical change causes an alteration in the molecular structure of the next section of membrane, which in turn becomes depolarized. So an impulse travels rapidly along the nerve fibre.

Nerve cells are remarkable because they can communicate with each other. An excited neurone sends messages, in the form of the tiny, rapid pulses of electrical activity described, along its axon, to the synapses which link it to other neurones. The electrical impulses cannot themselves jump across the synapse, but the signal is transmitted by chemical activity. In the synaptic knob are vesicles—bubbles of a *neuro-transmitter* chemical—which burst when the electrical impulses arrive. This releases the neuro-transmitter on to the surface of the next neurone, which responds by developing impulses of its own.

When impulses arrive at a neuro-muscular junction, similar transmitter chemicals are released, causing the muscle cells to contract. Drugs—chemicals which affect the working of the body—are often very similar in action to neuro-transmitters and so have a profound effect on the nervous system. By interposing their effects at the synapses they interfere with the delicately balanced relationships between many thousands or millions of working cells, and affect the whole system profoundly.

Everything we do requires the mediation of the nervous system, from the very simplest flick of a finger to highly co-ordinated, sophisticated activities. Some simple responses use only selected parts of the nervous system. If you touch something very hot, you will pull your hand away quickly. This simple but essential response is called a *spinal reflex*, since impulses from the sensory nerve endings in the skin, passing along the afferent nerves, need only reach the spinal cord to be acted upon; impulses are generated within motor cells of the spinal cord, which pass back down the motor neurones of the arm and activate the muscles responsible for moving the hand. This reflex is *automatic*—it would happen in your sleep. And it is *unlearned*—a new-born baby would behave in the same way.

The behaviour of very simple animals is made up entirely of reflexes, but higher animals and man have greater freedom of action and can respond in a variety of ways to most situations. Reflexes continue to be important in emergencies and for maintaining such vital activities as breathing and blinking. But most human behaviour falls into another category; it is voluntary, learned, and non-reflexive. This kind of behaviour is made possible because the nervous system of higher animals is not just a machine which can work in only one way. It is in fact much more sophisticated than the most complex computer, learning from experience and directing its own activities from higher control centres than simpler animals possess. Since no two people have the same range of experiences, and no two brains are exactly alike, every human nervous system behaves in a unique way.

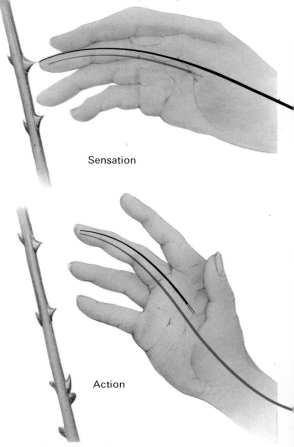

Sensation

Action

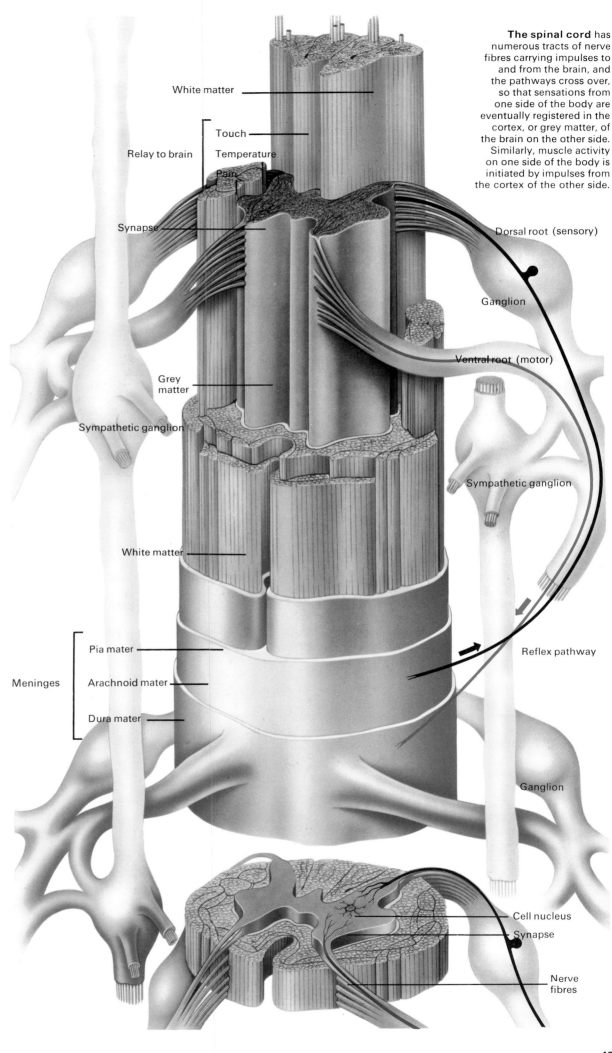

The spinal cord has numerous tracts of nerve fibres carrying impulses to and from the brain, and the pathways cross over, so that sensations from one side of the body are eventually registered in the cortex, or grey matter, of the brain on the other side. Similarly, muscle activity on one side of the body is initiated by impulses from the cortex of the other side.

White matter

Touch

Relay to brain

Temperature

Pain

Synapse

Grey matter

Sympathetic ganglion

White matter

Dorsal root (sensory)

Ganglion

Ventral root (motor)

Sympathetic ganglion

Meninges

Pia mater

Arachnoid mater

Dura mater

Reflex pathway

Ganglion

Cell nucleus

Synapse

Nerve fibres

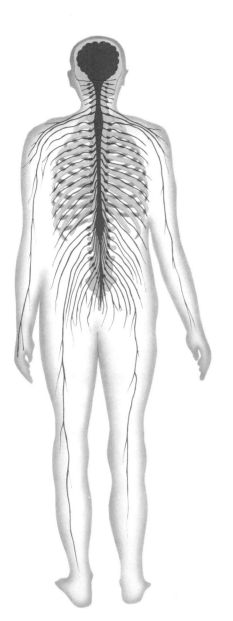

The nervous system

The brain may be looked on as an extremely modified, specialized and well-developed region of the spinal cord, together with it forming the *central nervous system*. To the brain are attached 12 pairs of cranial nerves, and from the spinal cord radiate 31 pairs of spinal nerves. Each spinal nerve is attached by an anterior (motor) root and a posterior (sensory) root, which fuse to form the individual, mixed nerve.

The *autonomic nervous system* forms a separate system of neurones, whose function is the automatic control of organs such as the lungs, heart and intestines. Together with the spinal and cranial nerves it makes up the *peripheral nervous system*. *Sensory* nerves carry messages from sensory organs to the brain, and *motor* nerves from the brain to effector organs—muscles or glands. Nerve impulses from a pricked finger travel to the brain through the spinal cord, and register as pain. But because sensory nerves connect with motor nerves at synapses in the spinal cord itself, the finger can be withdrawn reflexly before the brain even becomes aware of the unpleasant sensation. This ''short-circuit'' pathway is called a reflex arc.

The brain

Seen isolated from the bony, protective casing of the skull, the brain has a shape and surface rather reminiscent of a huge walnut kernel. The major part has two symmetrical and linked halves, with fissures, folds and wrinkles, and is covered with thin, membranous layers. But there the similarity ends. Without its shell, a walnut maintains its shape; deprived of the support of the surrounding cranium, the brain would sag and spread like soft fish roe or jelly. Built of more than ten billion nerve units, or neurones, the adult brain weighs nearly one and a half kilograms (the average is approximately 1380 grams in a man, and 1250 grams in a woman). Many of the units in this enormous concentration of nervous tissue have more or less the same function, so that an injury that destroyed several million at once might have little apparent effect. But this would depend, of course, upon the precise site of the injury. In some sites it could be disastrous. Intelligence does not depend primarily upon the size of the brain, but rather upon the complexity of its microstructure, the intricacy of connexions between its units, and its bio-chemistry. The brain might be likened to a large city, where the roads are nervous pathways, and the pedestrians · and vehicles are the electrical impulses. Intelligent behaviour results from sending vehicles down the right streets; learning consists, not in constructing new roads, but in putting up signposts and traffic lights at junctions, to direct the traffic flow. At birth the brain is almost fully developed in the complexity of its structure. It grows rapidly during the first five or six years of life, but this is due mainly to an increase in size of the cells already present, and growth of the *neuroglia*, connective tissue between the neurons that makes up some 40 per cent of the brain volume. After the age of 20 brain growth ceases. Unlike most other tissues of the body, brain tissue has extremely limited powers of regeneration following injury.

While all parts of the brain are ultimately connected, there are some major routes; the incoming sensory pathways and the outgoing motor paths are like motorways in comparison with the winding backstreets of the minor connexions within the brain.

The brain is not a homogeneous mass, but has several distinct parts. During our evolution from primitive animal ancestors new parts developed in the nervous system. The oldest parts—those responsible for the basic mechanisms that maintain life—are found at the base of the brain, joined to the spinal cord, while the newer parts—needed to elevate life from mere existence—are wrapped around the older areas. These new parts are deeply folded, and have a large surface area within the confined volume of the skull.

At the base of the brain, in the *brainstem*, is the *medulla*, which controls such essential activities as breathing, coughing and heart-beat. Behind and slightly above this is the *cerebellum* ("little brain"), which is important for the co-ordination of bodily movement and the maintenance of posture and balance. Although the cerebellum

The brain can be looked on as having three main regions—the *forebrain,* the *midbrain* and the *hindbrain.* The cerebrum (**1**) is the largest part of the forebrain. It is divided by a groove from front to back into two cerebral hemispheres, twisted and folded into many convolutions and connected in their lower central area. The cortex, or outer layer, is grey matter, composed of nerve cells (**2**). It encloses the white matter (**3**), nerve fibres that connect the cortex with other parts of the brain, and with the spinal cord. The cerebrum is responsible for receiving, storing and interpreting information from all over the body, and also for initiating voluntary movement. Deep in each hemisphere lie the caudate (**4**) and lentiform (**5**) nuclei, which co-ordinate muscular movement, and the thalamus (**6**), through which incoming information is channelled into the cortex. In the midbrain is the hypothalamus (**7**), one of the most important control centres in the body, and a regulator of appetite, water balance, temperature and sleep. Through the pituitary gland (**8**) below, the brain exerts control over many of the hormone systems of the body. In the hindbrain is the cerebellum (**9**), which monitors muscle tone and co-ordinates physical activities. Its lobes meet at the bulge called the pons (**10**). Below it is the medulla (**11**), through which information passes to and from the spinal cord (**12**).

Twelve pairs of *cranial nerves* enter and leave the brain: (**I**) *olfactory* (smell); **II** *optic* (sight); (**III**) *oculomotor,* (**IV**) *trochlear* and (**VI**) *abducens* (eye muscles); (**V**) *trigeminal* (sensation from scalp and face, mastication); (**VII**) *facial* (facial expression, taste); (**VIII**) *auditory* (hearing and balance); (**IX**) *glossopharyngeal,* (**X**) *vagus* and (**XI**) *accessory* (sensation and movement in numerous organs and muscles down as far as the colon); (**XII**) *hypoglossal* (movement of the tongue).

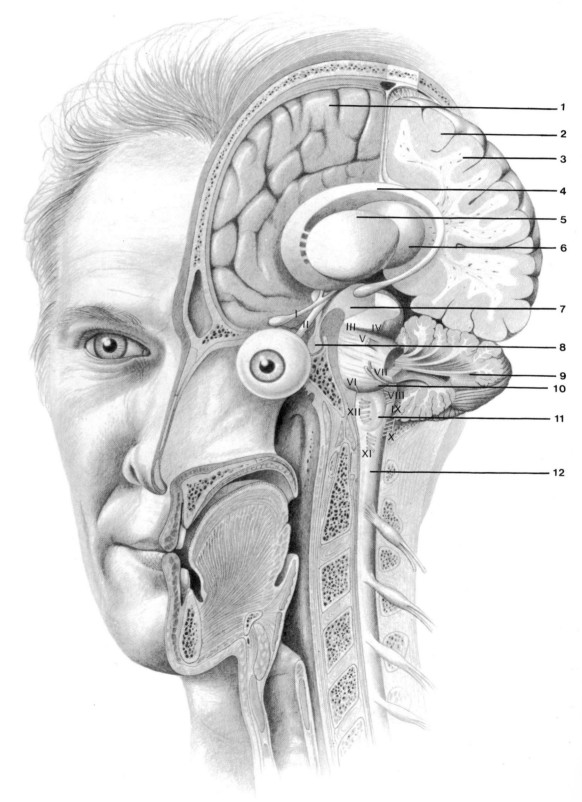

does not itself initiate movement, it is responsible for the smooth and balanced execution of movements, the maintenance of a degree of tenseness and preparedness for action in muscles (*tone*), and the integration of different movements into activities that may be merely repetitive, such as walking, or extremely skilled, such as playing the piano. The two sides of the cerebellum are united by the *pons* (bridge), which can be seen as a bulge in the brainstem. Through the brainstem runs the *reticular formation*, a network of fibres that carries the sensory pathways from the spinal cord into the brain. This diffuse area monitors incoming information from the body's sense receptors and regulates the level of a person's arousal from, at one extreme deep sleep to, at the other, a state of intense excitement.

In the middle of the brain, and grouped around the fluid-filled cavities called the *ventricles*, are areas that control the motivational aspects of daily life. The *hypothalamus* allows us to feel hungry or sated, thirsty or quenched, and triggers shivering when we feel cold, and sweating when we feel hot. By controlling the activity of the pituitary gland, and the "trophic" hormones that it produces, it is indirectly responsible for controlling many other hormones.

Forming a loop around the hypothalamus is a collection of structures together forming the *limbic system*—the *septum*, the *fornix*, the *amygdala* and the *hippocampus*. These are apparently involved in emotional responses such as fear and aggression, and interact closely to produce the many subtle changes in mood to which we are susceptible in different circumstances.

Also in the middle of the brain is a relatively large structure called the *thalamus*. Sensory information from the eyes, ears, nose, mouth and skin is sent first to the thalamus and then relayed to the *cerebrum*, which, in lobed left and right halves, the *cerebral hemispheres*, encloses it. The cerebrum forms a larger proportion of the brain in man than in any other animal. Its outer layer, the *cortex*, is the "grey matter" of common parlance, and is responsible for the many intellectual skills of which man is supremely capable. It has a convoluted appearance; its ridges are known as *gyri* and its furrows as *sulci*. The cortex can be divided into several different functional areas. Those parts that receive sensory messages through the thalamus, and from which stem the motor pathways, are termed the *primary cortex*. Curiously, the sensory and motor pathways cross below the brain, so that messages to and from the left side of the body are dealt with by the right side of the brain, and vice versa.

The various senses send information to different areas of primary cortex. Information from the eyes is relayed to the *occipital* lobe at the back of the brain, while that from the ears reaches the upper part of the *temporal* lobe, at the side. The senses of taste and smell, relatively poorly developed in man, are represented by small areas of cortex buried between the *frontal* and temporal lobes. The sense of touch has an area of cortex along the boundary between the frontal and *parietal* lobes. Because this area is also involved in the initiation of movements, incoming information about the body's position can be rapidly correlated with its movements.

The remaining areas of cortex—those at the anterior end of the frontal lobes, at the posterior ends of the parietal lobes and in the lower part of the temporal lobes—are collectively known as *association cortex*. These areas receive inputs from primary cortex and are necessary for understanding, learning, thinking, planning and the use of language. At the very front, anterior to the motor areas of the cortex, lie the *prefrontal* areas of the brain, often termed the "silent areas", because damage to them apparently produces no physical disability. However, they are concerned with intellect and personality; operations to isolate the prefrontal lobes are sometimes resorted to in cases of severe mental disorder.

Covering the brain are three layers of membranous tissue, called, from the outside inwards, the *dura mater*, the *arachnoid mater* and the *pia mater*. These are collectively known as the *meninges*, and are continuous with the coverings of the spinal cord inside the spinal canal. Within run numerous blood vessels, and circulating in the intercommunicating channels and spaces between the arachnoid and the pia is clear *cerebrospinal fluid*. Cerebrospinal fluid also fills the ventricles within the brain, and the central spinal canal; its main function is protection.

The brain is richly supplied with blood through branches of the internal carotid arteries and the vertebral artery, which have communicating vessels and form a circle around the base of the brain—the *circle of Willis*.

The cerebral cortex

The cerebral cortex, or "grey matter", forms the outer layer of the two cerebral hemispheres, and is fissured and convoluted so that there is a large surface area for the volume of cerebrum contained. (It has been estimated that the amount of cortex lining the fissures is about double that visible on the outside.) The cerebrum is divided into lobes—*frontal, parietal, temporal* and *occipital*—the divisions being for the most part demarcated by deeper fissures. The shallower fissures are known as *sulci,* and the convolutions they divide as *gyri*; many have individual names. The *sensory areas* of the cortex are found behind the sulcus that divides the parietal from the frontal lobe. Here are registered sensations from different regions of the body, in specific areas that can be mapped out with some precision. In area (**1**), for example, sensations from the trunk are received, in area (**2**) those from the face, and in area (**3**) those from the tongue. Sounds are registered in area (**4**), and vision has its own area back in the occipital lobe (**5**). Adjacent to each area is *association cortex,* concerned with the building up of sensations into the more complex patterns that we call concepts— ideas of what the messages received really mean. In front of the sensory areas, in the frontal lobe, lies *motor cortex,* where movement of specific parts of the body is initiated, and which can again be mapped into areas corresponding to the different parts of the body. Area (**6**), for example, controls movements of the fingers, and area (**7**) of the tongue. The temporal lobe seems to have functions related to memory and the process of recall; electrical stimulation can produce both illusions and hallucinations. The pre-frontal cortex, in the frontal lobe, is associated with emotions, excitement and behavioural response.

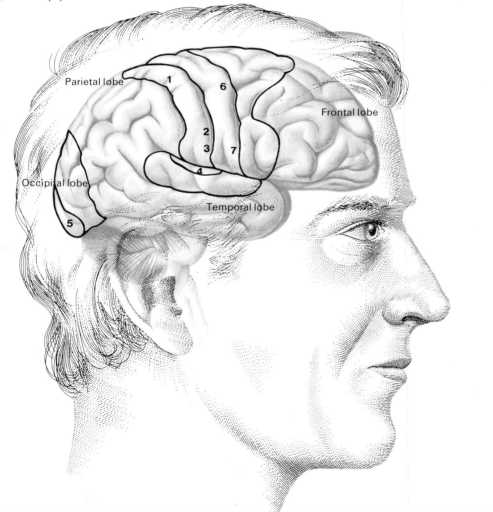

Parietal lobe · Frontal lobe · Occipital lobe · Temporal lobe

Mental activity

The brain is active all the time, even when we are fast asleep. Electrical activity in the brain—"brainwaves"—can be demonstrated and recorded by attaching electrodes to the scalp and using amplified signals from the brain to guide a pen from side to side across a roll of moving paper. The record that is produced is called an *electro-encephalogram* (EEG). The pattern of the EEG varies with the level of consciousness; generally the more alert one is, the higher the frequency of the EEG pattern. The main exception occurs in what is known as "paradoxical sleep", the state of sleep in which dreaming takes place. Here, although the subject is asleep, the EEG shows a high frequency pattern reminiscent of the consciously aware state. Normal sleep is associated with a low frequency EEG. Although the difference between states of relaxation and concentration can be observed on the EEG, it is not possible to identify the patterns which distinguish different mental activities.

There are many ways in which we can "know" something. We may perceive events or objects in the outside world, or remember things which have already happened. Deduction, inference and intuition are procedures we use in understanding what is going on around us, while language and thought are methods of symbolizing and structuring knowledge so that it can be used in mental processes. Imagination is the re-ordering of knowledge to produce novel or inventive ideas. Perception is the link between external reality and the ideas in the mind. We perceive people, objects, and events either directly through our own senses, or indirectly through descriptions, in which case we draw on concepts already familiar to us to build up a picture of the person or object in question.

Perception also depends on the context and expectation surrounding the sensory information fed to the brain. For example, we may "know" what a drawing portrays when, in fact, it consists only of a few lines in two dimensions. What we perceive through our senses is an arrangement of lines; reviewing our store of concepts we find what the arrangement most resembles, and say that the drawing represents a boat or a man. It is also possible to ignore something about which sensory information is available. For instance, we might overlook a misprint, or fail to distinguish between two similar objects. Dreams, hallucinations and some drug-induced changes in awareness can be considered as states of perception in which the contribution from the sensory information is minimal, but the contribution from other mental processes such as imagination, memory and so on is large.

Just as perception is not wholly dependent on what is happening in the outside world, so memory does not correspond completely with what has actually happened. Many events are forgotten completely, and cannot be recalled. Other events are remembered vaguely, or in a contracted or even completely different form. Why things are forgotten has not yet been discovered. Many of the difficulties encountered in remembering are problems of retrieval rather than storage. Repression is a psychological state in which unpleasant or disturbing knowledge cannot be retrieved from the memory store. In stressful situations, such as under examination conditions, we may also find it difficult to remember the things that we most want to. Under hypnosis, an exceptionally co-operative state of mind, repressed or "lost" memories can often be brought out. It is not true, however, that a hypnotized person can remember everything that ever happened to him.

There are at least two major stages involved in forming a memory. Short-term memory, which lasts only for a few minutes, is easily disrupted by electric shock, a blow on the head, or anaesthesia. It is supposed that at this stage the memory exists as electrical activity within the brain. This type of memory may be converted into long-term memory. Because long-term memory cannot be destroyed by events which upset the electrical activity of the brain, it is thought that this type of memory is stored chemically or structurally in the brain. However, it is not possible to say in which part of the human brain each memory is stored.

What we perceive, and hence what we may remember, is dependent on attention. One could think of the brain as consisting of a hierarchy of filters, which block the passage of unimportant or repetitive messages to the higher centres,

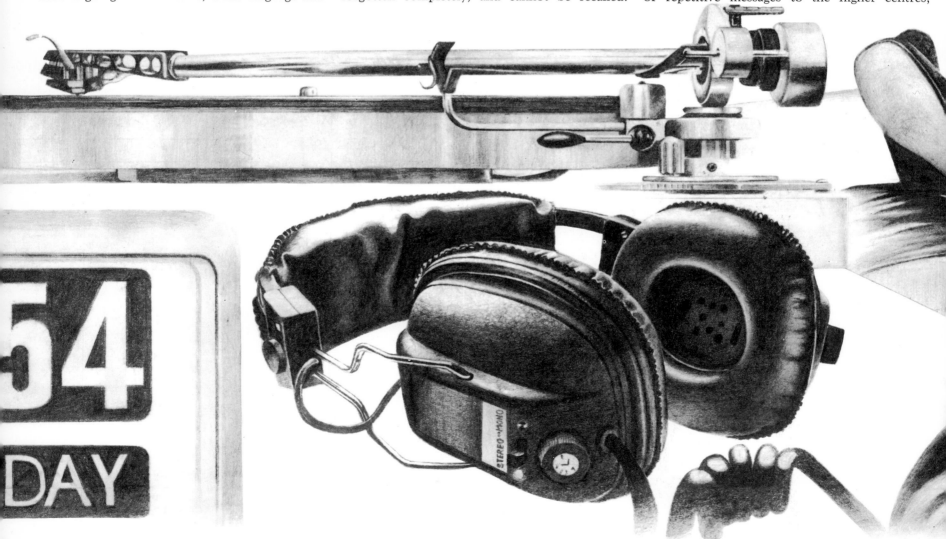

leaving them free for thinking processes, although important sensations immediately break through to conscious awareness. If one concentrates on one activity, it is possible to cut out the countless other sensory data that are constantly fed to the brain. A man reading will concentrate on his book, perhaps visualizing the events and characters described and will be only subliminally aware of other noises, sights, sounds and smells.

In order to think and form concepts beyond the perception of ongoing events, we symbolize previous events as memories and relationships as grammar and formal logic. The use of symbolic language, which is unique to human beings, makes the capacity for thought almost limitless. By enabling the individual to learn from the experience of others, language is the basis of cultural heritage and as such forms probably the single most important difference between man and animals.

But knowing, or cognition, is almost invariably accompanied by feeling (affection) and wanting (volition). Together, these determine the way we behave. Desires, which push us into action, are often related to bodily needs. Through the activity of the hypothalamus and the lower brain centres we are motivated to eat, drink and sleep, and also to avoid pain, discomfort and extremes of temperature. Emotions are states of mind which may be "rewarding" or "punishing". They thus direct our behaviour by determining which activities we seek to repeat and which to avoid. We develop the desire for love, security and approval which forms the basis of our personal relationships and social structure of our communities.

The autonomic system

The body regulates its activities in response both to external and to internal changes. Two control systems are involved—the *autonomic nervous system* and the *endocrine system*. The autonomic system looks after short-term changes, for example alteration of pupil size in response to change in light intensity, and the control of breathing and heart rate. The endocrine system generally organizes more long-term bodily changes, such as the menstrual cycle, growth rate and sexual maturation, but is also responsible for certain rapid responses such as an increase in the blood sugar level during physical activity. The two linked systems work in smooth co-ordination, usually without our knowledge or interference, and keep our internal affairs in order and our internal environment as near as possible constant; they only occasionally need to be overruled by conscious effort when something goes seriously wrong.

The autonomic system controls the actions of the muscles over which we have no conscious control; movements of the stomach and intestine, hair erection, control of the diameter of blood vessels and of air passages in the lungs, rates of secretion of glands, and ejaculation during sexual intercourse, all come within the scope of the autonomic nervous sytem.

The system works through the balanced antagonism of two subdivisions. These are the *sympathetic* and the *parasympathetic* systems. Both originate in cell bodies within the central nervous system, and are linked by axons with other cell bodies in ganglia outside the brain and spinal cord. Many organs have fibres from both systems; one system activates or stimulates the organ to action and the other inhibits it; one dilates or expands it, the other constricts or contracts it.

Fibres of the sympathetic division leave the spinal cord with the spinal nerves, but soon form a separate chain of 20 or so ganglia, on either side of the spine, from which grey, unmyelinated nerve fibres run to all parts of the body. Sympathetic nerves supply the iris muscles in the eye, the sweat glands, muscles in arterial walls, the heart and lungs, the liver, stomach, intestines, kidneys, adrenal glands (medulla), the bladder, the genitals and other organs of the abdomen. Fibres from the last few ganglia in the chains supply arterial muscles and other structures of the legs and the lower trunk.

Parasympathetic fibres also issue from the central nervous system, but only from the two ends of it — some from the brain, and the rest from the last part of the spinal cord. Fibres which originate in the brain leave the skull with the cranial nerves, while the lower group link to form the pelvic nerves, to supply the gut, bladder and genitalia.

Autonomic nerves work by secreting chemical *neurotransmitters* from their endings—*noradrena-line* from the sympathetic and *acetylcholine* from the parasympathetic. Generally, the sympathetic system is used in emergencies, when energy is needed quickly. Signals from the sympathetic increase the heart and respiratory rates and dilate the air passages. Blood flow to the muscles is increased at the expense of the supply to the skin and gut. Sugar is released from store in the liver, to be used by the muscles, and the entire action of the digestive system is temporarily inhibited. While the body is at rest, the parasympathetic system takes over. Heart rate and respiration rate decrease, and blood is diverted from the now inactive muscles to promote digestion.

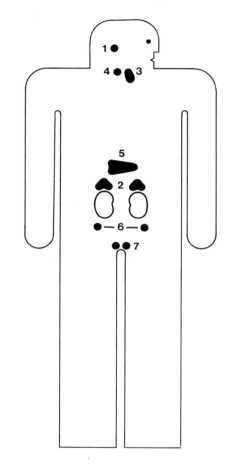

The endocrine system

Endocrine glands are secretory organs which release hormones, potent chemicals with specific actions, directly into the bloodstream. The system as a whole maintains chemical stability within the body. The amount of hormones the glands produce varies from time to time. Most are produced continuously, but the levels fluctuate considerably. The "fright, flight or fight response" is due to a sudden increase of adrenaline in the blood; the menstrual cycle depends on fluctuating levels of sexual hormones over a longer period. Endocrine glands often work in harmony, output from one influencing output from others. In some cases "target" glands produce hormones which then inhibit the output of the controlling gland, a "negative feed-back" system that helps to maintain a constant level of output.

The master-gland that controls most hormone systems is the *pituitary* (1), a pea-sized gland, surrounded by bone, attached beneath the hypothalamus, part of the brain itself. It is composed of both nervous and secretory tissues and its close affinity with the brain is reflected in a close relationship between hormonal levels and mental state. The pituitary has two parts. The anterior pituitary produces hormones that affect the thyroid and adrenal glands, and the reproductive organs, and control ovulation and sperm production. It also produces a growth hormone (*somatotrophin*), which promotes growth in the young, and in adults helps to balance energy output and tissue repair. The posterior pituitary releases two hormones—*vasopressin* and *oxytocin*. Vasopressin acts on the tubules of the kidneys, to maintain water balance. Oxytocin is released by women during labour, when it assists uterine contractions, and by nursing mothers during suckling, when it stimulates the expulsion of milk.

The *adrenal glands* (2)—small, triangular glands immediately above the kidneys—also produce a range of hormones. The outer layer, or cortex, of each produces small quantities of sex hormones, augmenting those produced by the gonads themselves; they also produce chemicals called glucocorticoids, important in the metabolism of carbohydrates and proteins. Production of these hormones is controlled by *adrenocorticotrophic hormone* (ACTH) from the anterior lobe of the pituitary gland. In addition the adrenal cortex produces *aldosterone*, a hormone which controls water balance by affecting the kidney. The central part of the adrenal glands—the medulla—is controlled by the sympathetic nervous system. In a situation of stress the medulla produces adrenaline, which assists the sympathetic nervous system in preparing the body for emergency activities.

Under direction from the hypothalamus and *thyrotrophic hormone* from the anterior lobe of the pituitary, the *thyroid gland* in the neck (3) produces the hormone *thyroxine*. This regulates rates of metabolism all over the body, and maintains levels of heat production. The *parathyroid glands* (4), nearby, control the metabolism of calcium and phosphorus in the body.

The *pancreas* (5) produces two important hormones, *glucagon* and *insulin*. Glucagon encourages the breakdown of glycogen in the liver, thereby raising the blood glucose level. Insulin lowers the level of glucose in the blood by facilitating its uptake in the muscles.

The gonads, *ovaries* (6) in the female and *testes* (7) in the male, secrete sex hormones (see pages 62-65). The hypothalamus controls the production of *gonadotrophic hormones*, which travel in the bloodstream from the anterior pituitary gland and stimulate both sperm production and the release of another hormone, *testosterone*, from the testes. Testosterone is responsible for male bodily characteristics. In women *gonadotrophic* hormones control the release of ova from the ovaries, and also the production of the hormones *oestrogen* and *progesterone* by the ovaries, and the complex changes of the menstrual cycle, involving growth and development of the uterine wall.

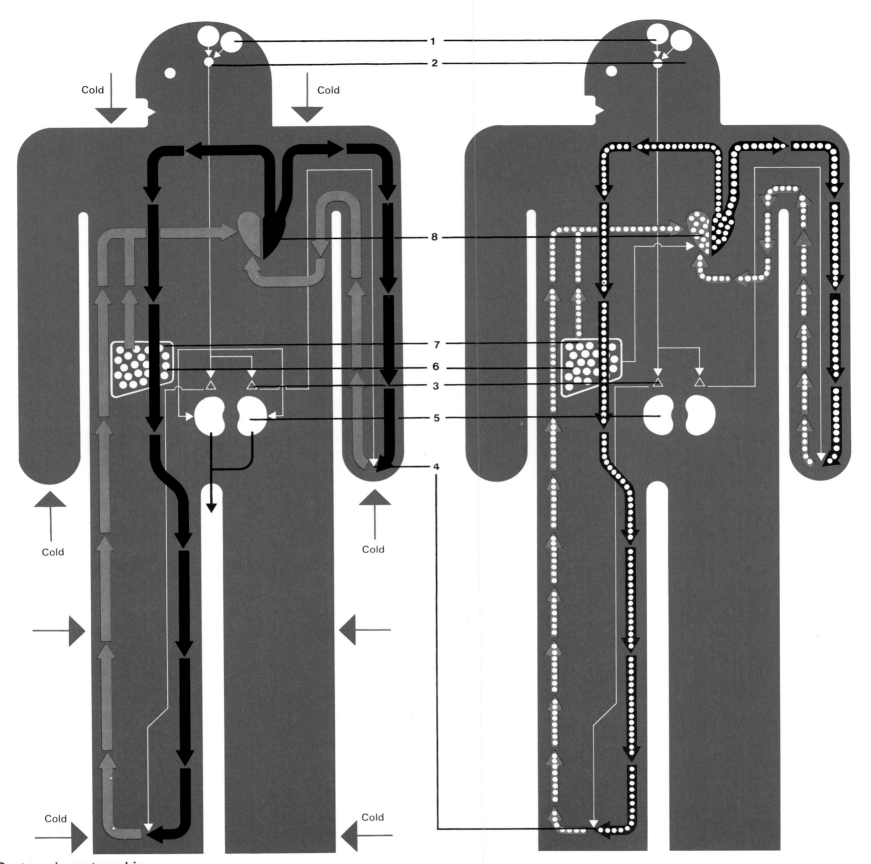

Systems in partnership

The autonomic nervous system and the endocrine system work in unison to control the automatic functions of the body—respiration, digestion, water balance and the regulation of body temperature. The hypothalamus (1) controls both systems via the pituitary (2), to which it is connected by a system of nerves and blood vessels. A diagrammatic representation shows the interaction of the systems in response to a cold situation, working together to prevent heat loss and to encourage heat production within the tissues. Cold first affects the skin, cooling the blood in the peripheral capillaries. The chilled blood circulates, eventually reaching the carotid artery, which supplies the brain. The drop in temperature is registered by a thermo-sensitive area in the brain, and a message sent to the hypothalamus to activate the systems. A nervous impulse travels to the medullae of the adrenal glands (3), stimulating the release of adrenaline, which causes constriction in the peripheral blood vessels (4), preventing heat loss from the skin by convection. Constriction also inhibits the function of the sweat glands, preventing heat loss by evaporation. The kidneys (5) are stimulated to produce more urine, concentrating the blood to make more oxygen available to the tissues for oxygenation—burning up to release heat and energy. Simultaneously, the hypothalamus is regulating the endocrine response. The pituitary is stimulated to increase its production of the hormone thyrotrophin, which in turn stimulates the thyroid to secrete more thyroxine, a hormone which speeds up oxygenation. Glycogen (6), stored in the liver (7), is mobilized and transformed into glucose to provide additional fuel. The heart (8) beats faster, sending concentrated blood containing oxygen and glucose quickly to the tissues where they are needed.

The menstrual cycle

The sequence of changes in the female reproductive tract that repeats every month is known as the menstrual cycle. It occurs as a result of many complex hormonal actions and interactions—all directed to the production of egg cells (*ova*) from the ovaries, their release into the Fallopian tubes, and the preparation of the lining of the womb for the reception of an ovum that has been fertilized by a male sex cell (*spermatozoon*). The time that menstrual cycles commence is called the *menarche*; it is usually at about the age of ten years, but varies from country to country and race to race. There has been a gradual decrease in the age of onset. Menstruation is one of the indications of puberty.

Menstruation ceases, at the other end of a woman's reproductive life, at the *menopause*. After this, child-bearing is no longer possible, although of course a woman's sexual life is by no means over. The menopause usually occurs at about the age of 45, but is variable.

Ova are produced in the ovaries by groups of cells called *Graafian follicles*, which grow and reach the surface of the ovary, there bursting to release just one ovum each month. The release of an ovum is called *ovulation*. The ovum is picked up by one of the tiny, hollow, finger-like projections (*fimbria*) of the Fallopian tube, and propelled through it and down the length of the tube by the movement of fine protrusions called cilia in the much-folded tube lining. If sexual intercourse has taken place, there may be millions of spermatozoa swimming in the Fallopian tube to meet the ovum, and one may meet and fertilize it. In this case the fertilized egg starts to divide and is then called a *blastocyst*; it passes into the uterus, settles in the lining (*endometrium*) and starts to grow there. This is the process of *implantation*.

The endometrium has been growing in thickness in preparation for implantation, and developing numerous blood vessels. If, after a while, a blastocyst has not arrived and become implanted, the endometrium breaks down, bleeding occurs from the uterine wall, and the contents of the uterus pass into the vagina, to be lost from the body. The cycle then begins again.

The length of the complete menstrual cycle is in the region of 28 days, but sometimes more and sometimes less. Actual bleeding occurs over about five days, and ovulation approximately midway between periods of bleeding. The unfertilized ovum can live in the female genital tract for about 72 hours, while spermatozoa can survive there for about 48 hours. Thus, within one menstrual cycle, the maximum time during which a woman can be described as fertile is in the region of 120 hours. However, because the time of ovulation can vary slightly from one cycle to the next, the fertile period may occur at any time.

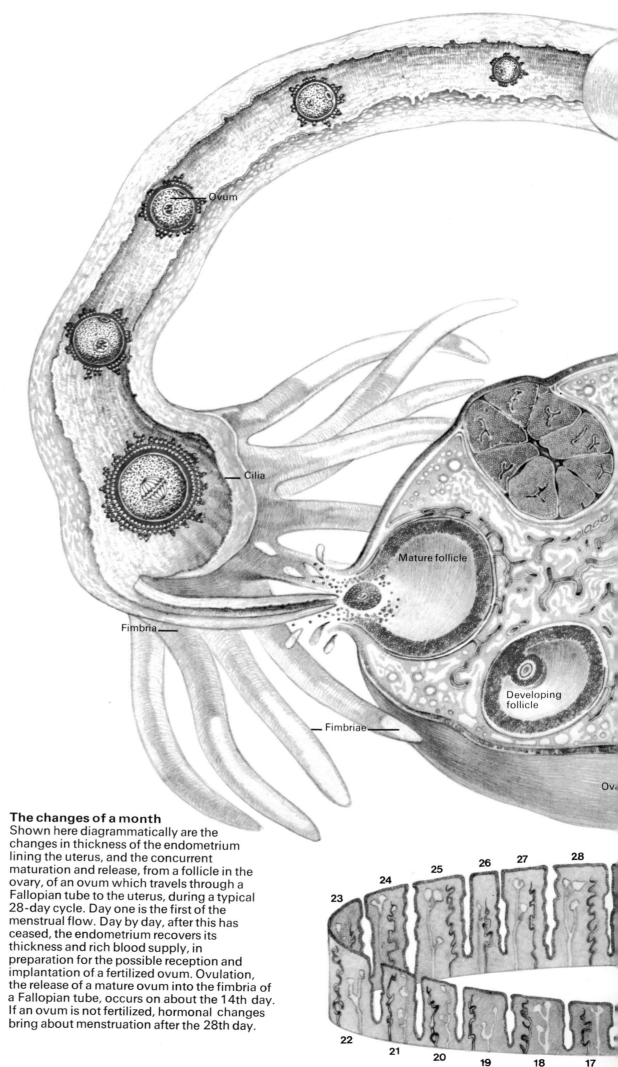

Ovum

Cilia

Mature follicle

Developing follicle

Fimbria

Fimbriae

Ov-

The changes of a month
Shown here diagrammatically are the changes in thickness of the endometrium lining the uterus, and the concurrent maturation and release, from a follicle in the ovary, of an ovum which travels through a Fallopian tube to the uterus, during a typical 28-day cycle. Day one is the first of the menstrual flow. Day by day, after this has ceased, the endometrium recovers its thickness and rich blood supply, in preparation for the possible reception and implantation of a fertilized ovum. Ovulation, the release of a mature ovum into the fimbria of a Fallopian tube, occurs on about the 14th day. If an ovum is not fertilized, hormonal changes bring about menstruation after the 28th day.

23 24 25 26 27 28

22 21 20 19 18 17

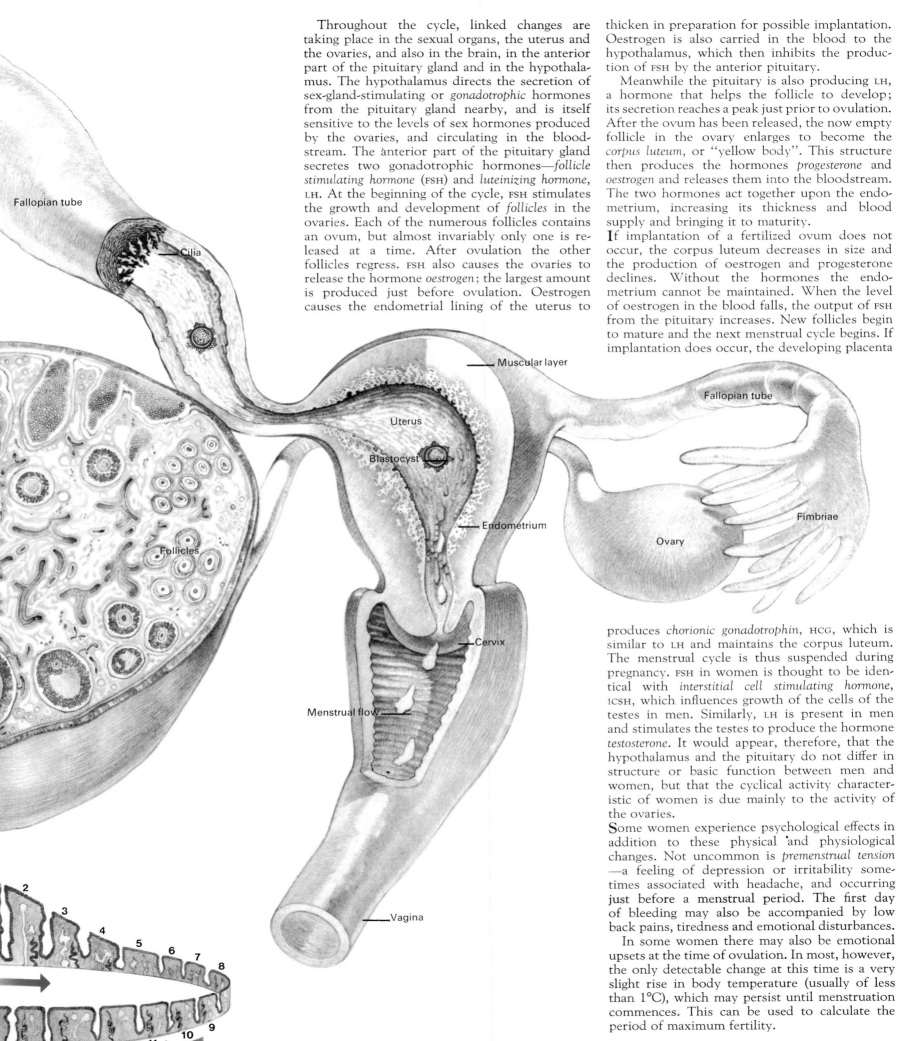

Throughout the cycle, linked changes are taking place in the sexual organs, the uterus and the ovaries, and also in the brain, in the anterior part of the pituitary gland and in the hypothalamus. The hypothalamus directs the secretion of sex-gland-stimulating or *gonadotrophic* hormones from the pituitary gland nearby, and is itself sensitive to the levels of sex hormones produced by the ovaries, and circulating in the bloodstream. The anterior part of the pituitary gland secretes two gonadotrophic hormones—*follicle stimulating hormone* (FSH) and *luteinizing hormone*, LH. At the beginning of the cycle, FSH stimulates the growth and development of *follicles* in the ovaries. Each of the numerous follicles contains an ovum, but almost invariably only one is released at a time. After ovulation the other follicles regress. FSH also causes the ovaries to release the hormone *oestrogen*; the largest amount is produced just before ovulation. Oestrogen causes the endometrial lining of the uterus to thicken in preparation for possible implantation. Oestrogen is also carried in the blood to the hypothalamus, which then inhibits the production of FSH by the anterior pituitary.

Meanwhile the pituitary is also producing LH, a hormone that helps the follicle to develop; its secretion reaches a peak just prior to ovulation. After the ovum has been released, the now empty follicle in the ovary enlarges to become the *corpus luteum*, or "yellow body". This structure then produces the hormones *progesterone* and *oestrogen* and releases them into the bloodstream. The two hormones act together upon the endometrium, increasing its thickness and blood supply and bringing it to maturity.

If implantation of a fertilized ovum does not occur, the corpus luteum decreases in size and the production of oestrogen and progesterone declines. Without the hormones the endometrium cannot be maintained. When the level of oestrogen in the blood falls, the output of FSH from the pituitary increases. New follicles begin to mature and the next menstrual cycle begins. If implantation does occur, the developing placenta produces *chorionic gonadotrophin*, HCG, which is similar to LH and maintains the corpus luteum. The menstrual cycle is thus suspended during pregnancy. FSH in women is thought to be identical with *interstitial cell stimulating hormone*, ICSH, which influences growth of the cells of the testes in men. Similarly, LH is present in men and stimulates the testes to produce the hormone *testosterone*. It would appear, therefore, that the hypothalamus and the pituitary do not differ in structure or basic function between men and women, but that the cyclical activity characteristic of women is due mainly to the activity of the ovaries.

Some women experience psychological effects in addition to these physical and physiological changes. Not uncommon is *premenstrual tension* —a feeling of depression or irritability sometimes associated with headache, and occurring just before a menstrual period. The first day of bleeding may also be accompanied by low back pains, tiredness and emotional disturbances.

In some women there may also be emotional upsets at the time of ovulation. In most, however, the only detectable change at this time is a very slight rise in body temperature (usually of less than 1°C), which may persist until menstruation commences. This can be used to calculate the period of maximum fertility.

Fallopian tube

Cilia

Follicles

Muscular layer

Uterus

Blastocyst

Endometrium

Fallopian tube

Fímbriae

Ovary

Cervix

Menstrual flow

Vagina

2 3 4 5 6 7 8 9 10 11 12 13 14

Sexual organs

Reproduction is the formation of new individuals on the pattern of existing ones. Man, like most other large, advanced organisms, propagates himself by sexual reproduction, a process involving a parent of either sex and resulting in variable offspring. Each parent provides special reproductive cells, or *gametes*—females produce egg-cells, or *ova*, and males produce *spermatozoa*—which cannot live on their own. Brought together in the female reproductive tract and allowed to fuse, the two form a single, fertile *zygote*, which grows into a new individual. The new organism resembles both of its parents in important issues, but differs slightly from them in detail; some of its characteristics may be copied faithfully from one or other parent; some may be a blend of parental characteristics; and some may be inherited from grandparents or more remote kin. The combination of different genes, which are the determining factors of all our characteristics, produces new individuals which are unique.

Irrespective of race, colour or creed, all human beings are divided into two groups—male and female. The most important single difference between the two is the structure and housing of the gonads (ovaries and testes)—the organs that form and nurture the reproductive cells—and the arrangement of internal and external accessory organs, the genitalia. The sexes also differ in body size and proportion, skeletal structure, the distribution of body hair, metabolic rate, temperament, and in many other ways. Some differences are entirely physical, dictated by the body itself. Others are largely or entirely cultural, imposed by the society we live in.

The sex of an infant is determined at its conception by the pattern of chromosomes contained in the newly formed zygote. Every normal human cell (other than a gamete) contains in its nucleus 46 chromosomes; in dividing cells these can often be seen arranged in 23 matching pairs. Forty-four of the chromosomes are autosomes, not directly concerned with sex determination. The remaining two are sex chromosomes, which form an identical pair in females (XX) but an ill-matched pair in males, one being shorter than the other (XY). The short Y chromosome is assumed to carry the male determining factor.

When gametes are being formed in the gonads, the specialized cells which produce them split into two, one half of each chromosome pair passing to each gamete. Ova formed in this way necessarily contain 22 autosomes and one X chromosome. Spermatozoa, on the other hand, contain 22 autosomes and either an X or a Y chromosome, because they are derived from male XY-endowed body-cells. Thus there is only one kind of ovum, but two kinds of spermatozoa. An ovum fertilized by an X-chromosome-carrying sperm will become an XX zygote and develop into a female embryo. One fertilized by a Y-chromosome-carrying spermatozoon becomes an XY zygote, which develops into a male embryo.

When the penis is erect, spermatozoa, produced in the testes, travel through the vas deferens, bypass the bladder and enter the ejaculatory duct, a muscular-walled tube. Here, alkaline secretions produced by two seminal vesicles (which supply solutions of fructose and ascorbic acid) and the prostate gland (which adds cholesterol, fatty acids, phospholipids and other nutrients), surround the spermatozoa, forming the greyish-white fluid known as semen, which transports spermatozoa out of the male body. Semen is an alkaline substance because spermatozoa survive longer in an alkali than in acid. The semen passes into the urethra and is forced out through its opening during ejaculation. In a male orgasm, about three to five millilitres of semen are ejaculated. Each millilitre may contain more than 60 million spermatozoa, each capable of fertilizing an egg inside a woman's body.

Seminal vesicle
Bladder
Prostate
Urethra
Spermatozoon
Corpora cavernosa
Corpus spongiosum
Epididymis
Seminiferous tubules
Vas deferens
Coronary sulcus
Testis
Glans
Scrotum
Urethral orifice

Penis and Testes
In the shaft of the penis, the urethra, through which urine or spermatozoa pass out of the body, is surrounded by the corpora cavernosa, tough-walled sacs containing spongy tissue which fill with blood under pressure during erection. The penis is covered with skin which forms a loose-fitting shroud over the sensitive glans penis.
A man has two testes, oval organs about 39 millimetres long by 27 millimetres wide, carried in a pouch of skin called the scrotum. Each testis is divided into lobules containing long, narrow coiled seminiferous tubules. Cells lining the seminiferous tubules form spermatozoa, releasing millions for temporary storage in the epididymis. When a man is sexually aroused, the spermatozoa pass into the vas deferens and on into the urethra.

The gonads

The gonads are the organs which form and nurture the reproductive cells. In a woman they take the form of ovaries, which produce the ovum or egg. The male gonads are the testes, which produce the spermatozoa. Fundamentally, the two systems are similar. In both sexes the two gonads are separate organs carrying out the same function. Both ovaries and testes are linked to the external reproductive organs—the vagina in the female and the penis in the male—by a system of ducts and sinuses. In the female, the individual ducts join to form the uterine cavity. In the male, they join at the beginning of the urethra, making one channel to the outside world. In the embryo, two pairs of tubes, the Müllerian and the Wolffian ducts, link the gonads to the area which will form the external reproductive organs. About two months after conception, the foetus assumes its sexual identity. If female, the gonads become ovaries, the Wolffian ducts degenerate, and the Müllerian ducts develop into the Fallopian tubes, uterus and vagina. If the foetus is male, the Müllerian ducts disappear, the Wolffian ducts develop into the seminiferous tubules and spermatozoa-carrying ducts, and the gonads develop into testes. At puberty, the gonads are activated by hormones released by the anterior pituitary to produce their reproductive cells and to secrete hormones of their own.

Sex hormones

Both male and female gonads serve a dual purpose, producing both reproductive cells and sex hormones. In the male, the testes secrete testosterone, the hormone responsible for the development of male characteristics, stimulating the growth of skeletal muscle, the production and distribution of body and facial hair, the deepening of the voice and the rapid development of both internal and external sexual organs. It is secreted in response to another hormone, the interstitial-cell-stimulating hormone (ICSH), which is secreted by the anterior pituitary. In the female, the ovaries secrete two hormones, oestrogen and progesterone. In the first week of the menstrual cycle, the pituitary secretes follicle-stimulating hormone (FSH). Mature follicles secrete oestrogen, which is responsible for the development of female characteristics—the growth of the breasts, the distribution of fat and of body hair—and also stimulates the growth of the uterine lining. When the follicle is about to burst, the oestrogen level drops, causing the pituitary to secrete the luteinizing hormone (LH), triggering ovulation. The ruptured follicle becomes the corpus luteum, secreting progesterone, which prepares the lining of the uterus for the reception of a fertilized egg. If none appears, the level of both oestrogen and progesterone falls, beginning the cycle again.

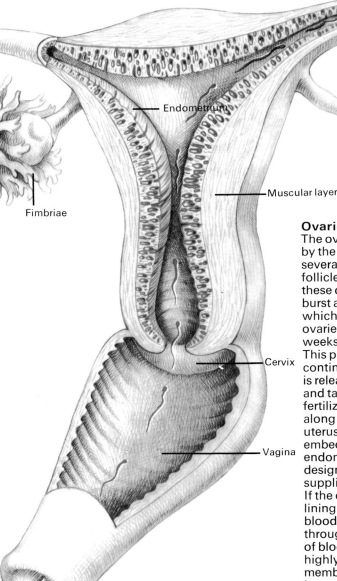

Fallopian tube

Ovary

Follicles

Ovum

Endometrium

Fimbriae

Muscular layer

Cervix

Vagina

Vaginal entrance

Ovaries and fertilization

The ovaries are situated within the basin formed by the pelvic bones. At birth, each ovary contains several hundred thousand minute sacs called follicles. Only between four and five hundred of these develop to maturity, when they are ready to burst and shed their ovum. Unlike the male testis, which produces millions of spermatozoa, the ovaries usually release one ovum about every four weeks ; the ovum may come from either ovary. This process begins just after puberty and continues for about 30 years. Each time an ovum is released, it is picked up by a frond-like fimbria and taken into the Fallopian or uterine tube, where fertilization normally occurs. The ovum is wafted along by the cilia lining the Fallopian tube to the uterus. If the ovum has been fertilized, it becomes embedded in the lining of the uterus, the endometrium, a mucous membrane specifically designed to receive and retain it, and richly supplied with blood to feed a developing foetus. If the ovum of the month is not fertilized, this lining breaks up and is washed away, mixed with blood from the vessels to which it was attached, through the cervix and vagina. This monthly flow of blood is known as menstruation. The vagina is a highly sensitive muscular tube lined with mucous membrane, which receives the penis during intercourse and conducts the ejaculated spermatozoa to the cervix, through which they pass into the uterus and up to the Fallopian tubes.

It is therefore the father's contribution to the zygote that determines the sex of an infant, and, in theory, equal numbers of each sex should be produced. In fact, Y-chromosome-carrying spermatozoa are very slightly smaller than X-carriers, and faster moving, and seem able to fertilize more than their fair share of ova. At the moment, boys outnumber girls at birth by about 21:20.

The reproductive organs appear early in the growing embryo as tiny knots of tissue close to the spine on the abdominal wall. Two pairs of tubes, the Müllerian and the Wolffian ducts, link the developing gonads with a small hollow—the urogenital sinus—at the rear end of the embryo. Up to the eighth week after conception, there is little to distinguish male from female. The presence or absence of the Y chromosome makes itself apparent later. In the female embryo, where both chromosomes are X-carriers, the developing gonads become ovaries, the Wolffian ducts disappear, the Müllerian ducts differentiate into the female reproductive tract—paired Fallopian tubes, uterus and vagina—and from the urogenital sinus develop the paired labia majora and labia minora and associated glands of the female. In the presence of both X and Y chromosomes in the male embryo, the gonads become testes, the Wolffian ducts become sperm-carrying ducts and tubules, and the Müllerian ducts degenerate. The urogenital sinus becomes part of the urethra, and the tissues on either side join along the midline to form the sac of the scrotum. This remains empty until the seventh or eighth month of foetal life, when the testes descend into it from the abdominal wall. The phallus is initially a small bump on the front edge of the urogenital sinus. In the male, it grows larger, acquiring two longitudinal masses of spongy, erectile tissue and the tube of the urethra, to form the penis—the erectile organ through which spermatozoa are transmitted from the male into the female reproductive tract. In the female, it is small, forming the sensitive and erectile clitoris.

Throughout early life, the reproductive organs remain small and non-functional, a source of mild interest and pleasant sensation to their owners. Shortly before puberty, gonadotrophic hormones produced in the anterior lobe of the pituitary gland cause the ovaries and testes to develop and secrete hormones of their own. These in turn stimulate the growth of the genitalia, and the changes of body form which are associated with adolescence. At the same time, the gonads start to produce their gametes, at first sporadically and then continuously. Girls begin to ovulate, settling eventually into a regular cycle in which a single ovum is released, and the reproductive tract made ready for pregnancy once every 28 days. In boys, millions of spermatozoa begin to form in the seminiferous tubules of the testes and a nutritious liquid medium for them is secreted by the seminal vesicles and prostate.

Not surprisingly, young people find these changes of body structure interesting and exciting, and very sensibly try out for themselves the range of new sensations associated with them. Most boys, and many girls, discover sexual excitement and orgasm through masturbation at this stage, learning to relieve their nervous tensions in a natural way.

Sexual behaviour

The behaviour of simple animals consists only of reflex responses to external stimuli. However, the behaviour of more complex species is also determined by the motivational system of drives and rewards *within* the animal. In humans, conscious awareness of our internal feelings and desires, and an understanding of our surroundings, allow us to choose the way we behave. This is true of sexual as well as of other kinds of behaviour. From the reflex behaviour of the simplest animals, a system of sexual drives and rewards has developed in higher animals; in humans, this system is elaborated further to encompass the pleasures we give and receive in family and social relations.

In the animal world the prime function of a sexual relationship is reproduction. Usually copulation occurs only when the female is producing eggs (ovulating) and therefore capable of becoming pregnant. Only at this time of *oestrus* is she receptive and attractive to the male. Changes in her behaviour, appearance or scent may stimulate the sexual drive of the male so that mating follows. In some species oestrus occurs at regular intervals throughout the year; in others there may be one or possibly two breeding seasons in the year.

Many species of *primates*—a group including monkeys, apes and humans—are unusual among animals because they are able to breed at any time of the year. Further, the females may be willing to mate at times when they are not ovulating. In these species sexual activity has achieved an importance beyond reproduction, within a group of animals serving both to unite pairs of animals in sexual relationships and to maintain the structure of the group as a whole. In the human situation, sexual relations form the basis of very strong and often permanent bonds.

This bond, which we call love, is basically a very simple system of exchanging rewards. In a happy family, children absorb the idea of love and the elements of the system from their parents, learning the important signals of touch, body warmth, facial expression and words, which convey feeling and concern and establish stable loving relationships between individuals. Well-loved children, practised in relating to each other and their parents, find it relatively easy to establish sensible relationships with others outside the family circle. During adolescence, when sex begins to permeate their lives, they come to relate readily to members of the opposite sex. The foundations of psychological well-being are laid in early childhood. However, the social inhibition which surrounds the discussion of sexual matters sometimes causes minor misunderstandings about sex to develop into serious sexual problems.

In many animals, including humans, mating is preceded by courtship. In order to mate, one animal must approach another, and so it is essential that sexual approach be distinguished from aggressive approach. Courtship serves the function of informing both individuals that their proximity is not dangerous, as well as preparing each for copulation. Since sex and aggression both involve close body contact and strong physical activity (at least in the male), it is not uncommon for courtship procedures to break down, and for one to be misinterpreted as the other. Sexual approach may be interpreted as aggressive, and result in fear and avoidance. Alternatively, aggression may be disguised as sex, as in rape and perversion. However, in the normal healthy situation, there is no connection between the motives of sex and aggression.

Sexual drives, like hunger, are determined by conditions within the body, though often triggered into action by external stimuli. Just why we feel strong sexual needs at some times but not at others is an important question which, for one reason or another, has never been properly answered. Levels of hormones in the blood, the hypothalamus and special centres in the brain are likely to be involved, but how they interact is not known. Some women are most sexually responsive during the week or ten days following menstruation. Men often reach their highest levels of activity in spring and early summer, and more conceptions occur in summer than at other times of the year. But these physiological rules, like the social rules and taboos surrounding sex, are readily broken when external stimuli are strong, and sexual behaviour can begin at any time.

Physiologists divide sexual responses into four phases—excitement, plateau, orgasmic and resolution—which follow each other in sequence. Excitement can be triggered by a wide range of stimuli, both mental and physical. Initial stages of excitement usually involve mental stimuli; there are few fields of human endeavour in which we seem more ready to use our imaginations freely, and some can advance almost to the point of orgasm through fantasy and imagination alone. Excitement is usually built up by sight, touch, scent or sounds, and human courtship practically always involves, at an early stage, the warmth of close body contact, kissing and touching—all relics of childhood days. In both sexes the skin of the genital regions is notably sensitive to stimulation by stroking and pressure. Other erogenous zones include the earlobes, breasts and flanks, but in the right circumstances almost any contact in love-making—indeed any stimulation by the partner, involving any of the five senses—can be acutely erogenous.

As a result of stimulation, excitement causes changes in the distribution of blood about the body, mediated by the sympathetic nervous system. The penis, clitoris, labia and internal pelvic organs become engorged with blood, the penis in particular growing to full size and assuming a suitable angle for penetration. With engorgement comes increasing awareness and sensitivity of the reproductive organs. The breasts enlarge, the nipples extend, and the skin flushes with blood, its overall sensitivity to touch increasing. Blood pressure and heart-beat rise. The vaginal walls secrete a thin lubricating liquid, and the labia too are moistened by secretions. The vagina lengthens and distends, the uterus pulling upwards out of the way. Once the organs have reached this stage of arousal, penetration is

usually easy, and further movement and stimulation carries excitement to the plateau phase.

Now blood vessels in the outer third of the vaginal wall become suffused with blood and the vagina contracts, tightening about the shaft of the penis. The tip of the penis expands slightly, and the testes are pulled inwards to the body. In the climax of orgasm muscle tensions which have built up all over the body relax; waves of muscular contraction propel semen from the ejaculatory ducts along the length of the penis, and matching contractions shake the vaginal wall. Finally, in the resolution phase, the organs return gradually to their normal condition.

Detailed surveys in the United States and Britain have shown that individuals vary widely in their need for sexual activity. Many people are well able to live full and happy lives with little or no sex. Others find sexual activity essential as a means of expressing themselves emotionally and physically, and often need the release from tensions which orgasm brings. It is not unusual for young people of either sex to want two, three or more orgasms per week; cultural and psychological background determines whether they achieve satisfaction through heterosexual or homosexual contacts, love-making, petting or masturbation, or suppress their erotic feelings altogether. Though love-making is primarily a social activity, its reproductive function has not disappeared. Those who are most active sexually often forget in the excitement and happiness of love-making that they may bring unwanted children into a society which cannot provide humanely for them. Although frequency of desire and orgasm fall slowly through middle age, variation between individuals remains wide, and some maintain a happy sex life well into their seventies and eighties.

Seen here in section are the male and female genitalia during sexual intercourse. From the ovary (**1**), an ovum released at the previous time of ovulation is propelled along the Fallopian tube towards the uterus (**2**). The penis (**3**) is the means by which spermatozoa, formed in the testis (**4**) and passed along the vas deferens (**5**), will be deposited in the female tract during orgasm. The seminal vesicles (**6**) and the prostate gland (**7**) add their own secretions to the seminal fluid, which is pumped through the ejaculatory duct (**8**) by waves of muscular contraction, and forms a pool near to the cervix of the uterus (**9**). The uterus, which during intercourse has moved up and away from the upper end of the vagina, now descends, so that the cervix dips into the pool of semen. Spermatozoa swim through the cervical canal and into the uterine cavity (**10**). Fertilization usually takes place in one of the Fallopian tubes.

Fertilization

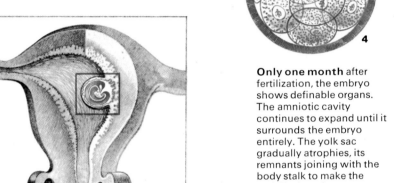

Fertilization is the union of a male germ cell (spermatozoon) with a female germ cell (ovum). Although this is the moment of conception, pregnancy does not become established until the fertilized ovum has become installed in the lining of the uterus.

Usually only one ovum is produced at ovulation. Very soon after it has been shed it is caught up by a fimbrium at the end of the Fallopian tube embracing the ovary, and carried slowly down the tube towards the uterus. The ovum may remain fertile for about two days, but fertilization usually occurs within twelve hours of ovulation in the outer third of the tube.

Four to five million spermatozoa are deposited in the vagina at coitus, but only about four thousand of these arrive at the site of fertilization, and only one actually fertilizes the ovum. When they are first released the spermatozoa are not very vigorous but they soon become active and start swimming in the alkaline fluid of the uterus; they travel at a rate of about two to three centimetres an hour. Their entrance to the uterus is probably assisted by a change in the cervical mucus to a thin watery fluid at the time of ovulation, and they may have traversed half the length of the cervical canal within 90 seconds of ejaculation. Many spermatozoa do not reach the Fallopian tubes, and some of them are lost in the tube that has no ovum present. Their active life is about two or three days but they gain the Fallopian tubes within a few hours of coitus, so that an ovum may be fertilized by a spermatozoon that arrived before ovulation occurred.

When the ovum comes into the vicinity of spermatozoa, the outer layer of cells surrounding it is dispersed by an enzyme, *hyaluronidase*, released by them. There is no attractive force between spermatozoon and ovum, and fertilization occurs as a random contact. As soon as a spermatozoon touches the ovum it adheres to it and becomes rapidly engulfed. Immediately, changes occur in the wall of the ovum that prevent the penetration of further spermatozoa. Once inside the ovum the head of the spermatozoon swells into a *pronucleus* and combines with the pronucleus of the ovum. This results in a restoration of the chromosome number to 46; the particular combination of the two sex chromosomes determines the sex of the new individual.

Throughout the process of fertilization the ovum is moving towards the uterus, and as its journey continues, the newly fertilized ovum divides a number of times and forms a mass of about thirty cells termed a *morula*. The morula reaches the uterine cavity about three days after fertilization, and since there has been little opportunity for its nourishment, its mass is no greater than that of the original ovum.

Meanwhile the endometrium of the uterus has continued to proliferate under the influence of the corpus luteum. When the morula enters the uterus, the endometrium is at its most active stage, with many glands and a rich blood supply. During the next three or four days the cells of

The first six days
After release from the ovary, the ovum travels slowly along the Fallopian tube, taking about six days to reach the uterus. Fertilization usually takes place high in the first part of the tube. Several spermatozoa may reach the ovum (**1**), but the first to meet the nucleus fertilizes the egg. The pronucleus in the head of the spermatozoon fuses with that in the ovum. Cell division now begins, the ovum splitting into two cells (**2**), four cells (**3**), eight cells (**4**) and so on, subdividing until it becomes a ball of cells called a morula (**5**). A fluid-filled cavity appears in the morula; the cluster of subdividing cells is now called a blastocyst (**6**).

Only one month after fertilization, the embryo shows definable organs. The amniotic cavity continues to expand until it surrounds the embryo entirely. The yolk sac gradually atrophies, its remnants joining with the body stalk to make the umbilical cord.

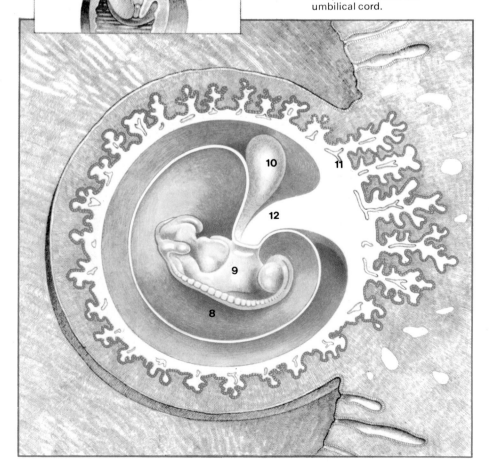

This is of course a splendid recipe for a self-duplicating system. In the dividing cell, when it becomes necessary for the chromosomes to duplicate, the DNA ladder splits along its weakest plane, which is the line of linkage between purines and pyrimidines, and the two halves fall apart. Each half ladder now proceeds to build up its missing portion from the stock of nucleotides lying to hand in the cell. Each half rung attracts to itself a nucleotide exactly like the one from which it was parted; thus arginines attract thymine-based nucleotides, guanines attract cytosines. With the rungs complete, the attached ribose and phosphate molecules link up to each other to form a new strut. Each half-ladder in this way builds itself up into a complete new ladder, and there are two identical DNA strands where before there was one. After the DNA has duplicated itself, the chromosomes (now formed of double strands) thicken into tight spirals and arrange themselves on a plane in the centre of the nucleus. A spindle of fine threads appears among them, stretching tightly across the nucleus at a right angle to the plane. The two strands of each chromosome part company, separate, and migrate in opposite directions along the spindle, gathering eventually in two clusters the length of the nucleus apart. Finally nucleus and cell body constrict and split into two new cells, each centred about its own set of chromosomes.

Chromosomes are clearly visible under any good laboratory microscope, and can be examined and counted with ease. It is even possible to link unusual chromosome patterns in man with particular physical abnormalities. *Down's syndrome* (mongolism) is shown by people with an extra fragment of chromosome, and some with a missing (or an additional) sex chromosome develop physical or mental aberrations.

Chromosomes carry the hereditary factors—called genes—which determine eye colour, tallness or shortness, shape of nose, blood grouping, and the dozens of other characteristics which go to make up an individual.

An important step in understanding heredity was made when the true nature of the gene was determined. A gene is no more than a length of DNA molecule, which acts as a template or pattern for the formation of a particular protein. The sequence of nucleotides making up a strand of DNA is in fact a code. Each set of three bases encodes a recipe for manufacturing a particular amino acid. So a single small protein molecule of fifty or so amino acids (for example insulin, a hormone secreted in the pancreas) takes up three times as many nucleotides along one side of the DNA ladder. The many thousands of proteins required by a growing human foetus—together with additional code groupings which start, modify and terminate the instructions—are catered for along the spirally-wound lengths of DNA in the chromosomes, which are estimated to carry some 16 billion nucleotides altogether.

The proteins are manufactured, not in the nucleus, but in the ribosomes which are scattered about the cell and gathered in large numbers on the endoplasmic reticulum of many secretory cells. The go-between which transfers the encoded instructions from the gene to the appropriate group of ribosomes is RNA (ribonucleic acid), a nucleic acid similar to DNA which is widely dispersed throughout the cell. Three separate kinds of RNA are needed before the correct amino acids can be assembled and strung together in sequence to form the protein.

It is not yet clear how particular genes are activated to issue their instructions. There is some evidence, however, that hormones and other chemical signals are responsible for spurring them at appropriate moments, so the secretions of one cell may stimulate genes in many other cells to direct the production of hormones affecting further sets of cells in other parts of the body. All the body's activities, including growth, may be controlled in this way.

Daughter cells
(23 chromosomes each)

Growth in infancy

Being born is the most shattering event most people ever experience. The baby is abruptly catapulted from a warm, serene bath of amniotic fluid in his mother's womb, the only surroundings he has ever known, into a cold, busy, strange environment. He emerges into the world breathless to the point of apoplexy, grease-covered, and spattered with blood. His head is temporarily misshapen by his forced passage through the birth canal. His skin is loose and wrinkled. His limbs are pathetically thin. His shoulders are hunched and his chest and hips are narrow to facilitate his entry into the world. He looks hopelessly fragile.

The new-born infant is, however, a good deal better prepared for life than he seems to be. He makes his first appearance already equipped with strong instincts for self-preservation, a sucking reflex to meet the need for sustenance and an already well-developed talent for crying to communicate pain or discomfort. He has a small but impressive repertoire of useful skills. He is sensitive to touch and to cold. He can taste, hear startling noises, and yawn and stretch his limbs to tone his fledgling muscles. The new-born infant can see, though not yet clearly, and he can squint to filter out bright lights. He can sneeze and cough to clear his air passages. He can clutch. His seemingly outsized head is already endowed with all the nerve cells he will ever possess. As for size, the average new-born infant is about 20 inches long and weighs about seven pounds. Some infants grow and shed body hair in the womb; many are born with long soft tresses which are gradually replaced by normal hair during the first weeks. The new-born baby's gut is small but his level of metabolic activity is high. As he comes to terms with his new environment, his body develops at an extraordinary rate and he needs feeding every few hours.

Crying is the infant's only means of communicating and he uses it unsparingly. He cries when he is hungry, tired, uncomfortable, needs burping or changing, or is simply fretful. The crying exercises his lungs and also weaves the beginnings of a fabric of contact with his parents; he learns of their concern for his feelings and the degree of their responsiveness to his calls for attention.

During the first four months of life, the infant sleeps most of the time. While he's awake, simple reflexes control his activities. But, asleep or awake, his body is astir. His cells are dividing; his muscles, bones, gut, liver and skin are growing and developing. His nerve cells are forming new, complex links for an ever-increasing range of purposeful activity. His food during the first few months is milk—his preference is for his mother's milk, which provides a nutritive, well-balanced diet.

Between four and eight months, the infant's birth weight doubles. The length of his body and limbs increases by a third. His eyesight and hearing sharpen. He begins reaching for things,

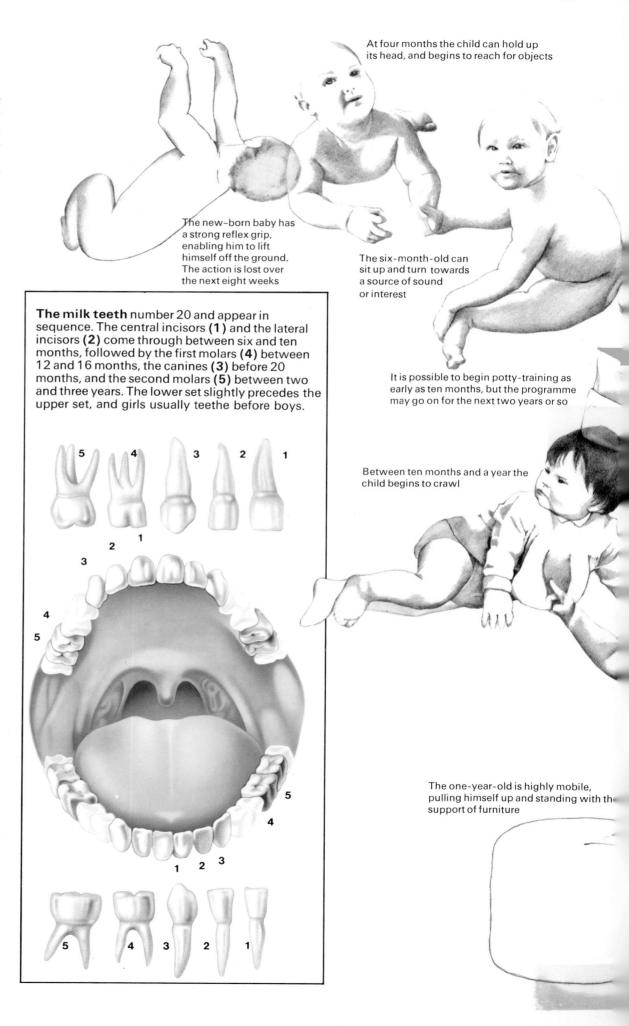

At four months the child can hold up its head, and begins to reach for objects

The new-born baby has a strong reflex grip, enabling him to lift himself off the ground. The action is lost over the next eight weeks

The six-month-old can sit up and turn towards a source of sound or interest

It is possible to begin potty-training as early as ten months, but the programme may go on for the next two years or so

Between ten months and a year the child begins to crawl

The one-year-old is highly mobile, pulling himself up and standing with the support of furniture

The milk teeth number 20 and appear in sequence. The central incisors (**1**) and the lateral incisors (**2**) come through between six and ten months, followed by the first molars (**4**) between 12 and 16 months, the canines (**3**) before 20 months, and the second molars (**5**) between two and three years. The lower set slightly precedes the upper set, and girls usually teethe before boys.

The three-year-old can run, climb and manage such complex toys as a tricycle

At eighteen months, the child can feed himself, and walk with minimal help

·becoming aware of the tantalizing world about him. He plays with his toes. He sleeps less and cries less. He laughs aloud, makes cooing noises and sings to himself. He begins sampling things with his fingers and mouth, and turns his eyes and head to follow moving objects. He can sit up with support. He can roll over on his stomach, and back again.

Before the infant's first birthday, his mental capacities grow more refined and individuality shows the first signs of emerging. A glimmer of comprehension becomes apparent. He responds when called by name. He reacts happily to physical contact with his parents and begins to recognize other recurring faces. Feeding, changing and bathing become significant social occasions, laying the groundwork for lifelong relations between infant and parent.

By the time he is one year old, the infant is crawling and trying to stand. He can push doors open and closed, and move toys from place to place. He experiments with words and sounds.

The development of the infant's mind as well as his body is now well and truly in motion. In his second year, he grows increasingly alert and imaginative. His thought processes and sensory perceptions grow more attuned. He is curious about familiar objects which are not in sight. He explores everything within reach, irrepressibly probing nooks and crannies; sometimes moving restlessly from nook to cranny, sometimes fascinated by one particular place and meticulously examining every aspect of it.

He can obey simple instructions but to match his expanding horizons, he begins constructing a workable vocabulary and is especially fascinated by the word "no". It's his first major assertion of conscious will and individuality. He learns new skills, largely by trial and error. As more of his nerve fibres become myelinated and linked to each other, his motor abilities increase. He can climb stairs, holding on to the railing. He can toddle and ride a tricycle. He can dress himself. The muscles controlling his bladder and bowels gradually come under his control.

The muscles of a two-year-old are slowly beginning to develop as instruments of energetic activity. He can run, throw and pick things up. He will soon be jumping and testing his skills on the lower reaches of a climbing frame. His speech pattern is growing more sophisticated; he can say simple sentences and enormously enjoys talking. He is curious about other children. He watches them with great interest but isn't likely to want to play with them until he is three. This is an age during which the infant consolidates the world he has come to know; he learns and plays happily alone, or with his parents.

Some babies are born with their first teeth already in evidence. Most cut their first milk teeth when they are about five months old. The remaining teeth make their appearance over the first years until, at the age of three, the child has a set of twenty and is capable of consuming the full range of adult foods. The three-year-old has also taken his first steps on the long road to maturity in other ways. He wants to know things; he endlessly asks his parents questions and the answers are meaningful to him. Though not yet ·at school, his formal education has begun. Playing with other children, he interacts with his first society of equals.

Growth

How, and at what rate, a child grows is controlled by three factors—genetics, hormones and diet. Genetic factors, carried on the chromosomes, and copied faithfully at each cell division, control the course of growth; they ensure that it follows the traditional patterns of the species and, more particularly, of the parents. So the human infant grows, in every minute detail of cell chemistry, into the human pattern. Children of tall parents tend to grow tall, those of stout parents run to fat, and facial and other features mature towards those of the parents. Hormones control rates of growth, which vary from tissue to tissue and stage to stage. Under the overall control of pituitary secretions, they are responsible for determining how energy, proteins and other resources are to be divided between the body's everyday needs and the manufacture of new tissues. At different times they promote the growth and maturation of brain tissue, deposition of subdermal fat, development of gonads and genitalia, and the striking growth of bones and muscles—the "adolescent spurt" which follows puberty. Food exercises an overall control of growth. Producing new tissue demands a ready supply of raw materials—fats, proteins, minerals, vitamins and carbohydrates—additional to those needed for everyday running and maintenance. When food is short, children are especially at risk. Those who are starved, or receive the wrong foods at critical periods of growth, show lasting effects; they remain undersized, develop poor physiques and poor resistance to disease, and may suffer a degree of mental crippling, never reaching their full intellectual capacity.

After the rapid growth of his first twelve months, the infant grows more slowly for the next three or four years. During the first year he has trebled his birth weight, and increased overall length by about one-third. It takes a further four years for him to double his weight again, and add a further third to his length. This is a period of consolidation, in which his brain develops, and he rapidly acquires new motor skills and learning. These appear in sequence as nerve tracts throughout the central nervous system acquire their coating of fat (*myelination*), and new nervous pathways are established between cells, increasing the range of activities open to him.

Between the ages of two and three he plays actively with objects around him, discovering sounds, colours, shapes, textures and flavours, learning to judge distances by eye, building and knocking down, losing and finding, experimenting with friction, gravity and other physical quantities, and generally discovering the limits of his world. This is a period when stability of family and home background are especially important to him; they are the baselines for his experiments, and their loss or change through family upheaval, removal, or travel may upset the model of the world which he is carefully building about him.

At four and five he throws himself into physical contact with the world, revelling in exercise and movement, and playing co-operatively with other children. Now skills of running, jumping, climbing and swinging develop, taking him outside the safe circle which he inhabited before. Contacts with other children and adults force upon him the need to communicate his ideas in words. Speech develops rapidly between the ages of three and five, and he learns to name familiar objects, express his own ideas and respond to the ideas of others. At this stage he stands in special need of interest and help from parents or play-school teachers. The trick of finding the right words for the objects and activities around him is a difficult one to learn, but most children find it exciting and rewarding if there is someone to respond to them. It requires the active co-operation of a willing, unharassed adult, who has time to listen to their prattle, and help them develop it into effective speech. Talking to children, helping them to find the right words and form sentences, brings them many benefits; they learn not only to talk, but also to develop and communicate their feelings, and gain the relief of being able to express themselves effectively from an early age. Parents under stress, without time or patience to talk to their children at this critical stage of development, prevent them from learning how to communicate; they may well be condemning themselves to a regimen, a few years later, of teenage tantrums and sullen silences.

Girls and boys show similar rates of development at these early stages. If allowed to, they play the same kinds of games and respond to each other in similar ways regardless of sex. However, adults usually contrive to encourage differences in behaviour, so that boys play self-consciously with manly toys and develop an element of roughness, while girls grow precociously feminine in an atmosphere of dolls and domesticity. So we prepare children at an early age for the roles which society traditionally reserves for them in later life.

Between five and seven both sexes enter their second period of rapid growth. The brain, which throughout early life has been well ahead of the rest of the body in size and maturity, has now reached almost its full adult dimensions, and the face is elongating rapidly to catch up. As the skull and jaws grow, the first permanent molars appear at the back of the mouth and, starting with the incisors in front, the milk teeth fall out one by one. This is a relatively painless process; as the crowns of the permanent teeth form under the gums, the roots of the milk teeth are gradually reabsorbed, and the new biting surfaces appear as the old ones topple away. From seven to nine the trunk and long bones continue to grow, both sexes reaching a leggy stage in which the bones seem to have outstripped the muscles. From about the ninth year the first indications of puberty appear in girls; boys wait two years or more, and may find themselves falling slightly behind girls in rate of growth during this short period.

Puberty occurs when gonadotrophic hormones of the pituitary gland stimulate the gonads into production of their own hormones. These cause the gonads to enlarge, and stimulate the growth and development of secondary sexual characteristics—which emphasize the differences between the sexes.

In girls, puberty begins with gradual development of the breasts and growth and darkening of the nipples. At about the same time coarse hair appears in the pubic region and armpits, the face rounds, the hips and thorax broaden, and the voice loses some of its higher tones. Internally

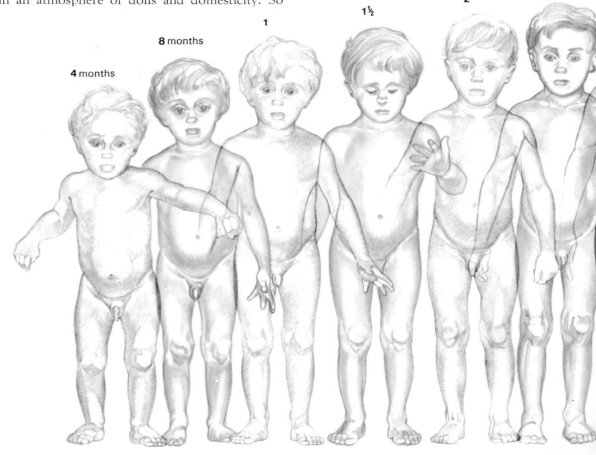

4 months   8 months   1   1½   2   3

the uterus and vagina develop, and the ovaries begin to release ova at monthly intervals, establishing the monthly or menstrual cycle. The labia of the external genitalia develop, and the clitoris and accessory glands mature. These changes may be spread over many months, menstruation often starting in the eleventh, twelfth or thirteenth year. Bone growth continues for two or three years after puberty, but then slows noticeably, and the girl may begin to store subcutaneous fat in embarrassing amounts under her skin. Hormonal imbalances may produce an oily skin and pimples, especially each month before menstruation, and emotional upsets often occur at the same time.

In boys the first signs of puberty usually appear at the age of eleven to twelve, when the testes and penis grow and circulation of hormones causes a sudden surge of growth in the long bones of the body. Pubic and armpit hair appears, the shoulders and chest broaden, and the accessory glands of the genitalia may begin secreting, causing frequent erections and occasional emission of semen at night. The skin coarsens and becomes oily, sometimes with facial pimples developing, and the moustache and beard put in their first tentative appearance. Growth continues through the next four or five years, activity usually ensuring that muscles clothe the bones and that fat is kept down to a minimum. The young man, made self-conscious by the rapid changes in his body, is all too often kept in a state of dependence at home and school. He usually finds it necessary to assert his manhood, contributing to the myth that adolescence must necessarily be a difficult period for children, teachers, and parents alike.

The later years of adolescence are a period of physical consolidation and emotional turbulence. Boys and girls between the ages of fifteen and eighteen tend to be perplexed by the imminence of physical maturity. They are often slow in adjusting to the concentrated growth and changes which accompanied the onset of puberty and early adolescence. They can be gawky and awkward, and profoundly aware of it. The mysteries of sexual awakening and the anxieties which often result from it compound their emotional ferment. They are deeply concerned about their looks and the judgments others make about them. They tend to be inherently rebellious—against parents, teachers and conventional behaviour—and this further shakes them loose from the stabilizing patterns which guided them through infancy, childhood and early adolescence.

Though their rate of bodily growth declines, their brains and central nervous systems continue to develop well into adolescence; no further cells are added, but the process of myelination is sustained until completion. A human is probably at his brightest, most receptive and most responsive in his late 'teens. He has a hunger for new experiences, new ideas and new abilities. In later years, he will find it harder to acquire new concepts, develop new thought patterns and learn new motor skills. Learning increases with the years, but rate of learning, and inclination to learn, usually declines.

Muscles develop steadily after puberty to catch up with adolescent growth. For most people, the years between the late 'teens and the mid-twenties are the most active. Muscle performance, including ability to operate continuously under conditions of oxygen debt, is highest. Heart, blood vessels, blood itself and lungs are all operating at their greatest efficiency. Athletes whose skills depend on instantaneous peaks of power output or prolonged levels of physical efficiency and performance are at their best in their early twenties. Endurance, persistence and

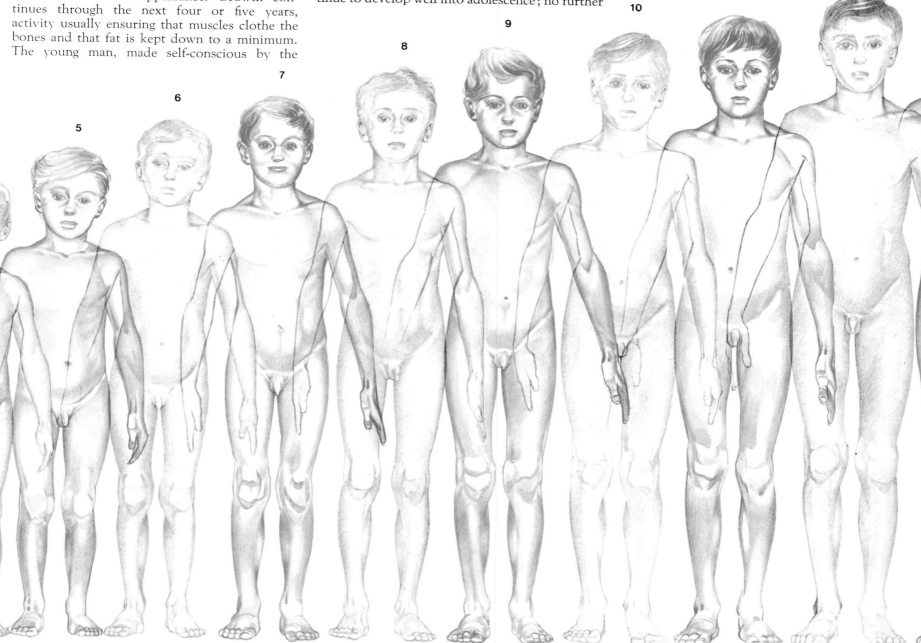

5   6   7   8   9   10   11   12

craft may improve later in life, but power output tends to decline from the mid-twenties.

The primary bones of the limbs, which grew rapidly during adolescence, reach their greatest length in the early-twenties. Linear growth ceases when the caps and shafts fuse, usually before the age of twenty-five. But the shape of many bones can be altered subsequently. Good posture and exercise can broaden the thorax and strengthen the bones long after linear growth has stopped; similarly, faulty posture can have a lasting adverse effect on the skeleton. The shape of bones which have ceased to grow can also be influenced by new habits of use following injuries.

The bones of the skull remain unfused well into the late thirties and forties. But the last molars usually appear at 17 or 18, sometimes trying to grow in an already overcrowded mouth.

In the young adult, the function of bodily growth is transformed; from that point on in life, it serves almost exclusively to replenish and sustain the body rather than develop it further. Worn cell surfaces and moribund cells are replaced, as are damaged cell tissue. The sophisticated bodily mechanisms and the bio-chemical agents for repairing the wear and tear of everyday activity and coping with infection are ceaselessly alert and operational.

Early adulthood is generally the period during which decisions are made concerning direction and purpose in life. The emotional and physical upheavals of adolescence have been left well behind. The lifestyle experiments, physical exuberance and frequently tormenting identity-seeking of the adolescent and post-adolescent periods may linger on, but, for the most part, they have already had their impact and have taught their lessons. The patterns of future sexual behaviour and emotional temperament are establishing themselves. So are eating habits which may prove critical to health later in life. Questions of career and ambition are raised, examined, decided upon and reconsidered. Marriage, parenthood and long-term direct responsibility for other individuals are distinct

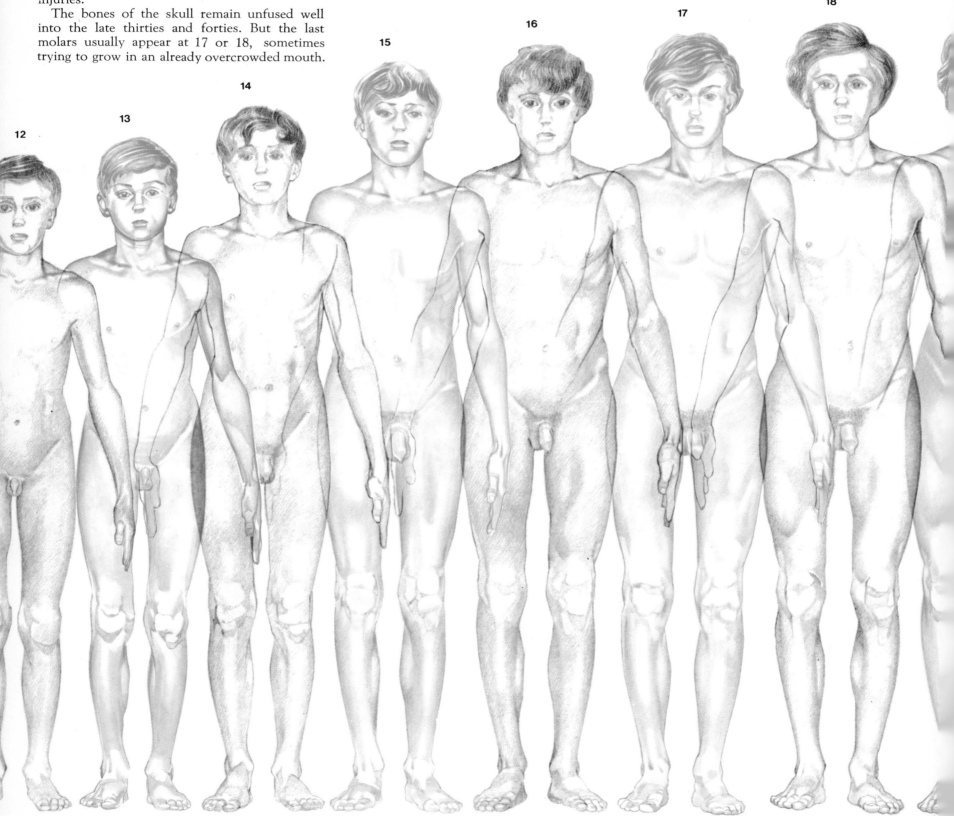

prospects if, in fact, they have not already materialized.

By the late twenties, there is a decline in the body's power output, a development most recognizable in athletes, with seemingly indestructible sports stars giving way to more youthful competitors in the full glare of publicity. But everyone is affected by this decline. It becomes more evident between the ages of thirty and forty. In subtle ways, the whole working of the body gradually slows down. Only those who have dedicatedly pursued a course of daily exercise will not be aware of it when climbing stairs or running for a bus. Blood vessels become less resilient and offer more resistance to the flow of fluid through them; they may also acquire a lining of fat which further reduces efficiency and opens the way to thromboses and strokes. Lung surfaces thicken and lose efficiency; it becomes more difficult for the body to take in oxygen or dispose of its surplus carbon dioxide. The blood loses a proportion of its red corpuscles and cannot circulate as much oxygen as before. Cells which once responded instantaneously to hormones grow less responsive. In middle age, people are susceptible to aches and pains.

Muscles toughen; the connective tissues which hold them together thicken and replace some of the active contractile cells. Muscle performance falls as less oxygen finds its way to the remaining cells and lactic acid and other waste products accumulate during prolonged use. Standard metabolic rate, an indicator of the body's background level of activity, falls steadily from adolescence onwards at a rate of five per cent or more per decade.

Nevertheless, a proper course of regular exercise, the right amount of the right food, enough sleep and an avoidance of stress situations can compensate the middle-aged body somewhat for the loss of youthful vigour. It can certainly contribute to greater resistance to illness and a healthier frame of mind. However, changes in muscle function and performance tend to discourage activity and induce a sedentary behaviour. Ironically, this development seldom impairs appetite to the same degree with the result that youthful figures give way to paunches. The approaching end of a woman's child-bearing abilities is signalled by menopause, generally in her late forties. The onset is marked by irregular menstruation, which ceases altogether over a period of about two years. During menopause, women often experience hot flushes, resulting from sudden rises in body temperature, as well as headaches and dizziness. These are symptoms of a change in the woman's hormonal balance and do not necessarily signify diminished capacity for or interest in sexual relations. Most women go through menopause without significant disturbance to their physical or mental well-being.

Life expectancy has increased dramatically and many who reach their sixties can now expect to live on to their eighties in a reasonable state of health and vigour. The problems which face them arise from the continuing reduction in metabolic rate and the slow accumulation of small metabolic defects which eventually prove overwhelming. Reduced metabolism is caused by many factors, including declining efficiency of lungs, heart, kidneys, circulation and possibly digestion, and loss of energy reserves. Old people feel cold more readily and are prone to hypothermia—loss of body heat—if they cannot keep warm. Growth and regeneration of tissues slows down, wounds and abrasions heal slowly and worn surfaces of the joints fail to maintain themselves in an efficient state. Metabolic changes, perhaps resulting from accumulated errors of transcription in many millions of cell divisions, are responsible for many of the more trying symptoms of old age, including lowered resistance to disease, loss of tissue resilience, brittle bones and high rate of fractures resulting from calcium deficiency, and arthritic conditions of the joints. Many elderly men develop prostate trouble. Many elderly people are accident-prone and suffer resulting injuries from which their bodies take longer and longer to recuperate. They also become more set in their ways, more resistant to change, more cautious and rigid; interests outside the fact of their advancing years are necessary for them to retain a degree of mental vivacity.

19
20
21

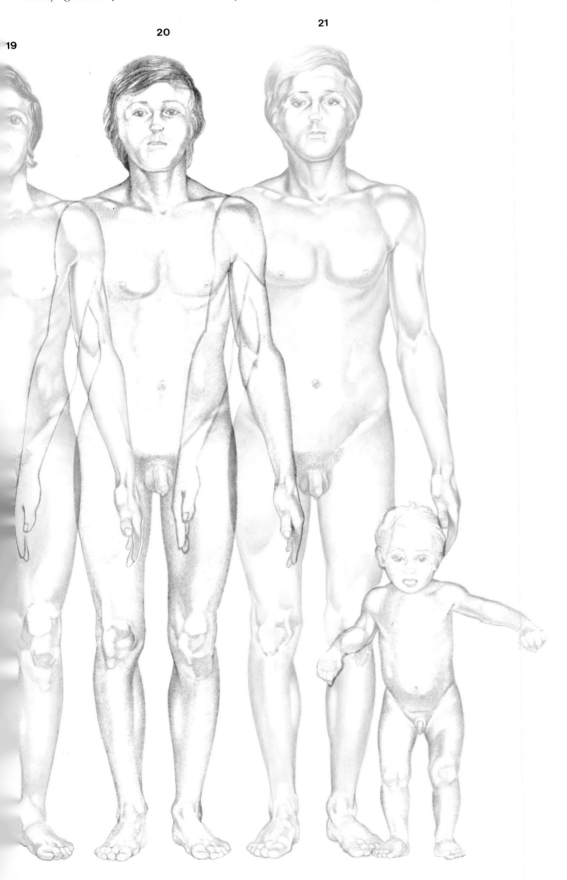

Disease

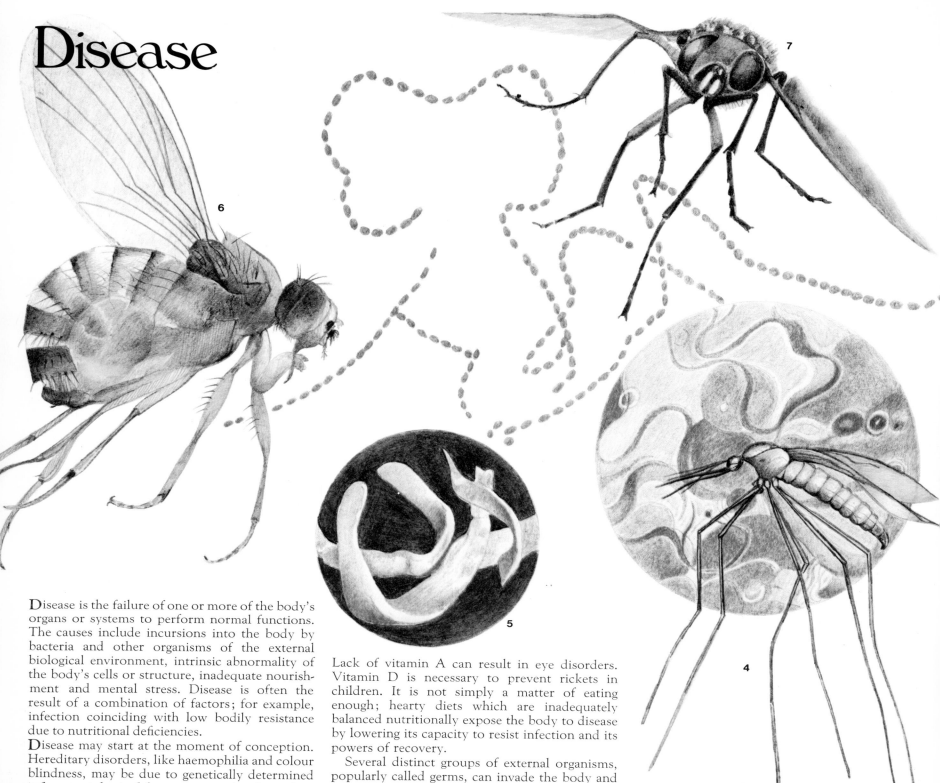

Disease is the failure of one or more of the body's organs or systems to perform normal functions. The causes include incursions into the body by bacteria and other organisms of the external biological environment, intrinsic abnormality of the body's cells or structure, inadequate nourishment and mental stress. Disease is often the result of a combination of factors; for example, infection coinciding with low bodily resistance due to nutritional deficiencies.

Disease may start at the moment of conception. Hereditary disorders, like haemophilia and colour blindness, may be due to genetically determined influences inherited from parents who themselves do not manifest the abnormality. Congenital diseases are those acquired during foetal development or in the process of birth. They may include malformation of limbs and heart abnormalities. Some metabolic defects, the roots of which may be present in infants, do not develop into such diseases as diabetes mellitus and gout (both of which result from malfunction of bodily chemicals) until much later in life, if at all.

After birth, health is at the mercy of the environment and the integrity of the various body systems, which, in turn, depend on adequate nourishment for proper development and maintenance. A lack of iron in the diet can, for example, contribute to the development of anaemia. Insufficient vitamin C at best leaves the body susceptible to colds, at worst causes scurvy.

Lack of vitamin A can result in eye disorders. Vitamin D is necessary to prevent rickets in children. It is not simply a matter of eating enough; hearty diets which are inadequately balanced nutritionally expose the body to disease by lowering its capacity to resist infection and its powers of recovery.

Several distinct groups of external organisms, popularly called germs, can invade the body and cause infection and disease. Bacteria are single-celled organisms which exist virtually everywhere; but only certain forms of bacteria can induce diseases, including whooping cough, scarlet fever, tuberculosis, tonsillitis, and gonorrhoea. Viruses are only a fraction the size of the microscopic bacteria but, unlike bacteria, they can only survive in body cells which they infect. Among the diseases for which they are responsible are influenza, colds, mumps, and chickenpox. Fungi are plant organisms, clusters of which are responsible for such afflictions as athlete's foot and thrush. Like bacteria, most protozoa, which are larger but still microscopic, are harmless. But certain kinds can cause such debilitating diseases as malaria, amoebic dysentery and sleeping sickness. Worms which invade the body are parasites of more complex structure. Tapeworms can grow up to ten yards in length within the intestinal tract. They can lead to intestinal obstruction and anaemia.

These various pernicious external organisms reach the body through any of several channels or agents; through contaminated food or water, through insects or animals, through the air, through persons already suffering from the diseases they cause, and through carriers who do not themselves show the symptoms. Measles, German measles, mumps, shingles, syphilis and diphtheria can be contracted through close contact with individuals already infected. Dysentery, cholera and salmonella can be transmitted by contaminated food or water. Flu, pneumonia, tuberculosis and the common cold can be trans-

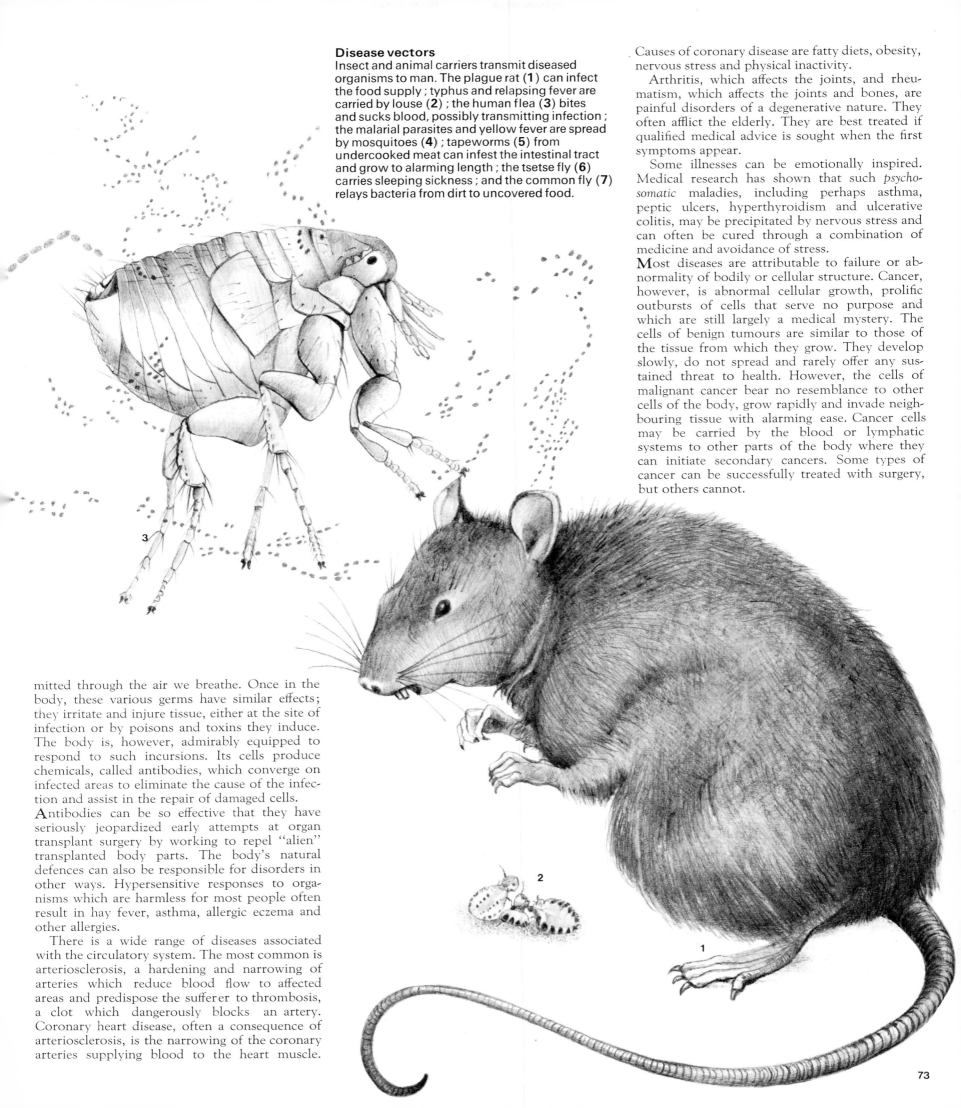

Insect and animal carriers transmit diseased organisms to man. The plague rat (**1**) can infect the food supply ; typhus and relapsing fever are carried by louse (**2**) ; the human flea (**3**) bites and sucks blood, possibly transmitting infection ; the malarial parasites and yellow fever are spread by mosquitoes (**4**) ; tapeworms (**5**) from undercooked meat can infest the intestinal tract and grow to alarming length ; the tsetse fly (**6**) carries sleeping sickness ; and the common fly (**7**) relays bacteria from dirt to uncovered food.

Causes of coronary disease are fatty diets, obesity, nervous stress and physical inactivity.

Arthritis, which affects the joints, and rheumatism, which affects the joints and bones, are painful disorders of a degenerative nature. They often afflict the elderly. They are best treated if qualified medical advice is sought when the first symptoms appear.

Some illnesses can be emotionally inspired. Medical research has shown that such *psychosomatic* maladies, including perhaps asthma, peptic ulcers, hyperthyroidism and ulcerative colitis, may be precipitated by nervous stress and can often be cured through a combination of medicine and avoidance of stress.

Most diseases are attributable to failure or abnormality of bodily or cellular structure. Cancer, however, is abnormal cellular growth, prolific outbursts of cells that serve no purpose and which are still largely a medical mystery. The cells of benign tumours are similar to those of the tissue from which they grow. They develop slowly, do not spread and rarely offer any sustained threat to health. However, the cells of malignant cancer bear no resemblance to other cells of the body, grow rapidly and invade neighbouring tissue with alarming ease. Cancer cells may be carried by the blood or lymphatic systems to other parts of the body where they can initiate secondary cancers. Some types of cancer can be successfully treated with surgery, but others cannot.

mitted through the air we breathe. Once in the body, these various germs have similar effects; they irritate and injure tissue, either at the site of infection or by poisons and toxins they induce. The body is, however, admirably equipped to respond to such incursions. Its cells produce chemicals, called antibodies, which converge on infected areas to eliminate the cause of the infection and assist in the repair of damaged cells.

Antibodies can be so effective that they have seriously jeopardized early attempts at organ transplant surgery by working to repel "alien" transplanted body parts. The body's natural defences can also be responsible for disorders in other ways. Hypersensitive responses to organisms which are harmless for most people often result in hay fever, asthma, allergic eczema and other allergies.

There is a wide range of diseases associated with the circulatory system. The most common is arteriosclerosis, a hardening and narrowing of arteries which reduce blood flow to affected areas and predispose the sufferer to thrombosis, a clot which dangerously blocks an artery. Coronary heart disease, often a consequence of arteriosclerosis, is the narrowing of the coronary arteries supplying blood to the heart muscle.

Epidemics

The incidence of disease within a population depends on a variety of factors. In the first instance the agent that causes disease must be present, but the extent to which people will be affected depends on the potency of the agent, people's susceptibility to it, and the way in which the disease is contracted or passed from person to person. An infectious disease provides the best illustration of the interaction of disease and the human community, but many of the principles apply to the other causes of disease.

When there is a constant source and incidence of disease within an area it is said to be *endemic*. Sudden increases in the number of cases of a disease or the appearance of a new disease affecting large numbers of people are called *epidemics*. Epidemics arise for three main reasons: a new organism to which few people have any natural resistance may develop, during a quiet period a number of individuals may accumulate who have acquired no immunity (this probably explains the epidemics of childhood illnesses such as measles), and thirdly, a disease may be endemic, but some change such as a natural disaster or an alteration in people's habits alters the status quo and allows the disease to expand. The recent enormous increase in venereal disease, especially gonorrhoea, could, for example, be explained by the introduction of the contraceptive pill,

The effect an organism may have on an individual depends on its virulence, the dose of infection contracted, and the person's susceptibility to it. In some people a particular organism may cause only a mild illness, whilst others are more severely affected. However, in both cases the infected person may acquire immunity to the disease and also pass it on to others. An individual's susceptibility to disease may be influenced by hereditary factors, his age, level of health and nutrition, and environment—especially extremes of heat and cold. He may also have acquired immunity to the disease.

Perhaps the most important factor in the incidence of disease is the mode in which it is spread. The transmission of disease involves its exit from an infectious person and its passage and entry into the next individual. The majority of infectious diseases leave and enter the body through the intestinal and respiratory tracts. Food and water are easily contaminated by carriers or infected persons, or indeed by an individual himself. Most of the infective diarrhoeas, tapeworms, poliomyelitis and infective hepatitis are acquired through ingestion. Epidemics of these diseases are usually explosive; large numbers of people are infected at the same time by contamination of water supplies or processed foods. Most diseases that involve the respiratory tract, such as the common cold, tuberculosis and many of the childhood infections such as measles and mumps are spread by 'droplet infection'.

The organisms responsible for these diseases are at one time or another present in the saliva, sputum or nasal mucus of the infected individual or carrier. When he coughs, sneezes or merely talks, a spray of fine droplets is ejected from his mouth or nose. Any of these droplets may infect another person or open wound. However it is the finest of these droplets that are most effective in spreading the organisms. While they are still in the air they evaporate, leaving tiny particles of dried mucus, some of which harbour viruses and bacteria. In a crowded place there may be many such particles floating in the air that may easily be inhaled by a susceptible person. Skin scales may also transmit disease in a similar way. Epidemics of respiratory diseases usually develop only as the organism is passed between susceptible persons, reaches a peak and dies away as the number of susceptible persons decreases.

It used to be thought that disease was spread solely by physical contact. In fact relatively few of the common diseases are truly contagious. Cold sores (herpes simplex) and glandular fever may be transmitted by kissing, and one group—the venereal diseases—are only transmitted by close physical contact, usually sexual.

The final route by which disease may enter the body is through the skin. Wounds may become infected, some parasites directly penetrate the skin, and many diseases are inoculated by other animals such as insects. Other animals may introduce disease to human beings either because they harbour it themselves or transmit it from another animal or man. The existence of diseases in other animals that can also infect man is important because animals can act as reservoirs of disease. Indeed, the continued existence of some diseases is entirely dependent on specific animal vectors or reservoirs. Malaria and yellow fever, for example, are only transmitted by certain mosquitoes, and schistosomiasis (bilharzia) can only remain in a region provided the appropriate species of fresh-water snails is present for the development of its larvae. The eradication of these animal vectors or reservoirs of disease is one important method of disease control.

From the foregoing account it will be apparent that both geographical and human factors may have a large influence on the prevalence of disease. There is a real increase in the incidence and variety of disease from temperate to tropical zones. The tropical populations of the world not only suffer from many of the common diseases of the temperate zones but are also afflicted with a great number of the diseases peculiar to the tropics, many of which are transmitted by insects. In addition their resistance both as communities and individuals is often reduced by overcrowding and poor housing, hygiene and nutrition.

Man himself is making profound changes in the geography of disease, not always to his advantage. In the "westernized" countries, prosperity and public health have largely banished the great endemic infectious diseases; cancer, circulatory disease and the degenerative diseases all characteristic of old age are now the main causes of death and illness. In tropical regions man's activities are changing the patterns of disease such as malaria and bilharzia.

Even on the smallest scale the study of the geography of disease may reveal surprising information about the patterns and causes of disease. Plotting the occurrence of a particular disease on a map of an area as small as a village or town may indicate such facts as the relationship between water supply and cause of arterial disease and cancer.

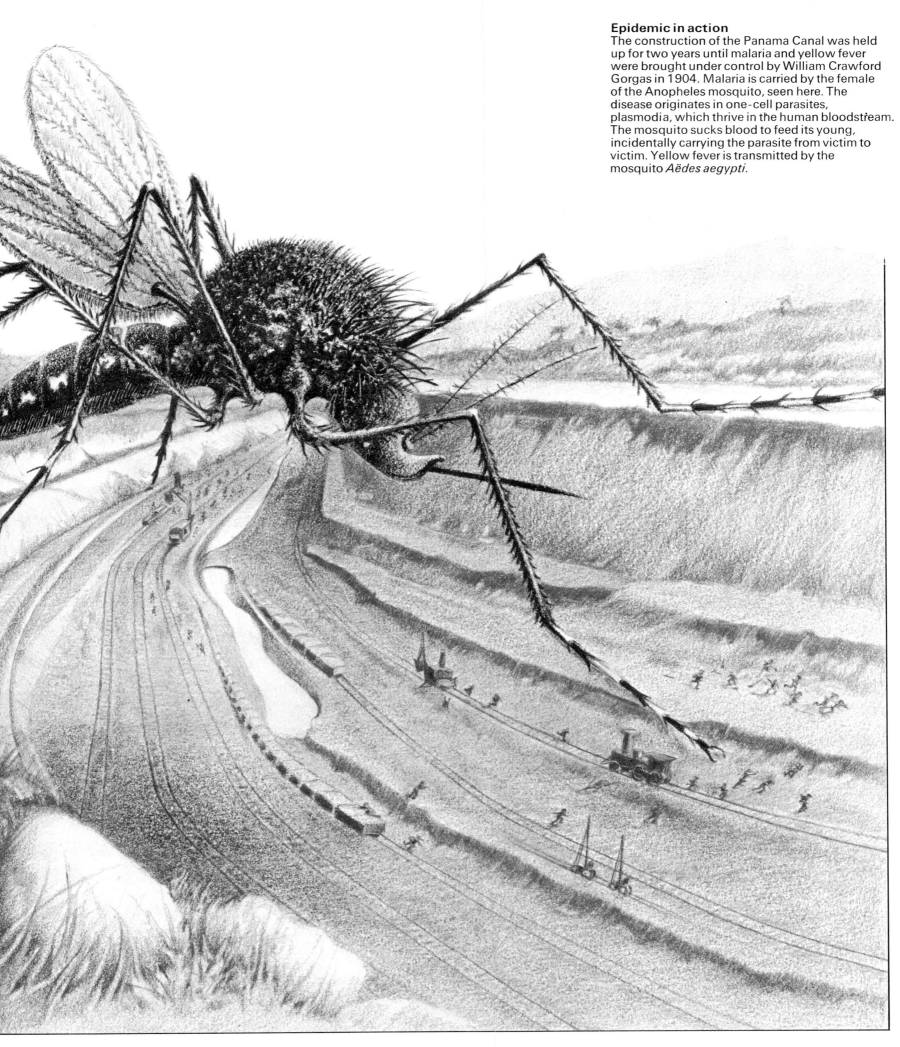

Epidemic in action
The construction of the Panama Canal was held up for two years until malaria and yellow fever were brought under control by William Crawford Gorgas in 1904. Malaria is carried by the female of the Anopheles mosquito, seen here. The disease originates in one-cell parasites, plasmodia, which thrive in the human bloodstream. The mosquito sucks blood to feed its young, incidentally carrying the parasite from victim to victim. Yellow fever is transmitted by the mosquito *Aëdes aegypti*.

Defence systems

Infections arise outside the body and have to penetrate our defences to become established within us. Inside, they run the gauntlet of our formidable defence systems, which are primed to attack any material which invades the body. We have three kinds of body surface through which invaders may enter—the skin, the lungs and the alimentary canal. The skin is a tough, waterproof membrane, with a slightly acid surface, which is constantly being replaced by new material from below. It is a cold and hostile barrier to potential invaders, which are geared for living in the warm moist environment under our skin. Sweat, secreted constantly by sweat glands in the skin, provides an additional hazard, for it contains an enzyme which breaks up bacteria and other organisms. Special areas of skin have special protection. The fine skin covering the eyes, the conjunctiva, is bathed constantly by tears from the lacrimal glands, which contain a chemical, lysozyme, which effectively destroys bacteria. Other delicate membranes, for example the lining of the vagina, are protected by acid secretions and even by the presence of harmless bacteria, which actively keep other, potentially harmful kinds, at bay.

The respiratory tract is protected primarily by the nose, a highly efficient filter and air conditioner. Hairs in the nostrils keep large, floating particles out and the air passages inside the nose are lined with mucus which traps all but the smallest particles, delivering them eventually for expulsion by coughing or for destruction in the stomach. Further down, the trachea and the bronchi of the lungs are protected by a mucous membrane, whose cilia waft mucus and particles upwards into the throat for swallowing. The respiratory tract is also protected by macrophage and lymphocyte cells, which wander over the surface of the mucous membrane, ingesting foreign particles, and acting as sentinels for the chemical immunity system.

Physical injury, which might temporarily incapacitate these defences, is generally warded off by the sensitivity of our early warning system of nerve endings and neuromuscular reflexes evolved especially to keep trouble away. Touch, irritation and ultimately pain warn us of impending damage to our surface areas; reflexes pull our hands from danger and close our eyelids faster than thought, and the cough reflex expels irritant objects from air passages without stopping to enquire what they are. The digestive tract is perhaps the most hostile entry port of all; stomach acidity destroys most invading organisms, and digestive enzymes destroy many which penetrate as far as the intestine.

Generally, invading bacteria cause disease only if they can accumulate. This is often prevented by the flow of materials about the body—the flushing action of the bloodstream through tissues, of saliva in the mouth, and urine through the kidneys, ureters and bladder. Where pockets

Repelling bacterial invasion

Bacteria (**1**) may invade from outside the body—from other people, animals or contaminated objects, or may migrate from other parts of the body where they are harmless. The threat of a bacterial invasion of any kind prompts the body's defence systems to action. If bacteria come from an external source, the skin (**2**) presents a formidable barrier, being waterproof, slightly acid and of a lower temperature than the optimum for bacterial survival. The usual entrance sites are therefore through wounds in the skin, or through the orifices which lead to the body's interior. Here, germs are checked by the lining of the digestive tract (**3**), which secretes powerful enzymes capable of destroying invaders. In the respiratory tract and nasal passages, cilia (**4**) constantly waft mucus either to the stomach to be destroyed, or back out through the mouth and nose in a sneeze or a cough, rejecting any unwelcome organisms or irritants the mucus has trapped. The mucous membrane is also patrolled by lymphocytes (**5**), produced by the nodes of the lymphatic system, which either engulf the invader, or produce antibodies to neutralize it. The destruction of bacteria often takes place within the lymph nodes, which are clumps of lymphatic tissue networked over the body. This causes the swollen areas under the arms or in the groin, which can be seen in particularly bad infections. The presence of an intruder stimulates the production of other white blood cells (**6**) by lymphoid tissue, the spleen and blood marrow. These also engulf bacteria and dead body cells. The delicate organs of the eyes are protected by a constant flow of tears

(**7**), which contain a bactericidal agent, lysozyme. Antibodies (here represented by arrows) are formed by the body in response to the presence of antigens—any material foreign to the body. Antibodies are formed on the lock and key principle, making a shape that exactly complements that of the antigen, so neutralizing it.

of bacteria lodge, trouble begins—for example in cracked tooth enamel, which saliva cannot flush out. In these situations, the body's internal defence systems come into action, responding specifically to the invasion of foreign material, and to the toxins which the invaders produce by their presence. Damaged tissues react characteristically in the way we recognize as inflammation. Outwardly, the affected area looks red, hot, swollen and tender. Inside, the blood vessels have dilated and their walls have become more permeable, allowing fluids and blood cells to pass outward into the tissues. The increased blood supply brings more oxygen, which many disease-producing bacteria cannot tolerate, and increased numbers of white blood cells, which engulf bacteria and remove dead cells and other debris from the scene.

Infection inevitably injures the affected tissues; following its victory over its invaders, the body must set about repairing the damage. Some infections cause little damage, but if cells have been destroyed, an ulcer or abscess cavity is left. The surface of the cavity is protected by a layer of tissue fluid, which is then invaded by capillaries and fibro blasts—special mobile cells which deposit strands of fibre. This forms a scaffolding into which cells grow from neighbouring tissues until the damage is made good.

Proteins in the blood also help to incapacitate bacteria and neutralize their poisons. When foreign proteins are detected, they are treated by the body as antigens; special proteins, globulins, produced by lymphocytes and by cells in the liver, spleen and lymphoid tissue are mobilized to produce antibodies, which act specifically against the antigens, effectively neutralizing them in one way or another. Some cause bacteria to clump together, hindering their spread; others disrupt the bacteria, or coat them with globulin material which makes them more readily ingestible by phagocytes. Yet others neutralize the toxins produced by the bacteria.

Viruses which enter the body are attacked in two ways. When an individual cell is invaded, it liberates a substance called *interferon* which diffuses into neighbouring cells and protects them against viral invasion. Lymphocytes armed with antibodies specialize in combating virus infection; in contact with an invaded cell, they cause it to disintegrate, and the virus, liberated into the body fluids, is mopped up by circulating antibodies. Anyone who has suffered from viral invasion acquires resistance or immunity to the particular organism responsible. In some diseases, such as measles and smallpox, immunity is lifelong; in others it lasts for weeks or months. Artificial immunity can be conferred by immunization, stimulating the body to produce antibodies by injecting appropriate antigens which have in some way been rendered harmless. New-born infants are immune to many forms of infection in the first few months of life because of ready-made antibodies which cross the placenta from the mother's bloodstream, giving them time to develop their own antibodies without having to suffer a succession of diseases.

With such a formidable array of defences at our disposal, it is hardly surprising that for most of our lives, we remain free from harmful, infecting organisms. A general state of good health is our best defence against disease.

Mental health

The terms "sane" and "insane", "sanity" and "insanity", implying as they do that there are two and only two ways of classifying the state of a person's mind, are today little used within the medical profession, although still in popular and in legal use. In fact a psychiatrist would be likely to use the words only when referring to the mental health of a defendant in a court of law—and then reluctantly, because states of mental health simply do not fit neatly into the labelled compartments which the legal profession would like. As our knowledge of mental illnesses and their causes has grown, so terminology has gradually changed. It is thought preferable to talk of "normality", "good mental health" or "good adjustment", rather than sanity, and of mental "abnormality", "disorder", "illness" or "maladjustment", rather than insanity or madness. Deciding whether the mind is healthy or disordered is a very different problem from diagnosing degrees of bodily health and bodily disorder. For the physical functions of the body there are reasonably clear-cut criteria of normality and abnormality that we can apply—normal organs carry out their functions properly and abnormal ones do not; healthy teeth do not ache or decay but diseased ones do; normal urine contains no sugar and there is a disorder somewhere in the body if the urine does contain sugar. It is a medical tradition that health is the absence of disease or disorder. For bodily health, this is a good enough definition, and it is tempting to say, by analogy, that good mental health is simply the absence of any mental disease. But then one has to define mental disorder, and when it comes to gauging the normality, or abnormality, of mental function, there are few straightforward criteria that we can go by.

Extremes of mental disorder are often readily recognized; it does not need a psychiatrist to diagnose abnormality if a person is suffering from severe hallucinations, behaving entirely irrationally, or has lost all ability to perform activities essential for his own continued survival. However, in many forms of mental disorder there are no such extreme symptoms, but merely exaggerations of the natural actions, reactions and expressions of the personality seen in people we regard as behaving normally—as we have come to expect them to.

It is difficult to say, for example, when suspicion, resentment and feelings of injustice—emotions explicable and justifiable in all of us from time to time—become so pronounced in a person that they would qualify as delusions of persecution. Or when, precisely, a person, shy, solitary and introspective by disposition, should be deemed mentally disordered because of his withdrawal into himself, and therefore in need of psychiatric help. The borderline between normal and abnormal, between what is acceptable and what is unacceptable, cannot be rigidly laid down, not only because standards of behaviour vary from generation to generation, and from society to society, but because we are all unique in our genetic make-up, background, intelligence and personality, and therefore react uniquely.

To attempt to distinguish between states of mental health and mental disorder, psychiatrists rely upon several different criteria for the normal. In everyday usage, normal infers doing what is expected—doing as the majority of us do. This has been called the "statistical" approach to defining normality, and has the disadvantage that it does not take into account the desirability or undesirability of being either "light" or "dark", as opposed to the neutral "grey" of the statistically average human being.

In measuring intelligence, for example, the criterion of the normal is the score of 100 in IQ tests. Persons who score much more or much less than 100 in this assessment of one aspect of mental function are statistically abnormal. But it could hardly be denied that having an intelligence greater than the average is a desirable trait, and having a lower than average intelligence an undesirable trait. Normality, using the statistical approach, implies conformity with an average, and does not take into account deviations that have positive value, both for the individual and for society as a whole—such as genius, creativity and heroism.

Opposed to the pure "statistical" approach, using an "evaluative" approach, psychiatrists try to take into account important personal and social factors that affect behaviour. In this approach, standards of adequacy and efficiency in the individual may be assessed. Is the person performing everyday activities at a level of efficiency lower than he is capable of, and has achieved in the past? Is he adequately fulfilling the role which his work or his position in society demands of him? We all vary in our levels of performance, doing things efficiently at times and less efficiently at others. If we consistently fail to reach the standards of efficiency demanded of us, the personal distress that our failings cause is indicative of a degree of abnormality. When a person's management of his everyday affairs deteriorates to an extreme degree, it is clear that psychiatric help is needed.

It is possible to analyse many different aspects of human behaviour, and attempt to set criteria for the normal and abnormal in each of them. But even if we analyse single features one at a time there are difficulties—psychological characteristics are not measurable to the same degree. There are no simple categories into which any of the aspects of human mental activity can be placed. People are not either intelligent or unintelligent, any more than they are either short or tall if their physical characteristics are considered. Intelligence, like height, must be measured on a gradual scale. And so it is with other psychological characteristics. There is a continuum between what is normal and what is abnormal.

It is safer to observe groups of characteristics—syndromes—rather than individual traits, and observe the overall picture in its particular context. What might be considered normal behaviour in one context can become abnormal—even dangerously so—in another. Aggressiveness in a person with a conscience may be controlled by reason, but in a person with no conscience is a menace to society.

The balanced mind

One sign of psychological health is happiness—contentment with an environment and mode of life, satisfaction in fulfilling the need for a partner in marriage and children, satisfaction in one's work, and satisfaction in relaxation or recreation. Every aspect of life cannot be expected to run smoothly, and the healthy mind shows resilience and adaptability to changing circumstances, and maturity—ordering behaviour appropriate to one's age and individual situation.

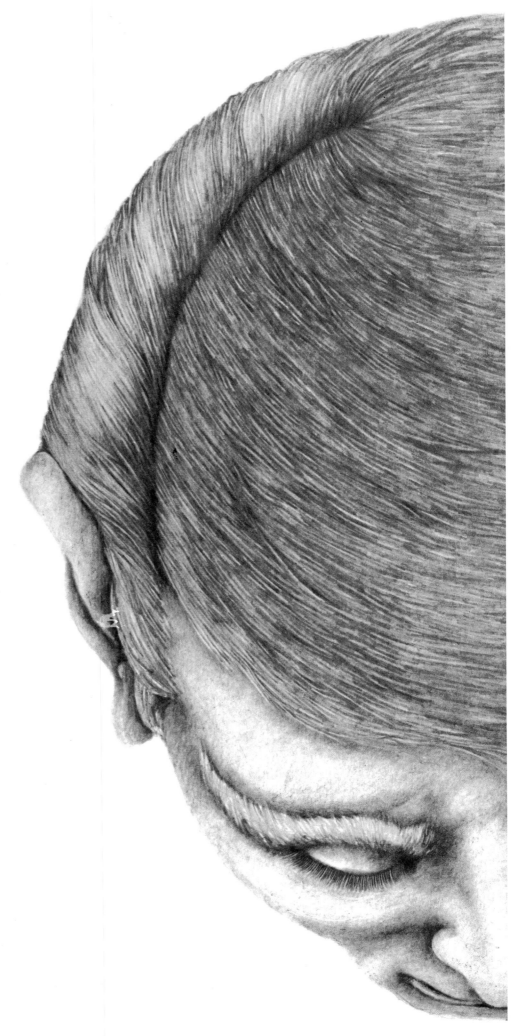

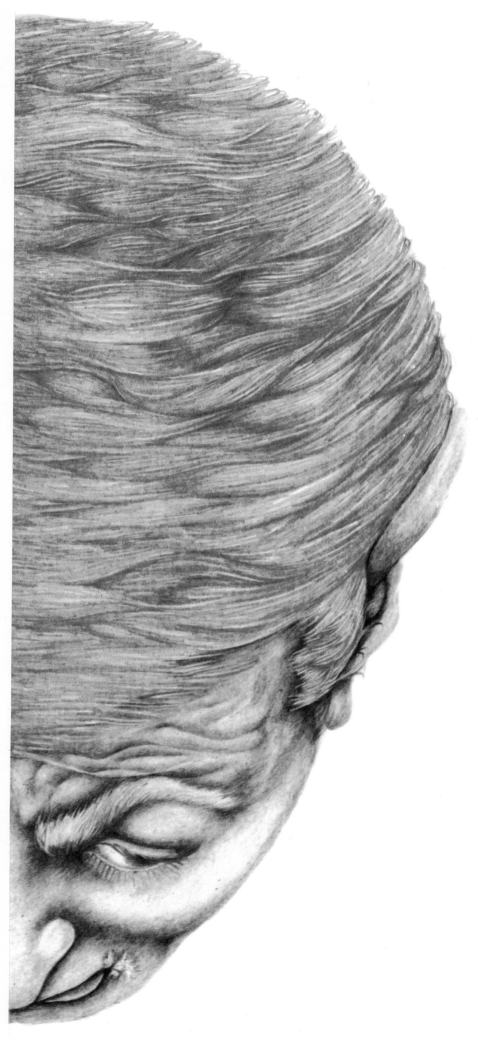

The unbalanced mind
Anxiety—"fear spread out thin"—is a major component in many mental disorders. All too easily, in the person lacking insight, anxiety, jealousy and suspicion mingle as a result of prolonged stressful situations. Delusions are an extreme result—unfaithfulness in a marriage partner is a common suspicion that may become overwhelming; financial worries distort family life; even minor worries such as an untidy garden turn into nightmares of inadequacy.

Mental disorder

Broadly speaking, mental disorders can be grouped into three categories; neurological diseases, genetic defects and psychoses.

Because the brain and the mind are so closely linked, damage or disease in the brain often has psychological as well as physiological symptoms. Brain damage may lead to a loss of sensation, for example blindness or deafness, or to a loss of motor ability such as paralysis, tremor or poor co-ordination; it may also cause a loss of the ability to use language, a decline in intelligence, or a state of confusion and disorientation known as *dementia*. Progressive damage such as that caused by a cancerous tumour in the brain may lead to a gradual change in personality and mental ability, while damage occurring at or before birth may lead to *mental subnormality*—a severe lack of intelligence, or to *spasticity*—a disturbance of movement and co-ordination. Sometimes also associated with brain damage is *epilepsy*. In this condition, either the whole or certain parts of the brain become overactive with results varying from fleeting changes in awareness to convulsions and unconsciousness.

Genetic disorders arise when certain genes function inadequately or not at all. Depending on which genes are faulty, the symptoms of these disorders may be physical, mental or both. Severe mental subnormality is often due to genetic malfunction, while a genetic predisposition may contribute to many mental illnesses.

However, mental disorders often occur without any obvious neurological or genetic cause. Where these conditions are such that an individual is unable to live a reasonably normal life, they may be termed psychoses. There are two main types of psychosis, the *manic depressive* disorders and the *schizophrenias*.

In manic depressive states, the person's emotional responses bear little relation to what is happening to him. In the classic case, the sufferer is alternately *manic*—overactive and excessively confident and enthusiastic—and *depressed*—unhappy, lethargic and apathetic. This pattern is repeated every few weeks, months or even years. More often, though, only the depressive or manic phase occurs, and between such episodes the individual shows appropriate emotional responses.

In the schizophrenic disorders, it is the person's cognitive or thinking processes which bear only an obscure relation to the real world. The disorder is characterized by *delusions*—ideas and convictions which have little basis in fact—*hallucinations*—perception of sights, sounds and voices which are not actually there, and behaviour which, while making sense to the schizophrenic, has little relevance to the outside world.

The causes of psychoses are difficult to determine, but the presence of several factors is probably necessary. A genetic predisposition towards the disorder may be important, since the identical twin of a psychotic person is more likely than another brother or sister to show the same disorder. Similarly, while it is not possible to ascribe these disorders to a specific neurological cause, the fact that the more bizarre symptoms can usually be controlled by drugs which act on the nervous system suggests that the brain may be acting in an unusual manner. Consideration of the personal circumstances of psychotics reveals that past experience, and in particular certain stresses in the family structure, contribute largely to the condition. However, the fact that children of the same parents brought up in the same environment do not necessarily suffer from mental disorders suggests that social factors cannot provide the whole explanation.

Mental health is not simply the absence of mental disease; it can only be assessed in the light of the individual personality in his individual surroundings.

Often classed as mental disorders are the various types of *neurosis*. It is difficult to say which types of behaviour should be termed neurotic, since behaviour which is normal and appropriate in one culture and at one time may be completely out of place in others. However, looking at behaviour of individuals in the context of their personal circumstances, it can be seen that some people make good use of the opportunities available to them. These people can be called well-adjusted or mentally healthy. By setting realistic targets for themselves they achieve success wherever possible, and by being flexible and adaptable in their attitudes, can cope with most of the difficulties and frustrations which they meet. On the other hand, there are people who, by the results of their own actions, must necessarily fail to achieve what they really want. They may set their aims so unrealistically high or so far in the future that they can never achieve satisfaction; or they may make their aims so low that they never make full use of their own potential.

A particularly common process that can be seen in neurotic behaviour is that of finding a trivial but immediate answer to a problem at the expense of a better, long-term solution. Thus a person who encounters difficulties at work may solve the immediate problem by changing his job. But if he persistently changes his job, his long-term ambitions will probably be thwarted. Heavy drinking, violence, and the apathy associated with depression are other examples of responses which are unlikely to improve the situation in the long run.

Fear or anxiety may be considered normal, and even useful, when it motivates a person to remove the source of his concern, but it may be a neurotic reaction when it is used as a substitute for finding a proper solution. The person seems to be hoping that a sufficiently intense emotional response will make the problems go away. Such *neurotic anxiety* may be divorced from the conflicts which originally caused it—when it is called *free-floating anxiety* — or it may be attached to a specific and often irrelevant object or situation, when it is termed a *phobia*.

Other neurotic reactions include *obsessional* or *compulsive* behaviour, where a person avoids confronting a source of conflict by persistently indulging in a distracting activity such as washing; and *conversion reactions* where a person develops the symptoms of a physical disease.

Man as a machine

The majority of men and women, despite the mechanization of industrial society, earn their living by hard physical work. Their survival depends on their ability to perform mechanical work. Man is essentially a machine and as with a machine the factors that limit physical performance are the quality of fuel, "engine" size and temperature control.

A man's productivity is determined by how hard he can work and how long he can keep his work rate up. In the long term, this depends on the quality of fuel or, in other words, the energy available to him in his diet.

Muscles are the motive power, or engine, of the human machine. Their contractions convert chemical energy into an equivalent amount of mechanical work and heat. Under normal working conditions energy is released by the continuing metabolism of food fuels—the "burning" of glucose and free fatty acids, using oxygen. The supply to the muscles is sufficient to maintain a steady work output. It is, however, common experience that extremely hard work is limited by a rapid onset of discomfort and exhaustion.

At the onset of exercise the respiratory and heart rates increase with the muscles' demand for oxygen. As the blood passes through the lungs it is fully saturated with oxygen, but the supply to the muscles depends on the output of the heart. When the heart is beating at its maximum rate (180-190 beats per minute in young adults, over 200 per minute in children and less than 170 in the elderly) the oxygen supply to the muscles can be increased no further and a maximum oxygen intake is reached. This is called *aerobic capacity*. Although muscle can continue to contract when oxygen is scarce, there is a rapid depletion of the high energy phosphates responsible for contraction and an overwhelming production of lactic acid. The accumulation of lactic acid disturbs the chemical balance in the cells, causing them to slow down or stop work. This *anaerobic* (oxygenless) metabolism results in an "oxygen debt".

The maximum heart rate varies little among people of the same age group, but there is a wide variation in aerobic capacity largely explained by differences in heart size. Normal young men have aerobic capacities of about three and a half litres of oxygen per minute and women some thirty per cent less because of their smaller body size. (Top class endurance athletes attain values of five to six litres of oxygen per minute.)

Few people can sustain work rates requiring maximal oxygen intakes for more than four or five minutes and even top class athletes for only fifteen minutes or so. Those who earn their living by physical work habitually operate at rates corresponding to about fifty per cent of their maximal oxygen intakes. It is found that below fifty per cent there is little lactic acid production but it increases rapidly at work rates exceeding sixty per cent. Furthermore, the muscles' fuel

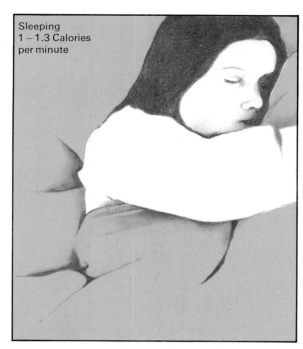

Sleeping
1 – 1.3 Calories
per minute

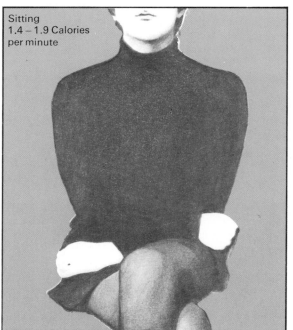

Sitting
1.4 – 1.9 Calories
per minute

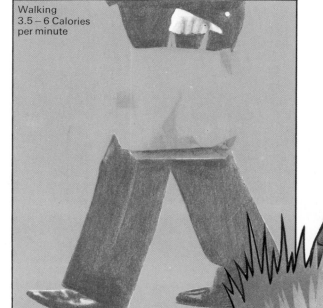

Walking
3.5 – 6 Calories
per minute

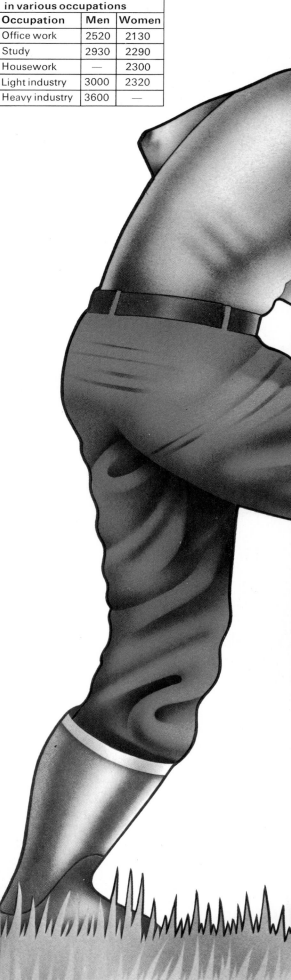

24 hour Calorie expenditure in various occupations		
Occupation	Men	Women
Office work	2520	2130
Study	2930	2290
Housework	—	2300
Light industry	3000	2320
Heavy industry	3600	—

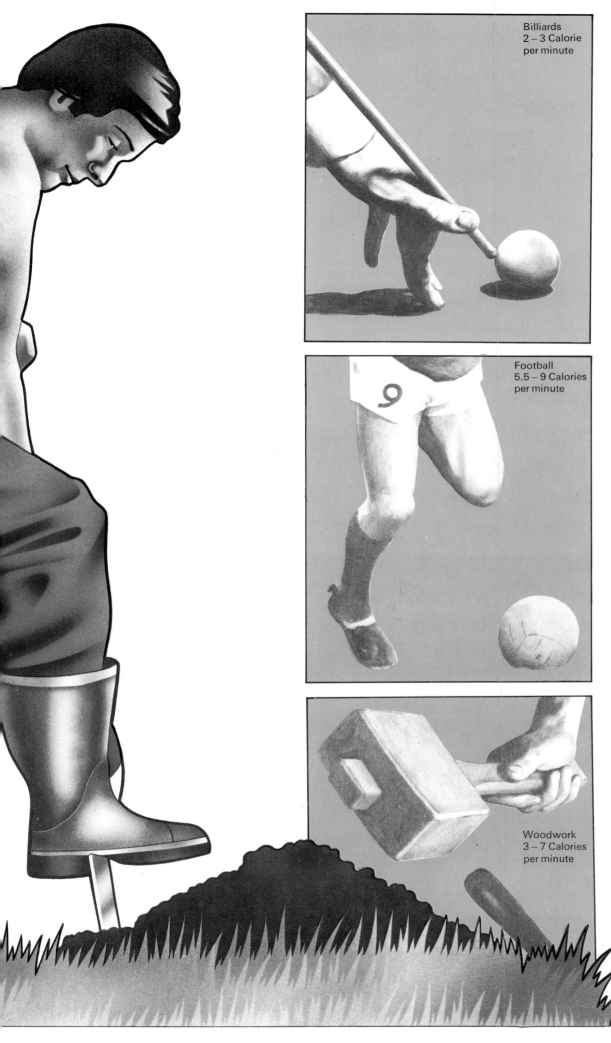

Billiards
2 – 3 Calorie
per minute

Football
5.5 – 9 Calories
per minute

Woodwork
3 – 7 Calories
per minute

economy is affected by the relative work rate. Most of the glucose metabolized comes from the glycogen within the muscle cells; the free fatty acids, however, are supplied by the blood from the fat depots. The ratio of glucose to fat used varies with the intensity of the exercise, and at high relative work rates glucose is the predominant muscle fuel. This results in depletion of the glycogen stores and during prolonged exercise they may become exhausted, leaving fat as the only available fuel. Although muscles continue to contract using fat as fuel, their power output is greatly reduced. The worker's limbs feel heavy and tired and he is unable to maintain his initial work rate. Endurance depends at least in part on the glycogen stores within the muscle cells. The efficiency of the body as a machine is about twenty-five to thirty per cent for most activities. That is to say that only this proportion of the chemical energy consumed is actually expended on mechanical work, the remaining seventy per cent or so being released as waste heat. This becomes very apparent during hard physical work. Some of the most important physiological responses to exercise are those concerned with temperature regulation. There is an increase in blood flow to the skin, the rate of sweating increases and the body surface becomes important as a "radiator" cooled by convection and the evaporation of sweat. Hence the red, perspiring face of exertion.

During physical activity the central body temperature rises by up to three degrees centigrade, depending on the relative work rate, to a new level. The skin temperature, however, remains closely related to the temperature of the surroundings, and is independent of the central temperature or work rate.

Both the control of sweating and the impression of a comfortable temperature are governed by a combination of skin temperature and central body temperature. On a cold day, though we are chilly standing about, we feel more comfortable with exercise because the rise in our central temperature allows us to better tolerate a low skin temperature. Hard work can be performed with little noticeable sweating. On a hot day the situation is very different: our skins are much warmer, any physical exertion makes us feel hot and we sweat copiously. Eventually if we feel too hot we either have to remove some clothing to lower our skin temperature, or reduce the work rate so that our central temperature falls, reducing our impression of hotness. When hard physical work has to be performed in the heat, prolonged sweating can lead to dehydration, and if water is not replaced a failure of temperature regulation and heat stroke ensue.

And so it is that the factors limiting human physical performance are very similar to those in other familiar machines. Working capacity depends on engine size—the maximal oxygen intake. The harder the work the greater the fuel requirements and importance of the optimal fuel —glucose. Adequate heat dissipation and temperature control are essential to prevent overheating and maintain thermal comfort. Finally, and this is where the analogy between man and machine ends, no person functions with maximum human efficiency without health, technical skill, motivation and courage to make the fullest use of his physiological capacity.

Health and efficiency

This book tells of the organization and day-to-day requirements of the body, and how it works. The integrity and harmony of this complex organism is good health—a priceless condition which it is in the interest of all of us to achieve and maintain. What can we do to keep ourselves in a state of good health?

Those of us who live in the "affluent society", and those who receive its benefits indirectly, are unlikely to die of any of the infectious diseases which remain the scourge of the poorer half of the world. Control of diphtheria, malaria, typhus, tuberculosis and other diseases, which at times in the past have reached plague levels, is a major achievement of modern medicine. However, we all die of something; in Britain and America and the more affluent parts of Europe, most of us die of coronary heart disease and strokes (mostly after-effects of atherosclerosis—"hardening of the arteries") or of chronic bronchitis or lung cancer. These diseases are a cause of concern because they may bring ill health and death in middle age, long before the approach of senility. Other cancers, various forms of rheumatism and psychological illness also account for a high proportion of medical practice.

Much of the ill health that afflicts modern society is cultural in origin, and on the whole preventable. Minor changes in life style could well extend our years of optimal health, and at least delay, if not prevent, the onset of fatal disease. Factors of everyday life known to influence our health include overeating, smoking and stress. Overeating, combined with lack of exercise and (often) wrong kinds of food, make us fat and predispose us to atherosclerosis and its after-effects—diseases of the heart and circulation. Many people are too fat. It would seem that the effect of prosperity on our diet has been to replace a healthy austerity in the intake of food with prodigality and overfeeding. By making food attractive, and equating rich diet with a feeling of prosperity, we tend to feed compulsively, far exceeding our dietary requirements. Obesity from overfeeding is virtually unknown in wild animals, who have simpler and less harmful ways of expressing satisfaction with the quality of their lives. Their body weight remains constant only so long as the energy intake in the diet exactly balances the energy output.

In most people natural appetite attends to this balance precisely; weight may fluctuate by one or two per cent from day to day, due to changes in body water content, but over a week or a month our weight can stay remarkably constant. To lose weight, the energy equation must be tipped in favour of expenditure, either by reduction in food intake or by increased expenditure—or both. Many people who are moderately overweight (as opposed to obese) are so simply because of physical laziness. A slight daily increase in activity, coupled with a moderate reduction in intake of fat-forming foods, would

bring them to better shape with little difficulty. Certain foodstuffs are suspected of predisposing us to atherosclerosis and diabetes. Animal fats contained in butter, meat, milk and eggs and refined carbohydrates (notably white flour and white sugar) fall particularly under suspicion, and most people could reduce their daily intake of these foods with benefit. Fish, fruit, vegetables and whole cereals are less suspect. Over-refined foods leave little roughage; many people feel better when their diet and gut contain substantial amounts of fibrous material, ensuring regular elimination of wastes.

Smoking, like the inhalation of any other noxious vapour, is a hazard to health. Cigarette smoking vies with breathing the chemical-laden and polluted atmosphere of industrial regions in the encouragement of bronchitis, and is now believed to be a prime cause of another killing disease, lung cancer. Perhaps the most serious of diseases which can be self-inflicted, it goes hand in hand not only with chronic and acute lung conditions, but also with heart disease and gastric ulcers. Heavy smokers put themselves seriously at risk. While we know a great deal about the ill effects of smoking, we have yet to discover what are perhaps the most important points of all—why do some people smoke heavily while others do not, and why do some smokers appear to become addicted while others smoke entirely through choice?

Competitive sportsmen presumably have the highest levels of physical fitness in the community. It seems probable that the specific qualities required for a high standard of athleticism are at least partly inherited; by training, the athlete merely improves the performance of an already well-endowed system. However, the biological effects of some kinds of training and exercise are probably beneficial to all of us, and it is worth examining how athletes improve their performance, to see if we could all benefit from a similar approach. The training effects of different types of exercise are rather specific. Some exercises improve mobility and co-ordination of the muscles and skeleton, increasing agility, and helping to prevent injuries and stiffness in joints and muscles. Other exercises involving maximal muscle contraction serve to increase muscle strength and size. Heart and lung functions are improved by vigorous activity, which makes heavy demands on the oxygen supply system. Activity of this kind also results in improved stamina and temperature regulation, and by using up energy, reduces the body's stores of glycogen and fats, to the benefit of the figure.

Muscular strength is in itself of no particular advantage to most people. But improved agility and stamina would be of great benefit to many who, through lack of any form of training or exercise, live out their lives with undeveloped physique, in what can only be considered a state of chronic ill health. On the whole, "physical jerks" tend to be unimaginative and of limited value to all but the enthusiast. To achieve a real and lasting impact on health, physical recreation must be enjoyable, and of sufficient intensity and regularity to have a training effect. Since the individual must return to it time and time again, it should also have some short-term aim or present a challenge—competition, or the acquisition of a skill.

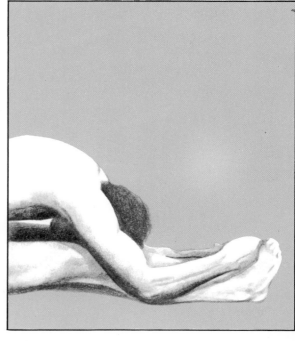

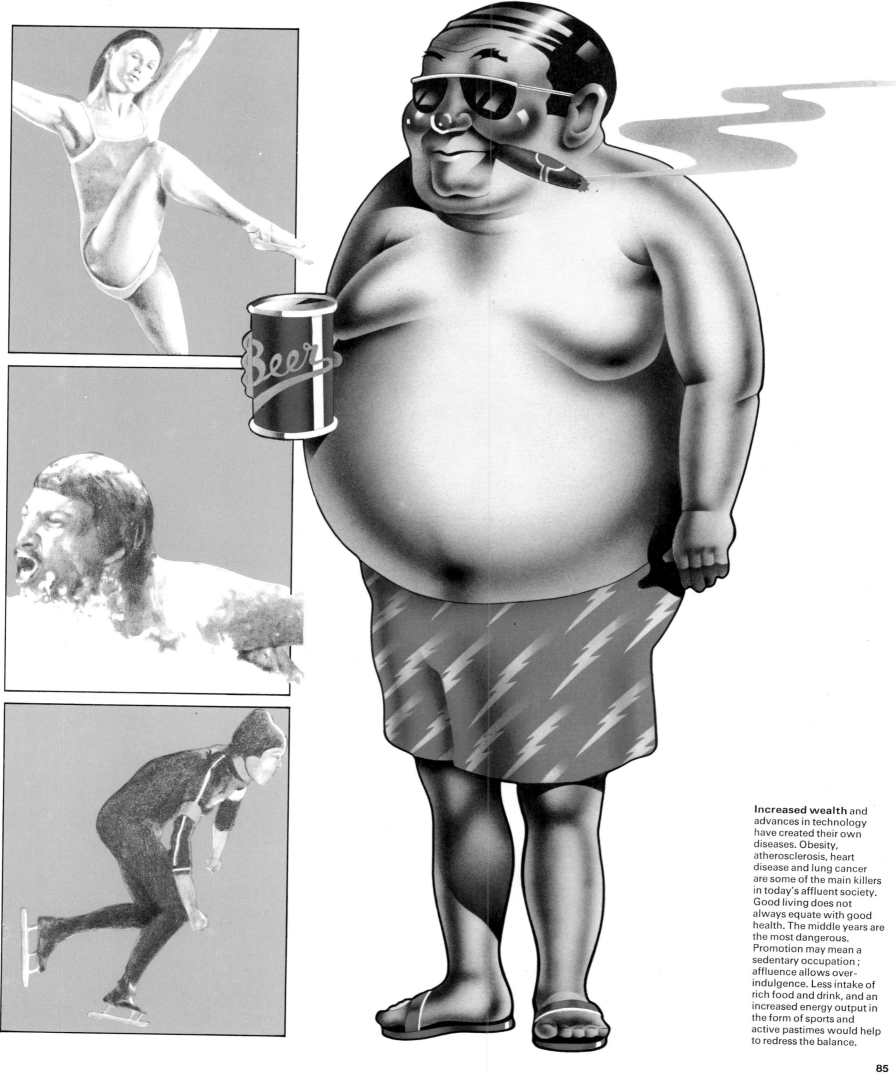

Increased wealth and advances in technology have created their own diseases. Obesity, atherosclerosis, heart disease and lung cancer are some of the main killers in today's affluent society. Good living does not always equate with good health. The middle years are the most dangerous. Promotion may mean a sedentary occupation; affluence allows over-indulgence. Less intake of rich food and drink, and an increased energy output in the form of sports and active pastimes would help to redress the balance.

Glossary

A

Abortion Accidental or deliberate expulsion of the foetus from the uterus before it has a reasonable chance of survival, conventionally taken as before the 28th week of pregnancy.

Abscess A localized collection of pus in the tissues following bacterial infection, usually surrounded by inflammation.

Acne An inflammatory disorder of sebaceous glands, affecting the face, chest and back, common in adolescence. The glands become plugged with excessive amounts of their greasy secretion, forming the typical blackhead or comedo. They may then become infected and develop into pustules. The exact cause is unknown, but hormonal imbalance appears to be involved. The spots should not be squeezed, since this increases scarring. The condition usually clears when puberty is over.

Acupuncture The relief of pain or treatment of disease by inserting needles through the skin at certain points, not necessarily close to the disorder. An important technique in Chinese medicine, now being investigated in the West.

Addiction The emotional or physical dependence on a drug, deprivation of which causes emotional stress and physical illness —withdrawal symptoms. It is acquired only by the repeated administration of the drug, and usually characterized by increasing tolerance to the drug, when larger and larger doses are required to obtain the craved-for effect. The chief drugs of addiction are powerful narcotics such as those derived from opium—morphine and heroin (diacetyl morphine) and similar drugs produced synthetically.

Addison's disease A rare disease due to deficiency of the hormones of the adrenal cortex (caused by its atrophy or disease), characterized by muscular weakness, lethargy, loss of weight, anaemia, abnormal skin pigmentation, and disordered metabolism. It is treated by hormone replacement therapy.

Adenoids A disorder caused by excessive size of the lymphoid tissue at the back of the nose (the nasopharyngeal tonsil), making breathing difficult. Together with the tonsils of the throat, this tissue grows in size during childhood, but regresses after puberty. If its growth is excessive, or it fails to diminish, it may be necessary to remove it surgically.

Albinism Inherited absence of melanin and other pigments that give colour to hair, skin and eyes. Albinos have white hair, and their skin and eyes appear pink because the colour of the blood flowing in them can be seen. Albinos cannot acquire a suntan, and find strong light painful to the eyes.

Albumin Simple water-soluble proteins occurring in blood, eggs, milk and muscle. They form the greater part of the blood proteins where their osmotic effect plays an important part in the control of fluid exchange between blood vessels and tissues.

Alcoholism An habitually excessive intake of alcohol. Not a true addiction because tolerance and withdrawal illness do not occur. Usually arises because the individual finds that he can cope with life more easily with the help of alcohol. Chronic alcoholism causes gastritis, cirrhosis of the liver and vitamin B_1 deficiency, resulting in degeneration of the brain and nervous system, and can lead to insanity. It is much more common than generally recognized. All forms of treatment ultimately depend on the desire and ability to control alcohol intake.

Allergy An abnormally strong immunity reaction or hypersensitivity to everyday substances such as pollens, dust, clothing and food. The antibody-antigen reaction causes an excessive release in tissues of the chemicals histamine and serotonin, responsible for the inflammation and characteristic symptoms: hay fever, asthma, rashes and digestive upsets. Drugs called antihistamines alleviate symptoms, and some cases may be treated by a course of desensitizing injections of the substance causing the allergy.

Alopecia A tendency to baldness. Early hair loss is commonly inherited. Other causes may be old age, infection, thyroid deficiency and some drugs, but often the cause is unknown.

Amenorrhoea Cessation of menstruation during the child-bearing age. Completely normal causes are pregnancy, lactation and the menopause. Other causes may be emotional upsets, hormonal disorders, malnutrition and general illness.

Amnesia Loss of memory due to emotional cause or head injury. Emotional amnesia is characterized by forgetting personal details. Amnesia following injury—retrograde amnesia—is of events immediately before the injury, which are never recalled; earlier memories are not affected.

Amoeba A mobile, unicellular organism of many different species that occurs in fresh water. Most are harmless, but some cause disease. *Entamoeba histolytica* causes amoebic dysentery.

Amputation Surgical or accidental loss of limb or part of a limb or other appendage.

Anaemia Deficiency of haemoglobin, the oxygen-carrying pigment in the red blood cells. The anaemic patient feels weak and weary, may suffer from headaches, and in severe cases shortness of breath on exertion. It can be caused by excessive loss of haemoglobin by bleeding or destruction of red cells, or defective haemoglobin production due to iron or vitamin B_{12} or folic acid deficiencies.

Anaesthesia Loss of sensation, due to a defect in the nervous system or induced by drugs. It may affect the whole body, or only a part of it.

Analgesia The relief of pain by drugs. Morphine and other narcotic drugs are powerful analgesics. Aspirin and codeine are milder, non-addictive drugs.

Aneurysm A bulging or ballooning of the arterial wall due to local weakening. It may press upon and interfere with surrounding organs, or rupture, causing serious loss of blood. Congenital aneurysms occur in the cerebral arteries and may press on nerves or bleed, causing a stroke. In the aorta, aneurysms may be caused by syphilis or atherosclerosis.

Angina Can be (1) a sense of suffocation; (2) acute infection of mouth or throat (Vincent's angina); (3) a severe crushing, or constricting pain of the chest which may radiate down one or both arms, generally related to physical exertion (angina pectoris). The last is caused by an inadequate blood supply to the heart muscle, generally due to coronary artery disease. Angina pectoris may be rapidly relieved by inhalation or swallowing of drugs which dilate the coronary blood vessels.

Anorexia A loss of the desire to eat, and a common accompaniment of many forms of illness. Anorexia nervosa is a condition, usually affecting young women, in which the patient refuses, and later becomes unable, to eat adequately, and so may become seriously emaciated. It occasionally starts with a desire to slim, which then gets out of hand, but may be due to adolescent emotional upsets; psychiatric treatment is needed.

Anthrax A very dangerous infectious disease contracted from farm animals and their products, especially hides and wool. Caused by the anthrax bacillus, which produces a severe localized inflammation of the skin, a "malignant pustule", or, in the lung, the pneumonia called "woolsorters' disease". Both are often fatal without immediate treatment with antibiotics.

Antibiotic A substance produced by living organisms—often moulds—which inhibits or destroys bacteria. The large group includes penicillin, streptomycin, tetracycline and chloramphenicol.

Anticoagulants Drugs used to prevent or delay blood clotting. Used in diseases such as coronary artery disease where there is a danger of thrombosis. The two main types are heparin, extracted from liver, and coumarin, derived from sweet clover. Both disrupt the sequence of chemical changes in clotting.

Antihistamines Drugs that prevent the effects of histamine. They alleviate the discomfort of insect and plant stings, and some allergic symptoms. Some are effective against travel sickness and may be sedative.

Antiseptics Chemicals used to destroy micro-organisms and prevent infection, without damaging human tissues.

Aphasia Defect or loss of the power to produce or understand words due to disease of the speech centre of the brain.

Aphrodisiac Any drug or agent that stimulates sexual desire.

Apoplexy *See* **Stroke**

Arm As an anatomical term, only that portion of the upper limb between shoulder and elbow, but more commonly the whole limb. The largest bone of the arm is the *humerus* (1), which articulates with the *scapula* (2) at the ball-and-socket shoulder joint, and with the *radius* (3) and *ulna* (4) at the hinge-like elbow joint. The joints between the radius and the ulna allow twisting of the former over the latter, so that the hand can be rotated through 180°. The lower end of the radius articulates with three of the carpal bones in the hand, at the wrist joint. The three main muscles of the upper arm are the *deltoid*, clothing the shoulder, the *biceps* at the front, and the *triceps* behind. Deep and superficial layers of muscle clothe the forearm and act on the hand and fingers. The arm is supplied with blood by the *brachial artery*, which divides into two at the elbow. Its nerve supply is from branches of the *brachial plexus*, a complex network of fibres from the lower part of the neck.

Arrhythmia Any irregularity in the heart-beat. In sinus arrhythmia the heart rate increases with inspiration and slows during expiration. Extra heart-beats and dropped beats are also common and do not necessarily indicate disease. They may be caused by a wave of contraction starting somewhere other than in the pacemaker. In pathological arrhythmias, due to disease of the heart muscle or conducting tissue, the heart's action may be seriously unco-ordinated, leading to inefficient pumping and even failure. Abnormal heart action may be corrected by drugs such as digitalis or quinidine, or electric shocks ("defibrillation").

Arteriosclerosis "Hardening of the arteries". A degenerative condition of the arteries in which there is thickening of the vessel wall, narrowing and loss of elasticity. It is often associated with excessively high blood pressure—hypertension. In atherosclerosis "plaques" of the fatty material cholesterol are deposited in the lining of arteries, especially the aorta and coronary and cerebral arteries, and may become calcified. The roughened surface predisposes to thrombosis, usual cause of heart attack and strokes.

Arthritis Inflammation of a joint. There are two main types. Rheumatoid arthritis is characterized by chronic painful swelling and considerable distortion of the smaller joints, of the hand, for example. Its cause is unknown. *Osteoarthritis* is a degenerative disease of larger joints such as the hip and knee, resulting in loss of cartilage and rough deposits of bone on the articular surfaces. The symptoms in both types may be alleviated with anti-inflammatory agents and analgesics. Many irreparably damaged joints can now be replaced with artificial ones of metal and plastic. (*See also* **Gout**.)

Asepsis Prevention of infection by excluding micro-organisms from surgical procedures. (*See also* **Sterility**.)

Asphyxia Suffocation, leading to a lack of oxygen in the tissues (*anoxia*) and a build-up of waste carbon dioxide. It may be caused by obstruction of the air passages, drowning, the presence of noxious gases or too little oxygen in the inspired air, or damage to the nerves controlling breathing movements. Unless the cause is quickly removed, death or irreversible brain damage ensues.

Asthma Difficulty in breathing, especially expiration, due to narrowing of the bronchioles of the lungs, and accompanied by wheezing. Not itself a disease, it is a symptom of an underlying disorder such as chronic bronchitis, allergy, or emotional upset. Status asthmaticus is a severe attack, prolonged for many hours and not responsive to treatment. Asthmatic attacks may be alleviated by drugs that dilate the air passages. Allergic asthma may be treated by desensitization. (*See also* **Allergy**.)

Astigmatism A defect of vision in which the focus of light rays on the retina in one plane differs from the other, because of uneven curvature of the cornea. It can be corrected with special spectacle lenses.

Athlete's foot (*Tinea pedis*) Fungal infection of the feet, especially between the toes, causing skin fissuring, inflammation and local itching. Several antifungal agents, usually dusted on as powders, are effective in treatment.

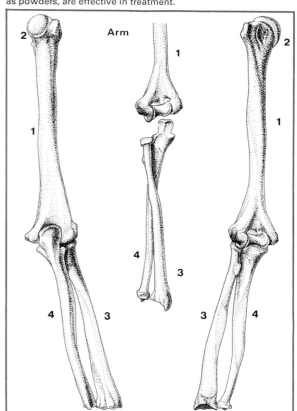

Arm

Atrophy Decline in size and function of a tissue or organ. Usually due to impaired nutrition or disuse.

Aura A premonitory sensation such as a strange smell, visual sensation or taste that may precede an epileptic attack, asthma or migraine.

Auscultation Examination of the functions of internal organs by listening to their sounds, usually with a stethoscope.

Autism A disorder of the mind of unknown cause, arising in childhood, in which the individual's senses and intelligence appear to be normal, but he is incommunicative and does not respond to his surroundings.

Autopsy (Post mortem) Examination of a dead body to ascertain the cause of death.

B

Bacteria Ubiquitous microscopic one-celled organisms, "germs", of numerous different types. They reproduce by simple division, extremely rapidly in favourable circumstances. Mainly involved in assisting decay and decomposition, the great majority are harmless to man; many are found on the skin, in the mouth and in the large bowel (they may be of benefit by producing amino acids and B vitamins). The numerous bacteria that do cause disease are termed pathogenic. Parasitic on tissues, their effects are caused by tissue destruction and irritation and by the poisons or toxins they liberate during their metabolism.

Balanitis Inflammation between the glans and foreskin of the penis, due to infection.

Bedsore (Pressure sore) Injury to the skin and underlying tissues caused by deprivation of the blood supply by prolonged pressure. It occurs in bed-ridden patients in areas where the tissues are compressed for long periods against the bones when sitting or lying. The sores may become infected and develop into huge ulcers requiring skin grafting. They may be prevented by good nursing: moving the patient regularly, stimulating the skin blood supply by gentle massage, and scrupulous cleanliness.

Bends Decompression sickness or Caisson disease. When the body is subjected to high pressure, as in diving and Caisson work, nitrogen dissolves in the blood. If the return to atmospheric pressure is too rapid, nitrogen comes out of solution, forming bubbles in the bones and joints causing the agonizing pain of "the bends". Bubbles in the spinal cord and brain may cause paralysis, mental disturbance, unconsciousness and even death, and in the blood vessels of the lungs ("the chokes"). The treatment is prompt recompression followed by *slow* decompression to allow gradual reabsorption of the nitrogen.

Beri-beri A disease caused by dietary deficiency of vitamin B₁, thiamine, occurring mainly in the Far East. There may be oedema due to heart failure, impaired sensation and muscle weakness caused by nerve damage, and deterioration in mental processes. B vitamins must be added to the diet to improve the condition.

Biopsy Removal of a sample of living tissue for diagnosis.

Birthmark (Naevus) A congenital abnormality of the skin. It may be pigmented—a mole—or a collection of dilated blood vessels, a "strawberry mark". Some disappear spontaneously; others may be hidden with cosmetics, or surgically removed.

Blackhead (Comedo) *See* **Acne**

Blood clotting Coagulation. One of the body's mechanisms for stopping bleeding. It is brought about by the conversion of the soluble blood protein fibrinogen into insoluble fibrin by the substance thrombin. Thrombin is not normally present in the blood, but is formed from a precursor prothrombin by the action of calcium ions and numerous other factors released by damaged tissues and blood platelets. The fibrin is precipitated as adhesive threads, which entangle the blood cells and stick to damaged tissues, thus stopping the flow of blood.

Blood pressure The pressure of the blood in the blood vessels measured in millimetres of mercury (mm Hg). The pressure in the larger arteries may be read with a pressure cuff on the arm, attached to a sphygmomanometer. The arterial pressure fluctuates during the heart cycle, being highest during the active pumping phase, systole, and lower during the relaxation phase, diastole. In normal adults the systolic pressure is about 120 mm Hg, diastolic 80 mm Hg.

Blood sugar The glucose circulating in the blood; its concentration or level depends upon the rates of intestinal absorption, uptake or release from the liver, and uptake by the tissues. In normal people, it is kept relatively constant at between 80 and 100 mg per 10 ml blood, by many complex mechanisms involving both hormones and the nervous system.

Blue baby A new-born child who looks blue due to lack of oxygen in his blood. The most common cause is a congenital "hole in the heart" defect, where some of the blood bypasses the lungs.

Boil (Furuncle) Infection and inflammation at the root of a hair with an accumulation of pus.

Bronchitis Inflammation of the small air passages or bronchi. It may be acute, due to viral or bacterial infection, or chronic (lingering). Chronic bronchitis (sometimes known as "English disease") is one of the commonest causes of death in Great Britain. It is a persistent inflammatory condition of the bronchi that results in progressive destruction of lung tissue.

Brucellosis (Undulant fever, Malta fever, Abortus fever) An infection by the *Brucella* bacteria that causes contagious abortion in cattle, sheep and pigs. It may be acquired by drinking unpasteurized milk from infected animals, or contact with them. The illness is characterized by intermittent (i.e. "undulant") periods of fever, headache and malaise alternating with relative normality, and may persist as a low-grade illness for many weeks. Treatment is with antibiotics.

Bruise (Contusion) An accumulation of blood in the tissues following damage to blood vessels. At first blue as the blood becomes deoxygenated, the tissues later become stained green-yellow as the bruise disperses and haemoglobin breaks down into other substances.

Burns Destruction of skin layers by extremes of temperature or chemicals. Superficial burns cause blistering and intense irritation but do not destroy the dermis; deep burns do, and tend to cause unsightly scars. The loss of body fluid from extensive burns seriously endangers life (destruction of more than one-third of the body's surface area is usually fatal without intensive care). Infection is also a grave danger. Replacement of the destroyed layers is by skin grafting.

Bursa A fluid-containing pocket of special tissue that reduces friction in an area where tendons or ligaments move over bone. "Housemaid's knee" is a form of bursitis—inflammation following excessive pressure and friction.

C

Caesarian section Assisting birth by the surgical operation of cutting through the abdominal wall and the uterus, and extracting the child. It may be necessary if the birth canal is too narrow, or in cases where the health of the baby or mother would be threatened by prolonged or even normal labour.

Calculus Any stone that forms in a hollow organ such as the kidney, bladder, gall bladder or a salivary gland.

Callus (1) Thickening of the skin in areas exposed to persistent friction or pressure. (2) A mass of bone-forming tissue that develops in and around the broken ends of bone following a fracture. It is gradually modelled and hardens into new bone during healing.

Calorie The heat required to raise the temperature of 1 gram of water by 1° Centigrade. In nutrition the energy value of food, and the energy exchanges of the body are expressed in Kilocalories or Calories. One Calorie = 1,000 calories.

Cancer The undisciplined and purposeless growth of groups of cells in the body, to its detriment, if not eventual destruction. Most cancer cells lose the function of the tissue in which they arise, and become in effect parasitic upon their normal neighbours, growing at their expense and hindering their activities. They spread by invading nearby structures, and, through the blood and lymphatic systems, establish secondary growths elsewhere in the body—*metastases*. Cancers of epithelial or surface tissues such as skin are known as *carcinomas*, and of deeper tissues as *sarcomas* (e.g. osteosarcoma, of bone). Not every tumour (which only means a swelling) is a cancer—only *malignant* tumours, which are invasive growths. We now know many causes (chemicals, irritation, radiation, viruses) of cancerous growth, and many ways in which it can be combated, including treatment by surgery, X-rays, radioactivity and hormones and drugs.

Carbuncle A collection of boils that forms a large abscess. It usually responds to antibiotic treatment.

Cardiac Pertaining to the heart, or the upper part of the stomach, the cardia.

Caries Dental decay. Probably initiated by acids produced in the mouth by bacterial fermentation of sugar, eating into the protective enamel and exposing the soft dentine to further bacterial attack. Sugar and sticky, sweet foods increase decay by encouraging the responsible bacteria; caries can be largely prevented by good oral hygiene and avoiding sweet foods between meals. Fluorides increase the resistance of enamel.

Cataract Opacity of the lens of the eye, causing impaired vision. Occurs due to congenital defect, following injury, or simply old age. The vision may be greatly improved by removal of the affected lens.

Catarrh Excessive mucus formation resulting from inflammation of a mucous membrane, especially in the respiratory tract.

Cauterization Burning tissues with heat, extreme cold or chemicals in order to destroy or cut the tissue without causing excessive bleeding.

Chickenpox (*Varicella*) A highly contagious virus infection spread by droplet infection or contact with open skin lesions. Usually a mild childhood affliction, it can, however, be extremely unpleasant in adults. A characteristic rash of small spots that rapidly become blisters and which are readily burst appears on the trunk, and more sparsely on the limbs. They eventually dry up, forming scabs which are still infectious. The same virus causes shingles.

Chilblains Swollen, itchy, purple-coloured areas of skin that appear on exposed parts such as the hands, feet and ears in cold weather. Fairly common in children and women, the complaint is probably due to an abnormal sensitivity of the arterioles in the skin to cold, which causes poor circulation.

Cholera An acute and extremely dangerous infection of the bowel, caused by the bacterium *Vibrio cholerae*, and spread by food or water contaminated by human faeces. It causes an extremely severe diarrhoea, with loss of water and salts from the body. It is this dehydration and disturbance of the body's chemical balance that may kill the patient. Treatment is by replacement of these losses and antibiotics.

Cholesterol A fatty substance present in most tissues and involved in the synthesis of bile salts and steroid hormones. Higher than normal levels of cholesterol are often found in the blood of patients with atherosclerosis, who may suffer heart attacks or strokes. The levels in the blood appear to be increased by high intake of animal fats; vegetable oils and fats may lower the levels of cholesterol in the blood.

Circumcision Surgical removal, for medical or religious reasons, of part of the foreskin.

Cirrhosis A disorder of the liver involving disorganization of the normal architecture, due to damage to liver cells followed by partial regeneration and scarring. The disorder may not necessarily involve ill health until it reaches an advanced stage. The common causes are chronic alcoholism, malnutrition (which may be an additional factor in alcoholic cirrhosis), viral hepatitis, congestive heart failure and schistosomiasis. Though it is a progressive condition if the causative factors are continued, it can be arrested by cessation of the cause.

Cleft palate and **Hare lip** Congenital defects in the formation of the face. In the embryo the upper jaw, maxillary sinuses and palate develop from two processes on each side of the head, which grow towards each other eventually and fuse in the midline. Failure to fuse leaves a gap which may only affect the lip, resulting in hare lip—or a gap in the palate between the mouth and the nose, cleft palate. The faults may be corrected by plastic surgery.

Cold sore *See* **Herpes**

Colic Painful spasm of muscle in a hollow organ, due, for example, to distention and inflammation as in colitis, or obstruction by a calculus, as in renal colic. The pain is intermittent, typically increasing to a peak then passing off again.

Colitis Inflammation of the colon or large bowel, usually caused by dysentery or food poisoning, and characterized by diarrhoea and colic. *Ulcerative colitis* is a severe chronic inflammation of the bowel, the cause of which is not known, but may have psychological aspects.

Coma A state of deep unconsciousness from which the patient cannot be aroused. Many of the reflexes such as pain and cough are depressed so that the patient is in danger of inhaling his own saliva or vomit. A patient in coma should always be laid on his side with his face slightly down so that any fluid drains out of his mouth and is not inhaled. The causes of coma are numerous; they include strokes, epilepsy, head injuries meningitis, poisoning by drugs or alcohol, suffocation due to gassing, shock, and lack of blood sugar—sometimes seen in diabetic patients.

Concussion Temporary loss of consciousness following a blow on the head that disrupts the normal working of the brain; there is usually amnesia for the events leading up to the incident.

Conjunctivitis Inflammation of the conjunctiva, usually due to viral or bacterial infection, but snow blindness and "arc eye", both due to excess ultra violet rays, are forms of conjunctivitis. The symptoms are painful watery eyes which feel gritty, and there may be photophobia; the eye appears red and bloodshot.

Convulsion Unco-ordinated muscular contractions over which the subject has no control. Often associated with a loss of consciousness. (See also **Epilepsy**.)

Corticosteroids The hormones produced by the adrenal cortex (*see* page 52), or synthetic chemicals with similar structure and effects.

Cowpox Infection of cows by virus similar to smallpox. Causes mild illness in human beings but confers lasting immunity against smallpox.

Cramp Painful spasm of muscles, often in the lower limbs. May occur when resting, or during or following severe exercise or heavy sweating resulting in salt depletion. Reduced blood supply and disturbed salt balance appear to be involved.

Cretinism Congenital deficiency of the thyroid hormone resulting in retarded mental development and growth.

Croup Laboured, noisy breathing accompanied by a characteristic barking cough. Most common in children, and caused by inflammation or abnormality of the vocal cords.

Cyst An abnormal space containing fluid. It may be due to congenital defects, or disease causing the blockage of glands and retention of fluid, the degeneration of tissues, or tumours that form secretions within themselves.

Cystitis Inflammation of the urinary bladder, usually due to bacterial infection. The symptoms are frequent and painful passage of urine.

D

Dermatitis Inflammation of the skin, usually due to an allergic disorder. There are two main types. A dermatitis characterized by itch and a mild rash may be precipitated by a definite allergy, emotional stress or for reasons unknown. Contact dermatitis is caused by an irritant such as oil, detergent or paint, and is a common occupational disease.

Detached retina Detachment of the retina from the supporting choroid, resulting in partial or complete loss of vision. It may follow injury, but more often occurs spontaneously. It is sometimes possible to replace the layer, or at least prevent the detachment spreading, by means of fine light beams (lasers have been used) which coagulate and "weld" the retina and choroid together in tiny patches.

Diabetes insipidus A rare disorder in which large volumes of dilute urine are excreted, due to abnormal functioning of the posterior lobe of the pituitary gland, which exercises hormonal control over the kidneys.

Diabetes mellitus The disease "sugar diabetes" in which there is an excessively high level of blood glucose (*hyperglycaemia*), due usually to a deficiency of the pancreatic hormone insulin, which, with other factors, normally regulates the amount of sugar in circulation, by promoting uptake by the tissues. Because of the high glucose level in the blood reaching the kidney, not all can be reabsorbed during urine formation, and the urine becomes in effect a sugar solution. Large volumes of water must be excreted to dilute and carry away the sugar, and this leads to dehydration and extreme thirst. Despite the abundance of sugar, the tissues are unable to take it up from the blood, and instead utilize fats for their metabolism. When fat alone is burnt as fuel, breakdown products related to acetone called *ketone bodies* are formed, and may build up to poisonous levels, causing coma and death. Degeneration of small arteries also occurs in diabetes, and may lead to impaired vision and nephritis, while degeneration of nerves may impair sensation and muscular function. Diabetics are more than usually prone to arterial disease and to infections in general. However grim this picture might seem, the outlook for diabetics is today very good. Diabetes can be controlled by regulation of diet, and by the administration of insulin and certain (*hypoglycaemic*) agents; many patients are able to lead a virtually normal life.

Diarrhoea Excessively frequent passage of excessively watery motions, due to irritation, inflammation or overactivity of the bowel, with many possible causes, including infection, parasites, bacterial toxins (as in food poisoning), drugs or poisons, ulcerative colitis or disturbances in the endocrine and autonomic systems. Diarrhoea can be controlled with drugs, but the treatment must include that of the underlying cause.

Diphtheria An acute and dangerous infection spread by droplet infection from patient or carrier. The inside of the throat becomes inflamed and covered with a dirty grey membrane, which may obstruct breathing. Toxins produced by the bacteria may affect the heart, kidneys and nervous system, and cause death. Diphtheria is now routinely prevented in many countries by immunization at an early age.

Diplegia Paralysis of both arms or both legs.

Diplopia Double vision, due to faulty co-ordination of the movement of the eyes through nerve or muscle disorder.

Dyslexia "Word-blindness". An inability, often apparently developmental but sometimes attributable to brain damage, to recognize, and distinguish between, the different shapes and patterns of words or individual letters. Although, otherwise, usually completely normal, the sufferer has extreme difficulty in reading and writing, and may be wrongly thought to be subnormal in intelligence.

Dyspepsia (Indigestion) Symptoms of stomach disorder, which may include an inappropriate feeling of fullness, abdominal discomfort, flatulence, nausea (and sometimes vomiting) and lack of desire to eat. The cause may be gastritis, peptic ulcer or some other gastro-intestinal disorder, emotional upset or psychological disturbance. Antacids will give relief in many cases and change in diet may help. But with chronic dyspepsia medical advice should be sought.

Dysmenorrhoea Pain associated with the onset of menstruation. The cause is not known, but hormonal and emotional factors may be involved. The condition often improves with marriage and rarely persists after pregnancy. Dysmenorrhoea of late onset may be due to a large number of gynaecological disorders and warrants immediate medical advice.

Dyspareunia Painful coitus in both men and women. In men usually due to inflammation or anatomical defects. In women there may be many causes, including inflammation of the vagina or bladder, anatomical defects, changes in the vagina after menopause or disease of the uterus. Dyspareunia not only involving pain but also difficulty in intercourse for both man and woman may also occur due to spasm of the muscles around the vagina. This may have an emotional cause and require patience and tact on the part of both partners to be overcome. Medical advice should be sought.

Dysphagia Difficulty in swallowing due to blockage or spasm in the throat or oesophagus.

Dystrophy Literally defective nutrition, but more usually degeneration or failure of organ development.

E

Earache Usually due to inflammation or irritation of the eardrum. The severe earache of *otitis media* is caused by the pressure of accumulated pus under the drum, which cannot drain down the blocked Eustachian tube. Earache may also be caused by foreign objects in the external ear. Pain may also be referred to the ear from the teeth or throat. Earache should always receive medical attention.

ECG Electrocardiogram. A recording of the electrical activity of the heart. Changes from the normal pattern may indicate damage to the heart muscle (as in coronary thrombosis), or other abnormalities in heart function brought about by disease processes, drugs and poisons.

Eclampsia Convulsions occurring during pregnancy due to toxaemia. (*See* **Toxaemia**.)

ECT Electroconvulsive therapy. Electric shock applied to the head sufficient to cause temporary disruption of the brain's activity, a treatment used sometimes to bring about improvement in severe mental depression and schizophrenia. It is being used less frequently with the increasing availability of drugs.

Eczema Dermatitis. Infantile eczema is an inherited allergic dermatitis that usually disappears in about the fourth year.

EEG Electroencephalogram. A recording of the electrical activity of the brain. There are characteristic patterns of activity during sleep and wakefulness, and during the different phases of sleep. The patterns may be changed by the presence of tumours and other abnormalities. It is a most useful technique for the diagnosis and identification of different types of epilepsy.

Effusion Abnormal accumulation of fluid in a body space due to inflammation.

Embolism Blockage of an artery by an embolus, a large or small mass borne in the bloodstream until it becomes lodged in a blood vessel too narrow to allow its passage. An embolus is commonly a clot, but may be fat, air or other material.

Emetic A drug used to induce vomiting.

Emphysema A condition of the lungs in which over-inflation of the alveoli and distortion of their structure produces increasing deterioration of lung function. It is a common sequel to chronic bronchitis.

Encephalitis Inflammation of the brain, often due to a virus infection. Epidemic encephalitis was once known as sleepy sickness.

Enteritis Inflammation of the intestine, usually due to infection allergy. The most common cause is food poisoning. When associated with inflammation of the stomach—gastritis—the disorder is called gastroenteritis. The symptoms are diarrhoea and abdominal pain, which may be accompanied by nausea and vomiting.

Enuresis Incontinence of urine. Control of the bladder during the day is usually acquired by the age of two and a half, and night control between the ages of three and five. There is rarely any physical abnormality to account for bed-wetting in children after this age; poor training, emotional upsets and transient urinary infection may be factors.

Epilepsy A disorder characterized by temporary loss of consciousness with or without convulsions. In *petit mal*, a mild form of epilepsy usually seen in children, there is a loss of consciousness so momentary that the child may not realize that anything has happened, and rarely falls. In *grand mal* the patient may have premonitory symptoms (*see* **Aura**); he then loses consciousness, goes rigid and increasingly purple in the face with oxygen lack. This is followed by severe muscular convulsions during which he may bite his tongue and void urine. The attack usually lasts for a couple of minutes, after which the patient may sleep or go into a trance-like state during which he may behave abnormally. Epilepsy is due to abnormal electrical activity in the brain, at first localized, but then spreading. In most cases there is no apparent cause, but in some it can be attributed to injury, tumour, stroke or infection. Epilepsy is not usually associated with mental or other defect. Many drugs are available for the suppression of attacks, allowing most epileptics to lead normal lives; however, in many countries they are not allowed to hold a driving licence.

Epistaxis *See* **Nosebleed**

Erysipelas A rapidly spreading acute skin infection caused by streptococci, in which the skin becomes red and swollen and highly inflamed. Once a very serious disease with high mortality, it is now readily controlled with sulphonamides or antibiotics.

Erythema Inflammatory reddening of the skin.

F

Fainting Loss of consciousness due to reduced blood flow to the brain. May be due to a nervous reflex resulting in extreme slowing of the heart, often caused by emotional shock. May also be due to pooling of the blood in the legs when standing still for long periods, the light-headedness sometimes experienced when standing up suddenly is due to a similar cause.

Fever High body temperature usually brought on by an acute viral or bacterial infection.

Fibroid A benign fibrous tumour of the uterus.

Flat foot Fallen arches. Dropping of the arches of the foot due to weakness in the supporting muscles and ligaments. May be overcome by exercises to strengthen the muscles in the sole of the foot.

Fontanelles The gaps between the growing bones of a baby's skull. At birth the bones of the skull have not finished growing and are not fully ossified and formed as in the adult. There are six fontanelles, the largest of which is found on the crown of the head. This is the last to close, at about one and a half years.

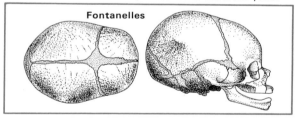

Fontanelles

Food-poisoning An acute intestinal illness (*see* **Enteritis**) developing up to 48 hours after the ingestion of contaminated food or water. Usually bacterial in origin, it may either be the result of infection, or poisoning by bacterial toxins. Infective food poisoning is commonly caused by the *Salmonella* group of organisms. The infection may be transferred by flies, or human carriers. Cooking kills bacteria but it may not destroy toxins produced by bacteria growing in the food before it is cooked. Other causes of food poisoning may be due to accidental contamination of food with poisonous chemicals during preparation, or the accidental ingestion of poisonous foods such as fungi.

Foot The foot is the final link in the system of levers of the lower limb. It serves three functions, bearing the weight of the body and providing a firm base for it when standing, and acting as a lever during locomotion. In order to meet these three requirements its bones are sturdy and arranged in arches tightly bound with ligaments. Only one, the talus (1) articulates with the leg in the ankle joint. This joint allows the leg to pivot over the foot. The talus rests on the calcaneum (2), the long bone that forms the heel and to which the calf muscles are attached through the Achilles tendon. The joint between these bones allows the foot to rotate in its own length, so that the foot remains in firm contact with the surface when walking on uneven ground. The remainder of the bones of the tarsus (3) and metatarsus (4) form two arches, one in the length of the foot and the other across it, drawing the sole into its characteristic vault. The weight of the body is mostly borne on the heel and the joints between the metatarsals and the phalanges (5) of the toes. There are a number of small muscles in the foot itself which probably have little purpose other than stabilizing the arches. The most important muscles acting on the foot are those in the calf and the outside of the shin, which are responsible for the movements of the foot and toes. During locomotion the muscles of the calf acting on the underside of the metatarsals and toes increase the arching of the foot, converting it into a rigid lever to transmit the thrust of the toes and move the body.

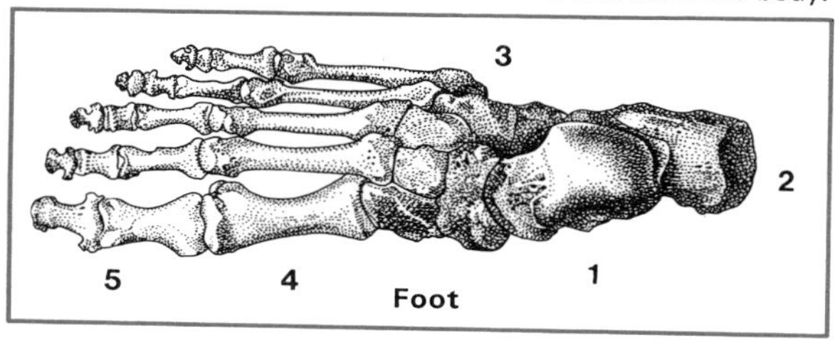

Fracture Break in a bone. Normal adult bone usually breaks cleanly, but a child's bone may bend and split in a greenstick fracture. Simple fracture denotes a break with little displacement of the bone and no open wound. A *compound* fracture is one in which the fracture is open to the exterior through a skin wound, and a *complicated* fracture one where other structures such as nerves and blood vessels have been injured by the broken ends of bones. In a *comminuted* fracture there are three or more fragments. Broken bones heal in the same general way as described on pages 76–77, but the scar tissue (*callus*) becomes calcified and finally fully ossified. Treatment of fractures consists of reducing the fracture, returning the broken bones are nearly as possible to their original shape, and holding the reduced fracture until the scar becomes rigid.

Frostbite Injury by freezing, in which tissues are damaged by the formation of ice crystals and deprivation of blood supply and may become gangerous. Frostbite should not be treated by rubbing, which increases the injury to already damaged tissue. The tissues should be thawed by slow warming, and then protected from infection and mechanical injury.

G

Gallstone A calculus formed in the gall bladder, usually composed of cholesterol, bile pigments and calcium salts. Gallstones are often symptomless but can cause pain and indigestion, and biliary colic if they distend the bile duct. They may obstruct the bile duct and cause jaundice. They are treated by surgery which includes excision of the gall bladder.

Ganglion A collection of nerve cell bodies, sometimes interconnected.

Gastritis Inflammation of the stomach. The symptoms may include anorexia, nausea, indigestion, heartburn and vomiting. Commonly caused by the ingestion of an irritant such as alcohol or aspirin. The symptoms may be relieved by antacids and bland diet.

German measles (Rubella) A virus infection. Usually a mild childhood illness, with a fine pink rash that starts on the head and spreads first to the trunk and then the limbs, with enlargement of the lymph nodes. A single attack confers lasting immunity. Infection during the first four months of pregnancy may cause congenital abnormalities in the child.

Gigantism Growth to an abnormally large size due to overproduction of growth hormone by the pituitary gland.

Gingivitis Inflammation of the gums, usually due to bacterial infection and poor oral hygiene. Also occurs in scurvy.

Glandular fever (Infectious mononucleosis) An infective disease thought to be caused by a virus. The symptoms may include tiredness, generalized aches and pains, sore throat, usually enlargement of the lymph nodes and occasionally a rash. There is a considerable increase of lymphocytes and monocytes in the blood. The illness usually lasts for a few days, but the patient may continue to feel ill, tired and depressed for some weeks, and it may be months before full vigour returns.

Glaucoma Abnormally high pressure within the eye, due to inadequate drainage of the aqueous humour constantly produced behind the iris and normally absorbed into veins in the *filtration angle* between iris and cornea in front, having circulated through the pupil. It may be caused by *iritis* (inflammation of the iris), by abnormality of the eye in which dilatation of the iris blocks the angle, or by factors unknown. Sudden, acute glaucoma may be intensely painful, but more common is chronic glaucoma, in which the high pressure within the eyeball may go undetected until optic nerve damage impairs vision. The condition may be relieved by drugs, or an operation to improve the drainage of aqueous humour.

Globulin A class of protein that occurs in blood and other tissues. Antibodies are composed of gamma globulin.

Glossitis Inflammation of the tongue, sometimes an accompaniment of anaemia or due to poor nutrition.

Goitre Enlargement of the thyroid gland. Simple goitre is due to dietary deficiency of iodine. Instructed by the pituitary gland, by means of thyroid-stimulating hormone, to increase the output of its own iodine—containing hormone thyroxine—the thyroid is unable to comply, but nevertheless enlarges, uselessly, and may attain great size. Large goitres may need surgical removal because of interference with other structures such as the trachea, and blood vessels and nerves in the vicinity, or simply for cosmetic reasons. In certain, mostly mountainous, areas iodine is lacking from the water and soil, and goitre is common. To reduce its incidence, iodine is now added to table salt in many countries. In *toxic* goitre, enlargement may be hardly discernible, but there is an over-production of thyroxine.

Gonorrhoea The most common venereal disease, caused by infection with gonococci—bacteria of the genus *Neisseria*, and readily transmitted by sexual contact. In men there is a discharge of pus from the urethra, and pain and sometimes difficulty in passing urine. In women there may be equivalent symptoms but very often none. If the infection is untreated it may cause scarring and narrowing of the urethra (stricture) in men, impairing urine flow and obstructing seminal flow. In women there may be chronic infection of the Fallopian tubes, resulting in subfertility. Gonorrhoea can also cause arthritis and inflammation of the eyes. The body does not become immune to gonorrhoea, which can be caught many times. Because women often have no symptoms they may not seek treatment, and they may unwittingly spread the infection.

Gout A disorder of metabolism resulting in excess of uric acid in the blood and its deposition in the tissues. The excess uric acid may be due to overproduction, or reduced excretion by the kidneys. The characteristic symptom of gout is a painful arthritis, often in a single joint. The uric acid crystals irritate the tissues around the joint, initiating an inflammatory reaction, but when the inflammatory phagocytes ingest the crystals they are damaged and release the substances that actually cause the pain in the joint. The kidneys are also damaged by uric acid crystals and nephritis may develop. A number of drugs that either increase the excretion of uric acid or prevent its formation are available for the treatment of gout.

H

Haematuria Blood in the urine, a symptom requiring immediate investigation.

Haemophilia An inherited and genetically determined bleeding disorder that occurs only in males but may be carried by females. It is due to failure of synthesis of one of the factors involved in blood clotting. Haemophiliacs bleed very easily, often from very mild injuries, and may bleed into their joints without apparent cause; bleeding may continue for some time. Transfusion with blood or plasma to provide the missing factor may be required to control severe bleeding.

Haemorrhoids (Piles) Enlarged veins at the junction of the rectum and anal canal. The veins become enlarged in much the same way as varicose veins in the legs. There is no known cause but there appears to be an heredity factor in many cases. They are often brought on by pregnancy. Piles may cause some discomfort, but the main risk is that chronic bleeding may result in anaemia. Piles may be treated by injection or surgical removal.

Halitosis Foul breath, usually due to bacterial action in the mouth or throat, which can be prevented by good oral hygiene.

Hallucination Perception of something that has no physical presence. "Hearing voices" or "seeing things". May occur in normal persons with fatigue. A characteristic of schizophrenia, and delirium tremens. May be caused by certain drugs.

Hallucinogen A drug that causes hallucinations. Cannabis, mescaline and lysergic acid diethylamide, LSD, are all hallucinogenic. Although these drugs have a reputation for abuse they are probably not addictive.

Hand The base of the hand is formed by eight box-like *carpal* bones (**1**), three of which articulate with the radius at the wrist. Beyond them are five *metacarpals* (**2**), which articulate with the *phalanges* of the fingers (**3**). The saddle joint at the base of the thumb allows this digit to be moved across the palm to meet the little finger—the movement of opposition, important in grasping. The fingers are flexed and extended by tendons from muscles in the forearm; delicate movements are controlled by muscles between the metacarpals and the phalanges. Two arteries supply the hand; they meet in an arch in the palm, giving off branches to the fingers. The muscles of the thumb are supplied by the *median nerve*; the other muscles are supplied by the *ulnar nerve*. Sensation is relayed by the *radial nerve* and branches of the other two.

Hare lip *See* **Cleft palate**

Hay Fever (Allergic rhinitis) An acute allergic inflammation of the nose. Characterized by sneezing and running nose and eyes. Commonly caused by pollens, but dust may also bring on an attack. The symptoms may be relieved by antihistamines, and desensitization to the allergen responsible may cure some cases. (*See also* **Allergy**.)

Headache A symptom common to many illnesses, especially infections. The causes of headache are not well understood but inflammation of the meninges the membranes surrounding the brain, or distention of the cerebral arteries may be responsible. The headaches associated with anxiety and fatigue appear to be due to tension in the muscles of the scalp, jaw and neck. Most headaches may be relieved with mild analgesics but medical advice should be sought if they persist.

Hepatitis Inflammation of the liver, usually due to a viral infection. The symptoms are those of a general infection but there is also jaundice. The virus may be contracted from other cases, carriers, or contaminated food or water. Infective hepatitis may also be transmitted by hypodermic needles that have been contaminated by the blood or serum of a carrier. Modern sterilizing techniques have greatly reduced this risk.

Hernia The protrusion of an organ or tissues through an abnormal opening, usually from one body compartment to another. The commonest types of hernia involve the alimentary canal leaving the abdominal cavity. The common "rupture" or inguinal hernia occurs through a weakness in the abdominal wall just to each side of the pubis. The intestine may also herniate through the groin into the top of the thigh. Occasionally part of the stomach passes into the chest through the same hole in the diaphragm as the gullet, forming a diaphragmatic hernia. Many babies have umbilical hernias at the navel which usually disappear, but umbilical hernias may develop in adults. Hernia may also occur through surgical incisions. Hernias can cause trouble by obstructing the intestines or reducing the blood supply of the tissues caught in them.

Herpes (1) *Herpes simplex* is the medical name for a cold sore, a virus infection of the skin that causes blistering around the nose and lips. The virus is always present in the skin and sores recur in very hot or cold weather. (2) *Herpes zoster* is shingles, an inflammation within the spine of sensory nerves from the skin, caused by the virus that also causes chickenpox. The condition may be extremely painful and causes blisters in bands around the body corresponding to the infected nerves. Apart from analgesics there is no specific treatment.

Histamine An inflammatory substance released from damaged tissues, and responsible for many of the symptoms of allergy.

Homoeopathy A system of medicine based on the dubious theory that small doses of drugs that cause symptoms similar to those of a disease will cure that disease ("like cures like"). It is also considered, for no good scientific reason, that the smaller the dose of the drug the greater will be its curative effect. The practice of homoeopathy depends upon a study of the symptoms of disorder in relation to the patient as an individual rather than eliminating the underlying cause.

Hydrocephalus Enlargement of an infant's head by accumulation of the fluid that bathes the brain and spinal cord (cerebrospinal fluid), produced by obstruction to or defective absorption of the fluid. If the fluid is not released the increased pressure damages the brain. The condition can be relieved by surgical

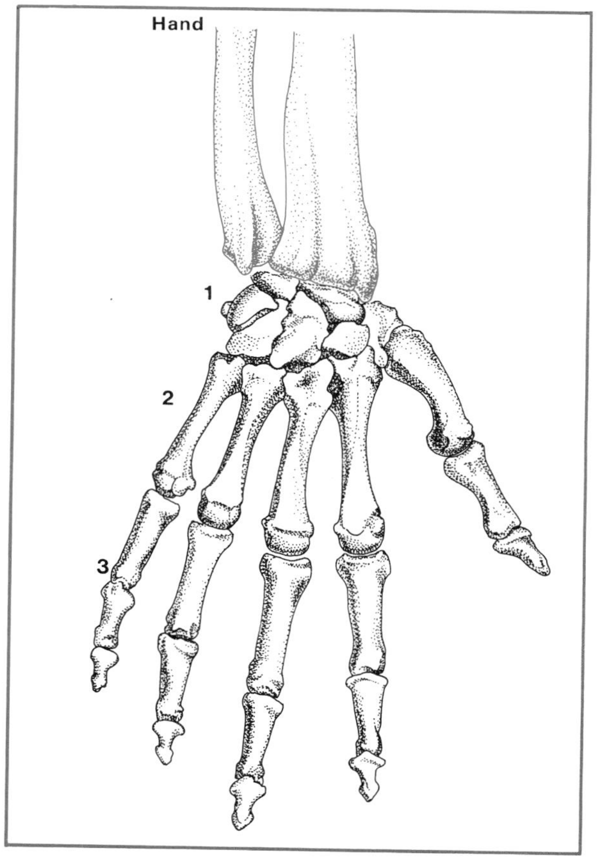

operation; a drainage valve is placed between the cavity in the brain and the jugular vein in the neck.

Hypertension High blood pressure. It may be caused by either kidney damage or disease, or occur without any apparent cause. Rare cases may be caused by hormone disorders. Many hypertensions are symptom-free for years, but eventually the disease causes cardiac failure due to overload on the head, strokes due to cerebral haemorrhage or thrombosis, and renal failure caused by damage to the capillaries in the kidney. High blood pressure also increases atherosclerosis and the incidence of its complications. It is treated by drugs that block the sympathetic nerve endings, preventing the constriction of small arterioles, and diuretics that reduce the circulatory blood volume.

Hypertrophy Increase in size of an organ or tissue brought about by enlargement of individual cells.

Hypnosis Trance induced by hypnotism. A state in which the hypnotized subject allows himself to come under the control of the hypnotist. When he returns to normal he has no memory of what occurred during the trance. Hypnosis may be induced quite easily provided the subject is co-operative and both he and the operator concentrate completely. It has been used to induce anaesthesia, in the treatment of neuroses and as an adjunct to psychotherapy.

Hysteria Not, in medicine, an uncontrolled emotional outburst, but a neurotic disorder in which the patient subconsciously reproduces the symptoms or signs of physical illness.

I

Impacted tooth A tooth that is prevented from erupting normally by an adjacent fully erupted tooth, usually because it is misaligned. Occurs most often to the third lower molar.

Impetigo An infection of the skin by streptococci or staphylococci, that occurs most commonly in children. Appears as scabby sores often around the nose and mouth or behind the ears. It responds to antibiotic treatment.

Impotence Inability to perform coitus. In men it is a failure to achieve an erection which may be caused by emotional factors, certain drugs, and physical illness. In women it is due to spasm of the muscles around the vagina which may have emotional causes, or be due to local abnormalities or disease.

Incontinence Failure to control the emptying of the bladder or rectum. Usually due to disorders of the nerves supplying them as in paraplegia, brain damage or senility.

Indigestion *See* **Dyspepsia**

Infertility The inability of a couple to have children. About ten per cent of couples are childless. In about forty per cent of the cases this is due to male infertility. Infertility in a man may be due to a low sperm count of less than two million per millilitre, or a high proportion of abnormal sperms. These deficiencies can be caused by hormonal disorders, defective spermatogenesis or obstruction to the seminal ducts (*see* pages 52–53), and may often be improved sufficiently to restore fertility. In women infertility may be due to failure of ovulation due to hormonal deficiencies, or abnormalities of the genital tract, such as obstruction of the Fallopian tubes following infection. Many of these abnormalities can be overcome by surgery. In some couples the secretions of the woman's genital tract is hostile to the man's sperms and destroys them before fertilization can occur. In many cases, what appears to be infertility is in matter of fact subfertility, and with assistance, that may range from education in the mechanics of sex to hormone treatment or surgery, many apparently barren couples may have children.

Influenza An acute infectious disease due to a virus that usually occurs in winter epidemics. Transmitted by droplet infection. Characterized by general illness and inflammation of the respiratory tract. A number of viruses may cause the disease and they change their nature periodically with the result that people are rarely immune to them and an epidemic occurs. The disease is often complicated by secondary bacterial infection resulting in pneumonia or bronchitis. There is no specific treatment for influenza. A number of vaccines effective against specific viruses are available.

Inoculation The introduction of weakened disease-causing organisms through the skin to stimulate antibody production and confer immunity against a disease.

Insomnia Inability to go to sleep, sleeplessness. May be caused by pain or other physical discomfort, but more usually emotional factors, particularly anxiety. There are many drugs available for inducing sleep, but understanding and treatment of the underlying cause is the best approach to insomnia.

Insulin A hormone produced by the pancreas, concerned with the control and use of blood glucose. It decreases blood glucose by increasing the uptake and breakdown of glucose by the cells and increasing the rate of conversion of sugar into fat by the liver. It also depresses the rate of addition of glucose into the blood by reducing the formation of new glucose from amino acids in the liver. In diabetes there is a lack of insulin resulting in excess glucose in the blood. Excess of insulin reduces the blood glucose to very low levels and may cause coma by depriving the brain of essential glucose.

Interferon A substance, produced by cells infected with virus, that prevents infection of other cells by virus.

J

Jaundice (Icterus) Yellow discoloration of the tissues by excess of the bile pigment bilirubin, caused by liver disease, obstruction of the bile duct or excessive breakdown of red blood cells.

K

Keloid A fibrous tumour of scar tissue that occurs in healing scars, especially those following burns.

Kyphosis Abnormal curvature of the spine in the forward/backward plane, with increased convexity of the back, due to deformities of the vertebrae caused by injury, infection, tumours, or abnormal bone metabolism. (*See also* **Lordosis.**)

L

Laryngitis Inflammation of the larynx and vocal cords, due to infection, irritation by smoke or gases, or over-use of the voice. The symptoms are sore throat, cough and hoarseness; the voice may be reduced to a whisper or completely lost. The most important part of treatment is to breathe warm moist air. Cough medicines and mild analgesics will also relieve the symptoms. Persistent hoarseness or change of the voice should receive medical advice.

Laxative A drug or other substance used to promote opening of the bowels, often as a remedy for constipation. Another term for a mild laxative is *aperient;* more powerful agents are *purgatives* or *cathartics.* Laxatives work by increasing the physical bulk of the faeces (bran or other vegetable roughage), by increasing their water content (magnesium sulphate—Epsom salts), by lubrication (liquid paraffin) or by chemical irritation (senna, cascara). Laxatives should never be used routinely, because the bowel may become "lazy", so that bowel movement relies upon their artificial stimulation. People who eat a good mixed diet, with plenty of roughage, drink plenty of fluids, and take reasonable exercise, should not need laxatives. Long-lasting constipation requires medical advice.

Leg The bones of the leg are the *femur* (**1**), or thigh bone, the *tibia* (**2**), or shin bone, the *fibula* (**3**), or splint bone, and the *patella* (**4**), or kneecap. The hip joint, between the head of the femur and the pelvic bones, is a ball-and-socket joint, and the knee joint, where the lower end of the femur meets the upper end of the tibia, acts as a hinge. The lower ends of the tibia and fibula articulate at the ankle joint with the tarsal bone of the foot called the *talus.* (In strict anatomical terms, only this part of the limb, between knee and ankle joints, is called the leg.) Acting on the thigh at the hip are the powerful *gluteal* muscles of the buttock, attached to the pelvis and femur, *adductors* inside the thigh, the *quadriceps femoris* at the front, and hamstring muscles behind. The quadriceps is attached, through the strong tendon at the front of the knee, to the front of the tibia, and straightens the knee. Within its tendon lies the patella. Below the knee there are three main groups of muscles: the *flexors* of the foot and ankle in front, *peroneal* muscles on the outside, and *extensors,* including the *gastrocnemius* and *soleus* muscles at the back, forming the bulk of the calf and attached through the Achilles tendon to the *calcaneum* or heel bone. The main artery to the lower limb is the *femoral artery*, in front of the hip joint, and the main nerve is the *sciatic nerve,* which enters behind the joint.

Leprosy A chronic infection caused by bacteria very similar to tuberculosis, and spread only by prolonged contact with infected persons. *Lepromatous* leprosy affects the skin, causing lumps and thickening and ulceration of the skin. *Tuberculoid* leprosy affects the nerves to the extremities. The long-term effects of the disease include paralysis, resulting in deformities of the limbs, especially the hands, ulceration and loss of fingers and toes. Ulceration of the mucous membrane may result in complete erosion of the nose. The disease may be treated by prolonged courses of drugs related to the sulphonamides, which at the same time render the patient non-infectious.

Leukaemia Excessive formation of abnormal white blood cells, leukocytes, and the tissues from which they arise. The cause remains unknown but it may be due to virus infection. In any one case of leukaemia only one of the different types of white blood cells is involved so that either the bone marrow or the lymphatic tissues are affected. The abnormal white cells never reach full maturity but continue dividing; these immature white blood cells are not able to function in the defensive reactions against infection. The white cell producing tissues encroach on the red cell forming marrow, so that leukaemic patients become anaemic and succumb easily to infection. With acute leukaemia the patient can only expect to live about six months; chronic leukaemia is usually fatal within three to four years. Leukaemia is most common in young children and after middle age. Very few cases of leukaemia are actually cured, but treatment may result in long periods of relatively symptom-free remission. Treatment is designed to reduce the leukaemic processes; radiation and cytotoxic drugs are used, both of which prevent the division of leukaemic cells.

Lordosis Curvature of the spine, increasing the concavities of the back commonly in the small of the back. Lordosis usually occures to offset the effects of kyphosis (q.v.), obesity and, temporarily, pregnancy, restoring the centre of gravity of the body.

Lumbago Ache in the small of the back. May be due to muscle tension or strains caused by faulty posture, or a slipped disc.

Leg

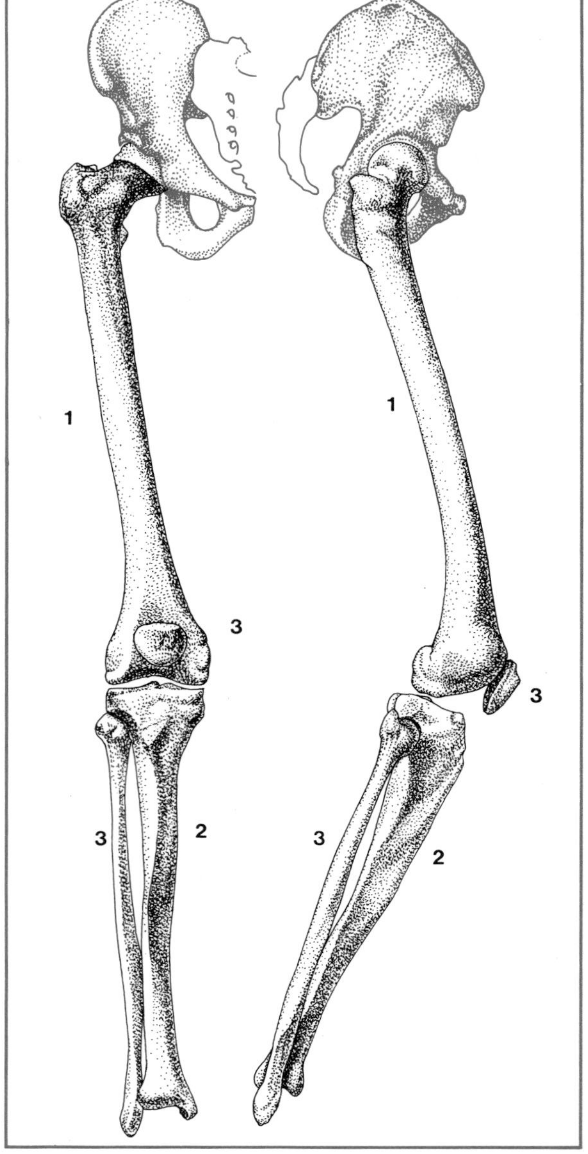

M

Malaria A disease caused by a protozoan blood parasite (*Plasmodium*) transmitted among humans by mosquitoes of the genus *Anopheles,* of warm countries. The parasites multiply in the liver without causing symptoms, but periodically they invade and mature in red blood corpuscles, eventually destroying them. Poisons liberated during mass breakdown of the blood cells cause intermittent chills and fevers; anaemia follows, with muscle pains and damage to spleen and liver. Drugs can be used to kill the parasites or lessen the severity of attacks, but some forms are difficult to eradicate once they are established in the body. Preventive drugs, taken daily or weekly in malaria zones, and local control of mosquito populations by spraying and draining breeding sites, offer the best long-term protection.

Mastitis A painful inflammation of the breast, due to several causes, including bacterial infection and hormone imbalance.

Mastoiditis Infection and inflammation within the spongy mastoid bone, situated behind the ear, usually a sequel to infection of the middle ear; a painful condition which, neglected, may lead to deafness.

Measles A virus disease usually of childhood, transmitted by vapour droplets. Starting with symptoms like those of the common cold, with sore eyes and sneezing, it develops into high fever, usually accompanied by tiny white spots in the mouth and followed by a rash of small red spots on face, neck and the rest of the body. Though not usually dangerous, it can occasionally lead to complications. It can be prevented by vaccination, and does not normally recur in adults.

Melanoma A dark pigmented spot on the skin which may appear spontaneously or develop from a previously existing mole. Any mole that changes its appearance or bleeds needs immediate medical investigation to preclude malignancy.

Ménière's disease A recurring condition of the inner ear, usually during or after middle age, with symptoms of sickness, dizziness and loss of balance during attacks. Drug treatment may alleviate the symptoms, and surgery has been employed.

Meningitis Inflammation, usually due to virus or bacterial infections, of the membranes covering the brain and spinal cord; symptoms include headaches, fever, muscular pains and stiffness in neck and back. A dangerous condition needing medical care.

Migraine A recurring condition of severe headaches (sometimes on only one side) often accompanied by nausea, dizziness and temporary defects of speech and vision. May be due to faulty metabolism of certain proteins, but stress, pre-menstrual tension and other physical conditions can bring on attacks.

Miscarriage Spontaneous accidental loss of foetus during the first seven months of pregnancy. (*See* **Abortion**.)

Mole A small pigmented spot on the skin, usually dark brown; normally harmless, but may become malignant. (*See* **Melanoma**.)

Mongolism A congenital condition (Down's syndrome) due to chromosomal abnormality; the mongoloid child usually has a short head, round face with slanting eyes, sometimes abnormalities of the hand, and heart defects. There is slight or severe mental retardation, but the child normally has a pleasant and affectionate disposition.

Multiple sclerosis A chronic condition of unknown cause in which small areas of the central nervous system degenerate. A wide range of symptoms result according to the sites of degeneration; usually slight but progressive impairment of activities, sometimes with remissions, lead to disablement.

Mumps A virus disease transmitted by droplets; mild fever is followed by swelling of the salivary glands. Usually passes off after two or three days, but may very rarely spread to involve the ovaries, testes or pancreas. A single attack usually confers lifelong immunity.

Mycosis Any disease caused by a fungus, such as athlete's foot, ringworm or thrush.

Myopia Short-sightedness, due either to too strong a lens or too long an eyeball; rays of light from distant objects focus in front of the retina. Remedied with diverging spectacle lenses.

Myositis Muscle inflammation, usually of unknown cause. Normally passes off without treatment, but severe myositis may lead to temporary or permanent paralysis of the muscle, and require medical treatment.

N

Naturopathy A system of health based on adherence to simple foods, regular exercise and natural (including herbal) remedies, and avoidance of drugs, unnatural stimulants and artificial living.

Nausea A feeling, often justified, of impending sickness. May be due to a wide range of causes, including bacterial food poisoning, alcohol, allergy, pain, tension, migraine, pregnancy, middle-ear troubles, motion or chronic digestive problems.

Neoplasm New growth of tissue or tumour; may be no more than a slight, harmless swelling (benign tumour), or may spread progressively to involve more and more of the neighbouring tissues (malignant tumour or cancer). Any unexplained swelling needs immediate medical examination.

Nephritis Inflammation of the kidneys, due to bacterial infection or poisons. Symptoms may include nausea, headache and fever, cloudy or dark urine, and oedema.

Nephrosis (Nephrotic syndrome) A condition of the kidneys in which the glomeruli and tubules gradually fail, resulting in loss of protein with the urine, and, often, retention of water in the tissues. (*See* **Oedema**.)

Neurone A nerve unit consisting of a cell body (**1**) with a nucleus, an axon (**2**) and dendrites (**3**). Impulses are fed into the nerve cell from the dendrites and leave via the axon. Where a nerve reaches a muscle, the axon terminates at a motor end

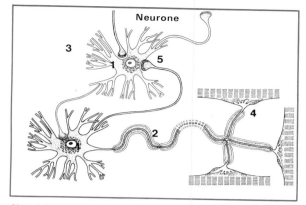

plate (**4**), passing instructions to its fibres. The point at which one nerve cell relays information to another is called a synapse (**5**).

Neuritis Inflammation of one or more nerves due to bacterial or virus infection or damage, as in shingles or Bell's palsy, etc.

Nosebleed Persistent bleeding from ruptured vessels inside nose. May be arrested by pinching the nostrils, rest and a cold, damp compress across the bridge of the nose. Frequent nosebleeds are sometimes associated with high blood pressure and medical advice should be sought.

Nystagmus Movement of the eyeball, under involuntary control of the balance centres, normally in co-ordination with movements of the head and visible objects; can occur inappropriately in Ménière's disease and other conditions of middle ear and brain, when it may cause vertigo.

O

Oedema Waterlogging of the tissues, due to excessive losses of tissue fluid from the blood, through the capillary walls. Often seen first around the ankles and face, but excess water may accumulate in the body cavity (*ascites*) and other tissues. Caused by increased pressure in the veins, due to obstruction or heart failure; or decrease in osmotic pressure of blood due to albumin loss, nephrosis or malnutrition.

Ophthalmia (Ophthalmitis) Inflammation of the eye and neighbouring tissues; includes conjunctivitis, iritis, glaucoma, trachoma, snow blindness and other conditions.

Osteoarthritis A disease of old age, in which bone gradually replaces articular cartilage at the joints, especially those of the legs, hips and spine. Radical treatment involves replacement of the joint by artificial substitutes.

Osteomalacia A condition resulting from shortage of vitamin D in adults. The symptoms include aching bones, muscular cramp and bone deformation.

Osteomyelitis Inflammation of bone due to bacterial infection, often from a source elsewhere in the body, with formation of an abscess. Pain, fever and general malaise occur suddenly, and require urgent medical treatment, usually by antibiotics and surgery at the seat of infection.

Osteopathy A system of treatment which involves the diagnosis and treatment (mainly by manipulation) of structural and mechanical derangements in the framework of the body. Particular attention is paid to spinal lesions, which are believed to have far-reaching effects on general health through their influence on the nerves and circulation.

Osteoporosis Weakening of bone, usually in old age, largely due to loss of calcium. May also occur in damaged or immobilized bones. The condition may be due to hormonal or dietary deficiencies.

Otitis Inflammation of the ear. In *otitis externa*, a mild condition, the canal of the outer ear is affected by fungi or bacteria, requiring antibiotic treatment. *Otitis media* and *otitis interna*, respectively inflamed conditions of the middle and inner ear, involve acute earache, fever and general malaise and possible vertigo; both require immediate medical attention.

Otosclerosis Formation of additional bone in the middle ear, which interferes with the action of the ear ossicles and causes progressive deafness. Surgery often improves hearing.

P

Paget's disease (1) A deforming disease of bone due to disorder of the hormonal system involved in laying down and reabsorbing bone salts. (2) A rare form of breast cancer, superficially resembling a rash on or about the nipple, which requires immediate attention.

Palpitation Unusual prominence of the heart-beat, which

may be due to emotion, exercise, shock or drugs; frequent spells of palpitation may indicate some physical upset, which should be investigated medically. (*See* **Arrhythmia**.)

Palsy Loss of muscle control due to local or regional disorder of the nervous system; may result in paralysis or tremors.

Papilloma An outgrowth of skin or mucous membrane; a wart, polyp or other form of benign tumour. May be due to mechanical or chemical injury, virus infection or unknown causes, and can usually be removed without difficulty. Any papilloma showing a tendency to change its appearance or spread requires medical attention.

Paralysis Loss of control of muscles, due to malfunction of the nervous system. May be due to infection (as in poliomyelitis or tertiary syphilis), injury to brain or spinal cord (paraplegia, hemiplegia), rupture or blocking of blood vessels in brain (stroke), or progressive diseases (multiple sclerosis, spinal or brain tumours). Local paralysis of fingers or limb may be caused by damage to a peripheral nerve, which may be permanent or recover with the restoration of the nerve fibres.

Paraplegia Paralysis involving the lower part of the body, and legs, resulting from injury to the spinal cord.

Parasite An organism (plant or animal) which lives directly at the expense of another. Parasites affecting humans may live externally on the skin (lice, fleas, bugs, ticks, mites, fungi, bacteria) or internally in the gut and body cavity (nematode worms, tape worms, flukes, hookworms, bacteria, protozoa); their livelihood is made by sucking or absorbing nutrient materials (blood, serum, cell fluids, part-digested foods) from the host, and using the energy to make more individuals of their own kind. They harm the host not only by robbing him of nutrients, but often by setting up local irritation, releasing poisons into his bloodstream, or transferring other parasites to him; thus lice suck the blood of their host, and may also transfer typhus to him. There are specific treatments for most forms of parasite, and the body often develops natural defences.

Parathyroids Endocrine glands (there are usually four, close to the thyroid gland in front of the neck) that produce the hormone parathormone, responsible for controlling metabolism of calcium. Excess secretion causes calcium to be dissolved from the bones and shed in the urine; shortage causes muscle spasms and twitching.

Parkinsonism (Parkinson's disease) A chronic, progressive form of palsy affecting patients in late middle age, associated with degeneration of the basal ganglia (central controlling movement) in the brain; co-ordination of movement is impaired, muscular tremors affect the hands, and other skeletal muscles twitch spasmodically or become sluggish. The mind remains active and clear but speech may be impaired. Parkinsonism often responds to drug therapy coupled with massage and exercise, and brain surgery has also proved successful.

Pellagra A deficiency disease due to shortage of nicotinic acid or niacin, part of the vitamin B complex, common among underfed people whose staple food is maize. Rashes, sore tongue and mouth, diarrhoea and mental disturbance are the symptoms; the cure is a mixed diet containing adequate niacin.

Pelvis The weight of the trunk is transmitted through each sacro-iliac joint (**1**) to the pelvis, which consists of three bones, the ilium (**2**), ischium (**3**) and the pubis (**4**) which lock together. The head of the femur (**5**) articulates with the cup-shaped *acetabulum* (**6**) at their junction. At the centre of the pubic arch is the symphysis (**7**).

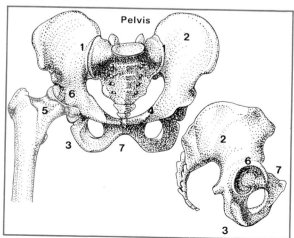

Penicillin An antibiotic derived from the fungus *Penicillium*, with strong bactericidal properties. Many forms of penicillin have now been derived to cope with particular forms of bacterial infection. A very few patients sensitive to penicillin-based drugs develop a rash or more serious symptoms under treatment.

Peritonitis Inflammation of the peritoneum or lining of the abdominal cavity, due to an abdominal wound or perforated intenstine which allows bacteria to enter the cavity. Symptoms include a painful, tender abdomen, fever, vomiting, and rigidity of the abdominal muscles. This is a dangerous condition, demanding immediate medical attention; antibiotics, surgery, and good nursing over a long period are usually needed.

Phenylketonuria A rare metabolic disorder due to inherited inability to transform phenylalanine, a protein derivative; this substance accumulates and poisons the brain cells, causing mental deficiency.

Phlebitis *See* **Thrombophlebitis**

Photophobia Inability to tolerate bright light; sometimes a condition associated with migraine, but may also accompany conjunctivitis and other forms of eye inflammation.

Pica The habit of eating soil, coal and other unsuitable materials; it develops occasionally in small children and very occasionally in pregnant women. Believed to signify mineral deficiency, and may respond to broader diet, iron tonics, etc.

Piles *See* **Haemorrhoids**

Pineal gland A small glandular body on the upper surface of the brain. Its function in man is doubtful, but it may be concerned with sexual development and maturation.

Pleurisy Inflammation of the thin epithelium lining the pleural cavities, which house the lungs. Caused by bacterial or viral infection, often associated with lung infection; symptoms include chest pains during breathing and coughing and fever. Fluid accumulating in the cavity may reduce the pain, but excess fluid may make breathing difficult, and have to be drained off. Treatment involves rest, antibiotic therapy and pain-killing drugs.

Pneumonia Inflammation in the lungs, caused by viral or bacterial infection; it may be localised in the base of the lungs (hypostatic pneumonia), in a single lobe (lobar pneumonia) or in alveoli close to the bronchial tubes (bronchopneumonia). Often follows other illness, and generally indicates a lowered state of health; typically begins with a rasping cough, fever, breathing difficulty and blood-stained sputum. Treatment by antibiotics, with rest and careful nursing, is usually effective.

Pneumothorax Presence of air in the pleural cavity, through accident (stab wound) or as a result of lung disease or malformation. Air in this situation prevents the lung from expanding fully. When the prime cause is removed by suitable treatment, the air is usually reabsorbed naturally.

Poisoning Disorders due to the intake of noxious substances, usually through the gut or lungs, and, rarely, through the skin. Poisons may be corrosive (acids, alkalis, disinfectants), destroying living tissue and causing pain and shock, or metabolic (carbon monoxide, cyanide, snake venoms), which upset the chemical working of the body. Though some act instantaneously, others may take several hours to affect the body, and considerable after-care is needed in cases of suspected poisoning. First-aid treatment may be vital; for details see any good first-aid manual. Medical advice is essential; if the nature of the poison is known or suspected, the doctor should be informed so that specific remedies can be prepared without loss of time. Even minor cases of poisoning should be treated seriously and given medical attention until all possibility of danger is over.

Poliomyelitis (Infantile paralysis) A virus infection affecting motor cell bodies in the spinal cord; damage to the cells causes paralysis of the muscles under their control, and may result in permanent, total incapacitation. Paralysis may affect only a few muscles or many, and may be temporary or permanent. Treatment during an attack includes massage and use of hot packs. Vaccination is now used effectively in many countries.

Polyp An abnormal outgrowth, usually benign (non-cancerous), of the mucous membrane or lining of the intestine, nose, bladder or elsewhere. Often removed by simple surgery.

Premature birth Birth in which the infant weighs less than 2.5 kg (5½ lb), although the degree of development is more critical than weight. Infants born some weeks before full term are at risk because they lack subdermal fat and lose heat rapidly; they also tend to have breathing difficulties and usually need incubation and constant care and attention until the critical weight is reached.

Prolapse Displacement of an organ after strain, as of the rectum (in children) or the uterus (after several pregnancies). Usually due to weakened surrounding tissues; it may be remedied by supports, muscular training, or surgery.

Protozoa Organisms made up of a single cell, usually less than 0.5 mm across, often very much smaller. Include the parasites responsible for malaria and sleeping sickness, and the intestinal parasites responsible for dysentery.

Psittacosis A mild or severe pneumonia-like condition caused by a micro-bacterial infection of the lungs; the organism concerned also occurs as a gut parasite of parrots, budgerigars and poultry.

Psoriasis Mild but irritating and temporarily disfiguring condition of the skin, in which irregular scaly patches appear especially on the scalp, neck, arms and back; may be associated with slight itching and arthritic pains. The cause is unknown; some people seem predisposed to it by heredity, and it cannot be passed on by touch. Responds to drug therapy and sunshine, and relief from itching may be obtained through skin lotions.

Puerperal fever An extremely dangerous general infection following childbirth, usually resulting from bacterial infection of the birth passage. Formerly commonplace, it is now very rare in communities where normal precautions against infection are taken and antibiotics are available.

Pyelitis Inflammation of the renal pelvis—the collecting area for urine at the head of the ureter. Often involving other parts of the kidney as well (pyelonephritis), it is caused by invasion of bacteria from the bladder or bloodstream, and usually requires drug therapy.

R

Rabies (Hydrophobia) A rare but very dangerous virus disease of the nervous system, usually transmitted to man by the bite of an infected dog; many other animals may harbour the virus. The symptoms are high fever, delirium and muscular paralysis, leading to death. *Immediate* immunization of any person exposed to the risk of infection is life-saving, but once the disease is established death is inevitable. Strict quarantine regulations prevent spread from country to country.

Rash An area of spottiness or redness on the skin, usually associated with itching or a burning sensation. Many different conditions, including food poisoning, measles, chicken pox, allergy, nettle stings, produce characteristic rashes, which may be important in diagnosis; in most cases the rash disappears after a few hours or days. Scratching, which may break the skin and allow secondary infection, should be avoided. Calamine lotion or soothing creams usually alleviate the discomfort.

Raynaud's disease A condition in which the blood supply to the skin of the extremities is dangerously reduced by arterial spasm sometimes leading to the death of tissues—gangrene. The underlying cause is unknown. Attacks may be brought on by fear, shock, chill and other stimuli which affect the autonomic nerves controlling blood circulation. Drugs are now available to relieve the spasm, but sometimes it may be necessary to cut the nerves responsible.

Reflex An automatic, involuntary response to a stimulus, as in the rapid withdrawal of the hand from a hot surface or the rapid blink when an object passes close to the eye. Signals from receptor organs (for example, pain sensors in the hand) pass to nerve cell bodies in the central nervous system and are transmitted directly to motor cells controlling effector organs (for example, muscles of the arm). Impulses also pass to the brain, reporting pain and initiating follow-up behaviour, but the withdrawal movement is effected without interference or control from the brain. The body is equipped with many inborn reflexes which control such natural activities as breathing and swallowing. In addition it builds up a stock of learned reflexes, eg, the movements of walking and playing the piano, which can ultimately be done repetitively without thinking. Injury to brain, peripheral nerves or muscles may destroy reflexes which may then have to be replaced, for example re-learning to walk or speak after a stroke.

Rhesus (Rh) factor A chemical factor present on the surface of blood cells in some individuals. About 85 per cent of people are Rh+ (positive, i.e., possess the factor); 15 per cent are Rh—. Possession is determined by heredity, and the child of an Rh— mother may inherit Rh+ from his father. Towards the end of pregnancy, when proteins sometimes leak across the placenta, Rh+ cells from the infant's blood may enter the mother and set up a lasting antigen in her bloodstream. This may leak back into the infant's circulation (or that of a later Rh+ infant) and damage the blood cells. Forewarned by blood testing, doctors can decrease the danger by desensitizing the mother (destroying her antigen), or by draining and replacing the blood of the infant at or before birth.

Rheumatic fever An acute disease of young people involving fever, usually high and lasting several days, and swollen joints. An attack always follows infection by streptococci which give rise to scarlet fever, tonsillitis or sore throat; the rheumatic fever is believed to be caused by antigens produced by the body in response to the original infection. The fever runs its course in a few days and the joints return to normal, but the valves of the heart which also enlarge under the influence of the antigens, may suffer permanent damage and cause heart failure later in life. This condition can be averted if the original infection is treated promptly with antibiotics; should the fever develop, complete rest is essential during the period of swelling and recovery, to avoid taxing the heart. Attacks are likely to recur following further infection by streptococci.

Rheumatism Painful muscles or joints, usually due to rheumatic fever, neuritis, osteoarthritis, rheumatoid arthritis, or some other condition with these symptoms.

Rheumatoid arthritis *See* **Arthritis**

Rhinitis Inflammation of mucous membranes lining the nasal cavity, due to virus infection (influenza, common cold) or allergy (hay fever) or chemical irritants; the common symptom is a running or blocked nose.

Rickets A disease of children, rare in well-fed communities and sunny climates, due to vitamin D deficiency; in the absence of the vitamin growing bones fail to lay down calcium salts adequately, and those subject to pressure or weight tend to grow misshapen, producing characteristic bow-legs, knock-knees and pigeon chest. Fortifying the diet with vitamin D (fish-liver oils, enriched margarine) prevents further deformation, but the bone distortion is usually permanent.

Rickettsia Micro-organisms, intermediate in size between bacteria and viruses, responsible for many diseases transmitted by arthropods (mites, ticks, fleas, etc.), including typhus, Rocky Mountain spotted fever and Ricketssial pox.

Ringworm *See* **Tinea**

Rodent ulcer A form of skin cancer occurring only on the face and scalp; starting as a small tumour, it develops into an open sore which may spread, involving both skin and underlying tissues. Though destructive if left without treatment, the cancer does not spread to other parts of the body, and can usually be treated by drugs, X-ray therapy or surgery.

Rosacea Reddening of the face due to permanent enlargement of surface blood vessels in the skin; a progressive condition with an hereditary basis. Parts of the skin may thicken, e.g., that of the nose or cheeks. The cause is unknown, but people who flush readily in response to spicy foods, alcohol, climatic extremes or emotional outbursts seem most likely to develop the condition permanently. Drug therapy may be effective.

Rubella *See* **German measles**

Rupture Tearing or bursting of an organ, usually resulting from a blow; may also be due to weakening by infection or old age. (*See also* **Hernia**.)

S

Salpingitis Inflammation of one or both of the Fallopian tubes, resulting from bacterial infection; often a complication of gonorrhoea.

Scabies Skin itch caused by a mite which burrows in soft skin to lay its eggs. Favoured sites are the groin, elbow, wrist and hands and feet. Infection spreads readily from one victim to another, and scratching opens the skin to secondary infection by bacteria. Ointments containing benzyl benzoate and other mite-killing preparations are effective.

Scarlet fever (*Scarlatina*) An infectious fever, caused by streptococcal bacteria, and spread by moisture droplets or infected food. Symptoms include fever, sickness and headache, followed by a rash all over the body and a scarlet tongue; after a week or more the skin may begin to peel. Antibiotics bring a case quickly under control and prevent secondary damage to kidneys, ears, etc., which may otherwise follow.

Sciatica A painful condition in areas supplied by the sciatic nerve (lower back, buttock, thigh, calf); it may be due to strain, inflammation of part of the nerve, pressure from a slipped disc, or other causes. Rest, physiotherapy or drug therapy may be prescribed according to the diagnosis.

Scoliosis Lateral (sideways) curvature of the spine, which may follow partial paralysis of the back muscles, diseases of pelvis, hips or legs resulting in poor posture or many other conditions.

Scurvy A disease due to shortage of vitamin C (ascorbic acid) in the diet. The symptoms include painful, swollen joints, bruised appearance of skin, weakness, bleeding gums and loosening teeth, with a lowered resistance to infection. The remedy is to introduce fresh fruit, green vegetables and additional ascorbic acid to the diet.

Seborrhoea Unusually oily skin, due to overproduction of sebum (oil) by the sebaceous glands, and leading to various skin disorders.

Sedative A drug which calms and soothes, reducing anxiety and stress without loss of consciousness.

Sepsis Infection; the destructive effects of bacteria and their poisons on the tissues of the body.

Septicaemia "Blood poisoning". Widespread sepsis—usually the result of bacteria spreading through the circulatory system from a focus of infection.

Shingles *See* **Herpes**

Shock A serious condition which develops when the circulatory system fails; symptoms include muscular weakness (wobbly knees), cold, clammy skin with loss of colour, weak, irregular pulse, low blood pressure, shallow breathing, sickness and mental confusion possibly with loss of consciousness. Shock develops when the heart falters or weakens, when a large volume of blood is lost (by internal or external bleeding) from the system, when liquid is lost from the body through diarrhoea, excess sweating or extensive burns, or if there is a massive dilatation of blood vessels reducing overall pressure. First aid is aimed at removing the prime cause wherever possible, restoring the circulation and easing the flow of blood, especially to the brain. *Anaphylactic* shock may occur when a person is injected with a substance to which he is hypersensitive.

Silicosis A progressively incapacitating disease of the lungs caused by deposition of fine dust in the alveoli; the resulting scar tissue reduces the area of lung surface available for gas exchange, leaving the patient breathless. An occupational disease of miners, quarrymen, sandblasters and others, silicosis may predispose its victim to pulmonary tuberculosis.

Sinusitis Inflammation of the thin mucous membrane lining the facial sinuses (air-filled chambers in the bones of the face). Generally caused by the spread of virus infection from colds or influenza; other causes include hay fever, badly infected teeth or tonsils, and chronic irritation from smoke or dust.

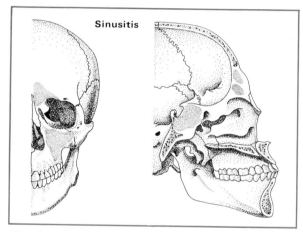

Sinusitis

Sleeping sickness A disease of tropical Africa caused by a protozoan blood parasite (trypanosome), which is introduced to man through the bite of an infected tsetse fly. In West Africa the disease is endemic and widespread. Infection is followed by fever and swelling of the joints and lymph glands, which passes off in a few days. In some patients there is no further effect, but in others the disease progresses to invade the nervous system months or years later, causing lethargy and death.

Sleepy sickness *See* **Encephalitis**

Slipped disc A disorder in which one of the pads of cartilage between adjacent vertebrae bulges (**1**) and presses on nearby structures (**2**). Pressure on a spinal nerve may produce pain and paralysis in the part it supplies—usually the leg. Treatment is by physiotherapy and immobilization. Surgery may be needed.

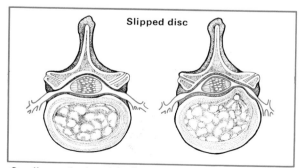

Slipped disc

Smallpox A virus infection, now mainly restricted to the poorer tropical countries; highly contagious and occasionally fatal, it often leaves heavy facial scarring. The symptoms are those of a bad dose of influenza, with fever and aching muscles; a rash appears about the third day, spreading from face and hand to body, and the spots spread to merge with each other as deep, scarring pustules. Vaccination gives certain protection.

Spasm Muscular contraction, usually sudden, uncontrolled

and painful; may be instantaneous (tic) or prolonged (cramps), and can be caused by infection, faulty circulation, disturbances of metabolism and many other causes. Prolonged or repeated spasms may require medical attention.

Spina bifida A congenital malformation in which the lower vertebrae fail to develop properly, exposing the spinal cord to damage. The damage may be slight or serious; in severe cases all nervous supply to the lower part of the body, including bladder and limb muscles, may be defective. Surgery shortly after birth may help to reduce the danger of further damage and improve the infant's chances of leading an active life.

Spondylitis Inflammation of the vertebrae, usually caused by injury or infection; symptoms include persistent backaches and stiffening of parts of the spine. X-ray and drug therapy may be effective in slowing down the progress of stiffening.

Sprain Injury to a joint involving damage to supporting tissues, such as tearing of ligaments, but without dislocation or broken bones.

Sprue Malnutrition resulting from failure of the small intestine to absorb fatty acids, calcium salts, vitamins D and K, and other essentials; symptoms include diarrhoea, anaemia and loss of weight. In tropical countries addition of folic acid (vitamin B complex) to the diet usually restores health. In temperate countries the condition may be due to gluten, a protein of wheat flour which upsets the digestive system of some individuals in this way. The remedy is a gluten-free diet.

Sputum Mucus coughed up from the air passages; in bronchial diseases, sputum may contain pus, blood and bacteria, all useful clues to the nature of the infection.

Squint (Strabismus) A condition in which one eye is misgalined in relation to the other. Usually congenital, squints detected early in life can often be corrected by exercises, corrective spectacles and other methods; it is important that this should be started as early as possible, before the child learns to ignore the information reaching his brain from the misaligned eye. A squint developing later in life is usually due to paralysis of one of the eye muscles, probably because of malfunction of the motor nerve responsible.

Staphylococci A group of spherical bacteria, identifiable by their habit of forming clusters rather than chains like streptococci. Responsible for skin spots, pustules and boils; in heavy infections their toxins can produce fever and septicaemia. The toxins are also responsible for some forms of food poisoning.

Stenosis Narrowing of a duct or opening in the body, usually as a result of disease. In *mitral stenosis,* flaps of the heart valve between the left atrium and left ventricle tend to stick together narrowing the duct through which blood passes at each heart-beat.

Sterility (1) Asepsis; freedom from living organisms, especially bacteria, attained by heating, use of ultra-violet radiation, antiseptics or other means. (2) Inability to procreate, usually as a result of a sterilizing disease or operation.

Steroids Organic chemical compounds containing linked rings of carbon atoms, important in living systems. Among those involved in body chemistry are the adrenal corticosteroids, vitamin D, cholesterol, and the oestrogens and androgens (sex hormones).

Stimulants Drugs which increase the rate of activity or sensitivity of the body, such as caffeine (present in tea and coffee), amphetamines, adrenaline and nicotine (present in tobacco and snuff). Many have harmful side effects.

Stomatitis Inflammation of the membrane that lines the mouth, usually due to bacterial infection following some other illness which has lowered the general resistance of the body. The condition disappears when general health is restored.

Streptococci A group of spherical bacteria, identifiable by their habit of forming chains rather than clusters, as do staphylococci. Responsible for sore throats, scarlet fever and wound infection, with a tendency to produce septicaemia rather than local abscesses when introduced under the skin. Streptococcal toxins may also be responsible for rheumatic fever and nephritis. Most streptococcal infections can be controlled by antibiotics.

Stricture A reduction in the aperture of a tube, stemming the flow of a liquid. An example is urethral stricture, in which the outlet from the bladder is constricted.

Stroke Acute loss of function of part of the brain, due to local rupture of blockage of arteries. Very mild strokes may pass unnoticed; serious ones cause death almost immediately. Normally, the patient loses consciousness and, on recovery, shows some sign of impairment—paralysis down one side, and loss of speech are common. Treatment includes prolonged rest and therapy, in which the nature and cause of the stroke can be established, remedial action taken, and efforts made to restore ability by physiotherapy, speech training and other means.

Stye A pustule on the edge of the eyelid, forming in the root of an eyelash. Frequently occurring styes need medical attention.

Subcutaneous Under the skin—i.e., in the layer of connective tissue between dermis and underlying muscles.

Sulphonamide Member of a family of drugs, all prefixed by the term "sulpha-", widely used against micro-organisms. They are especially effective in treating streptococcal infections, pneumonia, meningitis and genito-urinary diseases.

Sutures (1) The fine joints between the bones of the skull. (2) Stitches of catgut, fibre, silk or other material used to draw the edges of a wound together.

Sycosis Inflammation of the hair follicles of scalp or beard, caused by bacterial infection; usually mild, it can spread to form unsightly patches and scars. Treatment is with antibiotics.

Symptom Any physical or mental change indicating the presence of disease or disorder in the body. Strictly speaking, *symptoms* are changes reported by the patient; *signs* are changes discovered by the doctors in his examination.

Syndrome A group of symptoms and characters which together indicate a particular disease or disorder.

Synovium Membrane lining the non-articular surface of joints, which produces lubricating synovial fluid.

Syphilis The most serious venereal disease, caused by a spirochaete, usually transmitted by sexual contact through scratches or open sores on the skin, or mucous membrane lining the mouth or genitalia. The first indications appear one to twelve weeks after infection as a small lump under the skin, usually on or near the genitalia or mouth, and swollen lymph glands close by; the lump (chancre) may form a small ulcer. These symptoms do not last long, and may be missed altogether. Weeks to months later a rash appears, accompanied by a general feeling of slight fever and illness which may be mistaken for other conditions. Up to this point there is no permanent damage and the disease can be cured completely by antibiotics. Untreated, it continues by attacking tissues all over the body, including the central nervous system, heart and other internal organs over a period of several years; this damage is permanent, and may include paralysis blindness and insanity. Syphilis can be passed from an infected mother to an unborn child, who may be seriously handicapped from birth as a result. A simple blood test (Wassermann reaction) shows clearly whether or not the disease is present at any stage.

Syringomyelia A disease of the central nervous system in which small sacs of watery fluid appear in the spinal cord, upsetting both sensory and motor nerves and causing local pain or loss of feeling and weakness or paralysis in the limbs. The cause is unknown, and the conditon can often be relieved but not cured.

T

TAB A vaccine which gives immunity to typhoid fever and two forms (A and B) of paratyphoid.

Tabes dorsalis Locomotor ataxia. Loss of muscular control, involving partial paralysis and lack of co-ordination; due to damage inflicted by the syphilis spirochaete on the central nervous system.

Talipes (Club foot) Foot deformity caused by faulty development in the womb or later damage. Early orthopaedic treatment can do much to relieve the condition.

Tendinitis Inflammation of a tendon, often associated with tenosynovitis—inflammation of the tendon sheath. Occurs when muscles and their tendons are subject to unusual usage, for example in games players at the start of a season. Movement in the affected tendons is painful, and the area may be tender and slightly swollen. Rest, massage and local treatment by injection may be needed to restore normal action.

Tennis elbow A painful condition of the elbow, usually involving the muscles of the forearm, due to unaccustomed activity; not restricted to tennis-players—any similar twisting and repeated jarring may invoke the condition. Rest, massage and injections bring relief, though the pain is likely to recur if the activity continues.

Teratoma Literally a monster; grossly misshapen foetus, usually aborted well before full time, or a tumour involving several different kinds of tissue, suggesting a degree of organization.

Tetanus (Lockjaw) A disease caused by a bacillus which invading a wound and living anaerobically (without oxygen), generates a toxin that affects the nervous system causing painful spasm in muscles. Any deep wound contaminated with dirt, particularly manured soil, requires immediate medical treatment, which can include injection of anti-toxin and vaccination .

Tetany Muscular spasms caused by malfunction of motor nerves, usually due to a temporary deficiency of calcium from the body fluids. The spasms may pass off quickly, but recur until correct levels of calcium have been restored.

Thalassaemia A type of anaemia, occurring mainly in Mediterranean races, caused by a hereditary fault in the structure and life-span of red blood corpuscles and leading to weakness, disability and early death unless blood transfusion is performed regularly.

Thrombophlebitis Inflammation and swelling of a vein (phlebitis) linked with the presence of a blood clot (thrombus) which forms on the lining of the vein. Particularly prevalent in overweight people and in mothers shortly after childbirth, it may be associated with varicose veins, like them occurring especially in the legs.

Thorax The upper part of the trunk, above the abdomen, containing the lungs and heart and great blood vessels. It is a bony cage formed by the spine (**1**), the ribs (**2**) and the sternum (**3**), to which the ribs are attached by costal cartilages; above, the paired clavicles articulate with the sternum.

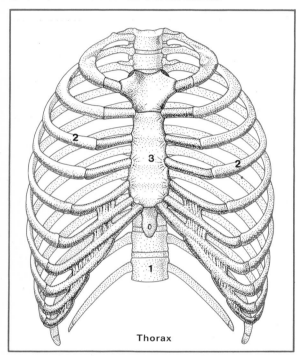

Thorax

Thrombosis Blockage of an artery or vein due to a blood clot, which may travel from a site of thrombophlebitis or other centre. Many clots can be circumvented by flow of blood through parallel vessels in the body's network of arteries and veins, but clots lodging in the coronary artery (which supplies the heart) may cause a heart attack, and minute clots in the arteries of the brain cause strokes, which may be seriously disabling or fatal. Injections of anticoagulants and enzymes sometimes help to disperse clots and discourage their formation.

Thymus Gland in the upper part of the thoracic cavity which is large at birth, grows until adolescence, then disappears slowly in later life. Intimately associated with the lymphatic system, it is responsible in early life for the production of lymphocytes and antibodies, two important lines of defence against disease.

Tinea A fungal infection of the skin. Several types of fungus are involved, including those responsible for ringworm, athlete's foot, dhobi itch and other local irritations. Contagious, and annoying rather than serious, most forms can be treated locally by fungicidal drugs and some antibiotics.

Tinnitus Sounds derived from disorders of the ear or auditory nerves; may be a constant and highly distressing accompaniment of otherwise total deafness, or little more than a background hissing due to too much wax in the outer ear passage. Some drugs may cause the condition, but in many cases the reason cannot be determined.

Tonsillitis Inflammation of the tonsils (patches of lymphatic tissue at the back of the throat) due to infection, often by streptococci. Symptoms include a sore throat with visible inflammation, which can usually be controlled readily by antibiotics. Chronically infected and enlarged tonsils may be removed in a simple surgical operation.

Toxaemia An illness due to the presence of toxins (poisons) in the blood. The toxins may be released by bacteria (especially streptococci in infected wounds, and those causing specific diseases, such as diphtheria, tetanus and typhoid) or due to diseased kidneys; some forms of bacterial food poisoning also

cause toxaemia. Symptoms usually include fever, but vary according to the particular toxin present. Toxaemia of pregnancy is a similar condition occurring occasionally during the last months of pregnancy, in which water accumulates in the body and the tissues swell. Though not serious in itself, this condition needs attention in case complications develop.

Toxin A poison produced by the body (and normally neutralized and eliminated) or by bacteria lodged either within the body or in food. Responsible for the symptoms of many diseases (see **Toxaemia**). Toxins are mostly proteins which act as antigens, stimulating the body to produce antitoxins which ultimately render them harmless.

Toxoid A toxin produced by bacteria but artificially rendered harmless by chemical processes, so that it no longer acts as a poison, but continues to evoke the immune response; when injected it causes the body to produce antibodies which confer temporary or permanent immunity. Anti-tetanus and anti-diphtheria toxoids are routinely used in this way.

Trachoma A widespread tropical disease caused by a microbacterium which attacks the conjunctiva and membranes lining the eyelids, causing inflammation and scarring; this may lead to permanent blindness. The disease is contagious, and common among the poorer populations of hot dry countries. It responds well to antibiotic treatment, though a badly infected cornea may remain opaque and require a graft before sight is restored.

Transfusion Transfer of blood or plasma from a donor to a recipient, necessary when a patient has lost blood in an accident or during surgery, or plasma through tissue seepage after extensive burns. A complete change of blood may be needed in some kinds of poisoning, and in infants whose blood has been damaged by Rh incompatibility (see **Rhesus factor**). Transfused blood must match the recipient's normal blood type.

Trauma Physical or mental injury. Physical trauma includes blows, burns, sprains, fractures and wounds. Mental trauma includes any event which seriously shocks or disturbs the mind.

Tremor Slight shaking due to the antagonistic tensions of muscles, which may be exaggerated in some neuromuscular diseases. Any progressive increase in tremor needs medical investigation.

Tuberculosis An infectious disease caused by a bacillus, which affects a variety of animals; only the cattle and human varieties are dangerous to man. Bovine (cattle) tuberculosis is contracted through the gut wall by drinking infected milk. This form is now rare in civilized countries, due to tuberculin testing of cattle and the widespread use of pasteurization of milk supplies. Human tuberculosis is spread by droplets, and infected sputum and food. Most people living in crowded conditions contract the disease at some time, but overcome it immediately and gain immunity. Those whose resistance is lowered by malnutrition, serious overcrowding, stress and by other infections may find tuberculosis more difficult to combat. In pulmonary tuberculosis (phthisis or "consumption") a small abscess forms in the lung and may spread to infect both lungs widely; symptoms include a persistent cough, blood-streaked sputum, flushed complexion, fever and loss of weight. In miliary tuberculosis the bacteria are spread through the body by the bloodstream, forming many small abscesses; in tuberculous meningitis the connective tissues covering the brain are involved. Infection may also spread to lymph glands, bones and joints, skin and internal organs. Treatment, effective if the disease is caught early, includes rest, good food, drug therapy and surgery.

Tumour A swelling or growth, caused by local multiplication of cells. Benign tumours and cysts (fluid-filled growths), apart from any pressure they may exert on surrounding tissues, may do little harm. Malignant or cancerous tumours grow and spread, individual knots of cells travelling via the bloodstream or lymphatic ducts to continue their growth in other parts of the body. Tumours and cysts may be removed by surgery. Benign tumours which show no signs of becoming malignant are usually left to themselves; malignant tumours are removed where possible, their offshoots (metastases) being treated by drugs or X-rays to reduce viability and growth. (See **Cancer**.)

Typhoid fever An infectious disease due to a bacterium which is transmitted through drinking water or food; people unaffected by the disease may be carriers capable of infecting others, especially if they are involved in nursing or handling food. The bacilli accumulate in lymphatic tissue in the small intestine, multiplying rapidly; from there they invade the bloodstream, their toxins causing high fever and a rash. Pockets of bacteria may gather in bones, joints or internal organs, but the most serious damage is done by those which weaken the intestinal wall, causing bleeding and peritonitis. This is often a cause of death. Antibiotics may be used to control the disease, and TAB is an effective vaccine.

Typhus Several serious infectious diseases caused by microbacteria of the *Rickettsia* group, transmitted to man by biting insects, mites or ticks, and causing high fever and rashes, sometimes complicated by pneumonia. Treatment is by antibiotics, and prevention by vaccination.

U

Ulcer An open sore on the skin or mucous membrane. Ulcers of the mouth and skin, often due to local infection, usually heal rapidly; any which persist should be examined by a doctor. Peptic ulcers form from time to time in the stomach and duodenum. Usually caused by autodigestion (the gut wall loses its protection against its own digestive juices), peptic ulcers cause abdominal pain, indigestion and nausea; they are especially prevalent in people suffering from stress and anxiety. If caught at an early stage they can usually be treated by dieting and drugs; neglected gastric and duodenal ulcers may need surgical treatment. Persistent stomach pains and indigestion are signs of trouble, requiring medical investigation.

Uraemia Excess of urea in the blood, due to partial failure of the kidneys, following damage, poisoning, circulatory disturbances, and many other conditions which affect the performance of the kidneys.

Urethritis Inflammation of the urethra, the tube which carries urine (and in the male, sexual products) to the outside world, usually due to bacterial invasion or diseases in which an irritant urine is produced (see **Cystitis, Gonorrhoea**); treatment of the cause, often by antibiotics, relieves the condition.

V

Vaccination A method of conferring immunity to specific diseases, by stimulating the body to produce natural defences (antibodies); more generally termed immunization. Treatment usually involves introducing harmless bacteria or viruses, or their products, into the bloodstream of the patient by a scratch on the skin or injection. The agents may have been especially bred from virulent ones (tuberculosis, yellow fever, poliomyelitis) or killed before introduction (measles, cholera, typhoid fever); poisonous products (tetanus, diphtheria) are rendered safe before use (see **Toxoid**). In every case the body responds as though infected, producing antibodies or antitoxins for varying periods afterwards. Some agents confer permanent immunity; with others it is wise to receive booster doses at intervals to ensure that the immunity is not lost.

Varicose veins Swollen, dilated veins, usually the large surface veins of the legs; due to faulty valves which prevent the normal flow of blood in the surface veins, and its inward flow from surface to deep veins. The condition is often accompanied by swollen feet and pain in the legs. The veins, often unsightly, may become inflamed, and there may be thrombophlebitis. Poor circulation may lead to the formation of ulcers when the skin breaks down. The condition is more common in fat people, expectant mothers, and those whose job requires them to stand still for long periods. Relief may be obtained by wearing supporting stockings, and both rest with the feet up and exercise. Once dilated, the veins are unlikely to grow smaller of their own accord, and troublesome ones must be reduced by injection or removed surgically.

Vector Carrier of a disease; usually an insect or mite, which picks up disease germs, harbours them, and transmits them to a new host.

Venereal diseases Infectious diseases which are transmitted almost without exception by sexual contacts. They include syphilis, gonorrhoea, chancroid (soft chancre) and lymphogranuloma venereum (LGV), and several minor irritant conditions. All respond well to antibiotics if treated early. Syphilis and gonorrhoea especially are potentially dangerous diseases, for which early and complete treatment should be sought.

Vertigo Dizziness, involving a sensation of whirling and loss of contact with the earth; due to a disturbed sense of balance, which may be caused by temporary falls in blood pressure, Ménière's disease, or many other conditions. Repeated attacks of vertigo require medical investigation.

Viruses Very small organisms composed mainly of nucleic acid, which cannot live independently but require a host tissue; many are responsible for diseases of man, including colds, influenza, poliomyelitis, German measles and hepatitis.

Viscera The internal organs, contained in the thorax (lungs, heart) and abdominal cavity (for example the stomach, intestines, liver, spleen and kidneys).

Volvulus Contortion and knotting of the intestine, which causes blocking of the tube and restriction of blood supply. The symptoms are acute abdominal pain and vomiting, and the only remedy is emergency surgery to untangle the knot.

Vomiting A powerful muscular reflex involving antiperistalsis (the reversal of normal peristaltic movements of stomach and throat) and contraction of the muscles of the diaphragm and abdomen. Controlled by a centre in the brain, vomiting occurs when the stomach is overfull, when certain poisons or irritants are present, when balance is upset, in obstruction of the small bowel and circumstances associated with danger (fear, shock).

W

Wart A small, persistent patch of rough skin forming a flat, shallow tumour, caused by virus infection. Warts usually occur on the hands, arms and legs, but may appear on the soles of the feet (plantar warts) or elsewhere; they often disappear spontaneously, but painful or unsightly warts can be removed by freezing, chemical treatment or surgery.

Whooping cough Infectious disease of children caused by bacterial invasion, affecting the bronchial tubes. Starting with symptoms of a bad cold and cough, the disease progresses after a few days; the cough worsens and at times becomes uncontrollable, with a characteristic whooping sound as the patient tries to draw breath. The coughing and the vomiting which sometimes accompanies it are distressing rather than dangerous, but children with whooping cough should be guarded against secondary infection and other complications to avoid irreparable lung damage, until well after the cough has ceased. Antibiotic treatment may shorten the disease.

Wounds Any breaks in the skin, including cuts, abrasions (grazing), lacerations (tearing) and punctures; contusions (bruises) are wounds in which the surface is unbroken but underlying tissues are damaged. Skin has a remarkable capacity for healing itself, if the body as a whole is healthy, the wound and underlying tissues are clean, and loose edges are pulled together by clips, stitching or plaster. Minor wounds need only cleaning with soap and water and the application of a clean, firm dressing. More extensive wounds, especially lacerations and puncture wounds, need careful attention to avoid infection and ensure sound healing.

X

Xanthoma A deposit of yellow fat in the skin, especially on the eyelids; often indicative of diabetes or certain blood conditions in which excess cholesterol is deposited in arteries.

X-rays Short-wave electromagnetic radiation capable of penetrating living tissues; because different tissues differ in their transparency to the rays, photographs or screened displays may be obtained in which internal organs appear as shadows. Clearer results may sometimes be gained by the use of opaque materials (for example barium sulphate "meals", iodine solutions, fine rubber tubes) which help to give organs a firm outline. Interpretation of X-ray pictures, radiology, is a highly-skilled branch of medicine. X-rays may also be focused at different depths in the body, and their concentrated energy used to destroy tissues, especially cancerous cells which cannot be reached in other ways.

Y

Yawning Like stretching, a comfort movement with both voluntary and reflex components. The most likely function of these movements is to apply pressure to lymphatic glands and promote circulation of lymph after a period of stagnation.

Yaws An infectious disease of tropical countries, closely related to syphilis but capable of living briefly outside the body; it can therefore be transmitted by any form of contact, not necessarily sexual, and by flies. Symptoms include outbreaks of ulcers on the skin, and deeper penetration of muscles and bones which may leave the victim crippled and scarred. Penicillin and other antibiotics control yaws, but early treatment is essential to avoid permanent damage.

Yellow fever A disease of Africa and tropical America, caused by a virus which affects other animals as well as man, and is carried by biting mosquitoes. In a mild form the disease resembles influenza, but outbreaks among people unaccustomed to it (for example city dwellers, labouring gangs) include more serious and fatal cases. Fever rises, heart, liver and kidneys are attacked, and the skin yellows with jaundice. There is no effective treatment for yellow fever, but the disease can be brought under control by mass vaccination and, where necessary, control of the mosquito carrier.

Z

Zoonosis Any infectious disease affecting both man and animals. Many disease-producing parasites are specific to a single host species whose body fluids, temperature and defence mechanisms they are adapted to deal with. Some are capable of living actively or passively in more than one kind of host; thus trypanosomiasis survives harmlessly in antelopes but causes sleeping sickness in man, and yellow fever virus is found in many apparently healthy warm-blooded animals in the tropical danger zones. Many parasites require alternate hosts to complete their complex life cycles; the tsetse fly is not just a passive carrier of trypanosomes, but a host in which important stages of their life cycle are completed. Involvement of other animals in the life cycles of disease-producing parasites sometimes makes it very difficult to eradicate disease from human communities; however, alternate hosts are occasionally more vulnerable than the disease germs themselves (mosquitoes carrying malaria or yellow fever) and control can best be effected through them.

Index